THE LONG PARLIAMENT OF CHARLES II

Peter Tillemans, *The House of Commons in Session*, oil on canvas, *c.* 1709–1710. Tillemans shows the Commons Chamber—formerly St. 'Stephen's Chapel—after Wren's alterations. All evidence of the Gothic structure is concealed, but the fabric of the chapel was largely intact beneath Wren's fixtures (Palace of Westminster).

The
LONG PARLIAMENT
of CHARLES II

❖

ANNABEL PATTERSON

YALE UNIVERSITY PRESS
NEW HAVEN AND LONDON

For information about this and other Yale University Press publications, please contact:
U.S. Office: sales.press@yale.edu   www.yalebooks.com
Europe Office: sales@yaleup.co.uk   www.yaleup.co.uk

Set in Baskerville by IDSUK (DataConnection) Ltd
Printed in Great Britain by MPG Books Ltd, Bodmin, Cornwall

Library of Congress Cataloging-in-Publication Data

Patternson, Annabel M.
    The long parliament of Charles II/Annabel Patterson.
        p. cm.
    Includes bibliographical references and index.
    ISBN 978–0–300–13708–8 (ci: alk. paper)
    1. Great Britain—History—Charles II, 1660–1685. 2. Great Britain—Politics and
government—1660–1688. 3. Great Britain. Parliament—History—17th century.
4. Great Britain. Parliament—History—17th century—Sources. 5. Charles II, King of
England, 1630–1685. I. Title.
    DA445.P33 2008
    942.06'6—dc22
                                                                                2008015555

A catalogue record for this book is available from the British Library.
10 9 8 7 6 5 4 3 2 1

Table of Contents

❖

Acknowledgments

The Long Parliament of Charles II required the steepest learning curve of any book I have attempted. My greatest debt, indubitably, is to the Mellon Foundation, from which I received an Emeritus Fellowship, part of a wise project to keep scholars intellectually alive and productive after retirement. It was large and flexible enough to see me through a radical change of plan, a good long stay at the British Library and the Bodleian, and the acquisition of copies of many manuscripts too dense to read *in situ*. Supporting me at every step of the way were Berny Lytton, the Director of the Koerner Emeritus Center, and Patricia Dallai, the executive secretary of the Center, which also provided a spacious office, computer support, and tea and sympathy. As a result, the book came together almost painlessly (until time came for the index, always a nightmare in the terrain of early modern parliamentary history, with all those names!)

But I could not possibly have managed that steep learning curve without the help of and instruction by a group of real historians, who took me under their wing. First, Paul Seaward, who with amazing generosity encouraged me to continue from where his *Cavalier Parliament* left off, found me the magnificent Tillemans painting, and read the entire manuscript with scrupulous care. Second, Kevin Sharpe, who actually read it twice, and made smart suggestions for reorganization and expansion, which led to a bigger and better book. Third, Mark Knights, who not only sent me his own list of manuscript newsletters, and his own notes on them, but also allowed me to test the book's hypothesis at the University of East Anglia. And fourth, Tim Harris, who shared his views of Charles II with me, and negotiated for me a pre-publication sight of Roger Morrice's *Entring Book*. Without these four historians, I might still be floundering.

Their truly substantial and selfless help was supplemented by that of Steven Pincus, now happily my colleague, who has brought the Restoration back into sharp focus; Nicholas von Maltzahn, whose brilliant edition of

Marvell's *Account of the Growth of Popery* I depend on, and who generously sent me his own copy of Daniel Finch's long newsletter to his uncle describing the 1677 session; Martin Dzelzainis, who shared his work on Restoration censorship; and Georgianna Ziegler, Head of Reference at the Folger Shakespeare Library, who introduced me to the Newdigate letters. Oliver Arnold's book on Shakespeare and parliament suddenly brought into focus the rule of secrecy of debate, which increasingly became unenforceable. Gabrielle Spiegel read the entire manuscript, which is way out of her medieval historian's territory, with enthusiasm and historiographical acumen. Claude Rawson supplied information about James Ralph. And Laura Seitveit Miles spared me footwork and hours of downloading the texts of manuscripts.

It is customary at this point to say that any flaws and errors that remain are my own. Of course they are. But I hope that my readers will care less about those they discover than about this new account of the second Long Parliament and the fresh approach to documentation it exhibits. The book was a pleasure to write; may it speak to the spirit of collaborative scholarship, once known as the republic of letters.

❖

Abbreviations

Account	Andrew Marvell, *An Account of the Growth of Popery and Arbitrary Government in England* ("Amsterdam," 1677)
BL	British Library
CJ	*Journal of the House of Commons*
CSPD	*Calendar of State Papers Domestic*
CSPV	*Calendar of State Papers, Venetian*
Collection 1776	*A Collection of King's Speeches* (London, 1776)
Dering 1	Basil Duke Henning, ed., *The Parliamentary Diary of Sir Edward Dering 1670–1673* (New Haven, 1940)
Dering 2	Maurice Bond, ed., *The Diaries and Papers of Sir Edward Dering* (London: HMSO, 1976)
Grey, *Debates*	Anchitell Grey, *Debates of the House of Commons 1667–1694*
HMC	Historical Manuscripts Commission
LJ	*Journal of the House of Lords*
Life	*The life of Edward Earl of Clarendon . . . in which is included a continuation of his History of the Grand Rebellion. Written by himself*, 2 vols (Oxford, 1857)
P&L	*Poems and Letters of Andrew Marvell*, ed. H. M. Margoliouth, 3rd edn. rev. Pierre Legouis, with the collaboration of E.E. Duncan-Jones, 2 vols. (Oxford, 1971)
POAS	*Poems on Affairs of State: Augustan Satirical Verse, 1660–1714*, vol. 1, ed. George de F. -Lord (New Haven, 1963)

PART ONE

METHODS AND SCOPE

❖

Introduction

It seems both proper and improper to begin with an image: the gorgeous representation of the House of Commons in session created by the Dutch painter Peter Tillemans in 1709 or 1710, as reproduced on the cover and as the frontispiece of this book. This was one part of a two-part commission, the pendant to a painting of Queen Anne in the House of Lords. I think we may therefore assume it was a royal commission. It is improper here because anachronistic. Yet the anachronism is forced upon me by the fact that no visual representation exists of any Restoration parliament, despite the efflorescence of images—of the king, his ministers, his mistresses—during this era. Is it only coincidence that historians have similarly left rather a large slice of Restoration parliamentary history blank? The Tillemans image is proper here, on the other hand, because its style, halfway between court painting and Dutch realist genre painting, gives us a more human sense of what it would have been like to sit in St. Stephen's Chapel in the late seventeenth century (even after Sir Christopher Wren's renovations had added the galleries and so reduced the crowding) than do the other, often-reproduced images of the early House of Commons, with their formidable rows of black hats and indecipherable faces.[1]

Much energy has already been devoted to editing diaries and debates of the Jacobean and Caroline parliaments, which have intense pertinence to our own debates about what caused the civil war of the mid-century. It is now time to move on to the Restoration parliaments, which have not hitherto seemed to carry such causal or constitutional weight. But honorable spadework has been done. The labors of scholars who contributed biographies of members to Basil Henning's *House of Commons 1660–1690*; the digitalization of the official parliamentary journals and Grey's *Debates*; and the deciphering and editing of Pepys's *Diary* and Roger Morrice's *Entring Book*—all have made available, even to non-specialists, mountains of material just waiting for interpretation, for the yet larger picture to be built around them. Meanwhile, there is still gold to be found in unpublished manuscripts. The fact that the reigns of the last two Stuarts have not been nearly so controversial in our time as those of the first two means, happily, that not every stone has yet been turned over—including the question of whether members of the Commons in the 1670s still wore their hats when seated, whereas according to Tillemans they had abandoned the practice by the early eighteenth century. Was Tillemans accurate? This is one of the many facts we don't yet have at our disposal.

This book focuses on what came to be known, even to itself, as the Long Parliament of Charles II. This parliament sat for eighteen years, without a general election, from 1661 to January 1679, and by 1675 it was already thought to be superannuated by many observers and some of its own members. The story of this Long Parliament has not yet been fully told. It is not a success story, either from the perspective of the king and his ministers or of the various ideological groups and factions that made up the membership of both Houses, especially the House of Commons. But later, in the eighteenth century, when its history was reconstructed and published, this Long Parliament came to be thought extremely important, not only in helping to bring about the replacement of James II by William III, but in resurrecting principles of royal accountability and parliamentary initiative that had been rendered unrespectable, for many, by the first Long Parliament.

I mentioned "non-specialists," and I must place myself in that category, as neither a parliamentary historian nor a historian proper. I got some practice for the job, however, in writing *Reading Holinshed's Chronicles* (1994), a book that challenged the then current historiographical assumptions about that late Elizabethan monument. Working on Andrew Marvell, particularly for the Yale edition of his *Prose Works*, locked me firmly into the Restoration era, and, given Marvell's long career as a member of the House of Commons, brought me to realize that a modern narrative of the parliament in which he served was overdue. Marvell's name will often appear in this study, but not, I hope, in excess of his importance.

Sometimes called the "Cavalier Parliament," sometimes the "Pensionary Parliament," this remarkable assembly was definitively called "The Long Parliament of Charles II," in conscious analogy to that of Charles I, by Wilbur C. Abbott, who wrote two long articles under that title in the *English Historical Review* in 1906. The only other major studies of this parliament, by D.T. Witcombe and Paul Seaward respectively, shortened their view. Witcombe called his book *Charles II and the Cavalier House of Commons*, and stopped the story in 1674.[2] This was understandable for a book that began as a dissertation, but it had the unfortunate effect of giving a more optimistic picture, at least from the crown's perspective, of this period of parliamentary history than is sustainable; for by not tackling the longest and most contentious session, of 1677,

Witcombe obscured the larger drama whereby a parliament that had begun in joyful subservience to the restored monarch became increasingly alienated and obstinate, not just in its unwillingness to grant him money.

This is even truer of Paul Seaward's extremely detailed study,[3] which restricted itself to the period dominated by Edward Hyde, earl of Clarendon, as chancellor. The period of Clarendon's management was marked by more or less congenial relations between king and parliament and, although there were struggles over money, Charles at least assumed that the system could be made to work. By 1673, however, when Thomas Osborne, later earl of Danby, first took over the management of the nation's finances, the Long Parliament was already questioning the royal prerogative in foreign policy. In 1677, in one of the longest sessions of the reign, the parliamentary Opposition, well enough defined to be called such today, actually managed to prevent Charles from aligning himself definitively with France. This session laid the psychological ground for what would be its greatest (though failed) challenge to the crown, an assault on the assumed succession of James, duke of York.

Of course, other major historians of the Restoration have addressed the subject of this parliament, but not as their exclusive focus, and not from its beginning to its end. Steven Pincus's *Protestantism and Patriotism* dealt in some detail with the sessions that authorized and then berated the conduct of the Second Dutch War, from 1664 to 1667.[4] His focus, however, was primarily on England's changing relations with the Dutch Republic and the newly imperial France of Louis XIV. Tim Harris, in *Restoration: Charles II and his Kingdoms*, not only took a broader, "three-kingdoms" approach, but in the case of England began his story with the Exclusion Crisis parliaments.[5] Both, interestingly, believed that the Restoration regime was in serious danger of collapsing *because* of parliamentary resistance to royal policy. Pincus saw this point reached in 1667–68, Harris in 1679–80. My own conclusion is that there were several such crises: 1673–74, 1675, and especially 1677–78.

The parliamentary sessions of the 1670s were, naturally, an important aspect of John Spurr's *England in the 1670s: "This Masquerading Age"* (Oxford, 2000), but, as its subtitle suggests, this book requires parliament to compete not only with social and cultural views of the decade, but with the inference that the institution itself was a form of masquerade. According to Spurr, "not even the most prosaic political dispute of this period . . . could be taken at face value. At times almost everyone seems to have been dissembling" (p. 2). However intriguing this thought, it tends to devalue the constitutional issues of the day, which were large; the risks members of parliament took to promote causes in which they believed or to stymie designs they suspected; and, more prosaically still, the hours and hours of patient sitting, drafting, amending, recording, and reporting to which Spurr's parliamentary chapters bear witness.

A new study of the whole of this Long Parliament is therefore worth undertaking, if only to finish a story partially told. But it is also time to *re-evaluate* the whole period—and this phase of the institution. By the dissolution in January 1679 it was clearly superannuated, but was it a disgrace? If so, by what standards? If we continue to call it the Cavalier Parliament (as does the excellent new edition of Roger Morrice's *Entring Book*), do we distort its later behavior, when the balance of opinion had shifted so as to produce quite different voting patterns? What would we have *wanted* it to do, and whom do we mean by "we"? And what would "we" mean by calling either the Long Parliament, or the Restoration itself, either a success or a failure?

Witcombe saw "success" from the king's perspective, and saw it as alternating continually with failure. Thus a series of his chapter headings reads as follows: "The Dominance of the Opposition"; "The Failure of the 'Undertakers' "; "The Cavaliers to the Rescue"; "The Dominance of the Court"; "The Court in Decline." The last chapter is entitled "Danby's Hopeless Quest." Had he continued to the dissolution, Witcombe's last chapter could have been called "The Royal Bull Survives to Fight Again." For Abbott, a Whig historian if ever there were one, it was the successes of the Opposition, not the recovery of Charles II and the Tory reaction, that marked the period as positive: "The king gave up his catholic and French policy and lived within his means; his opposition to Holland was abandoned with the marriage of William and Mary; his extravagance was curtailed, his army disbanded" (p. 284). More radical still was Abbott's conclusion:

> Not much of the real history of the time is to be found in the courtier memoirs on which so much stress has been laid. That . . . lies in the parliament and especially in the growth of the opposition in the commons; [which] leads one more and more to the conviction that the Revolution of 1688 was, as to its date, an accident, and that some such movement might well have come at any time in the preceding fifteen years. (p. 285)

Seaward's and Witcombe's versions, conversely, can now be recognized as a form of revisionist history, which during the second half of the twentieth century de-emphasized—indeed, tried to do away with—the concept of an Opposition, or of Court and Country parties, replacing it with the fluctuation of temporary alliances and selfish motives. Seaward was explicit in his revisionary aims, and hoped that Restoration history would "shortly end up being contested between the same two camps that have battled over the early Stuart ground"(p. 3). This is a historiographical disagreement rather than an ideological one, but beneath it may run an ideological undercurrent. Do "we" in fact believe that the Restoration was desirable, or simply the only possible outcome after the collapse of the Protectorate, and hence a necessary evil? At one extreme, Pincus, Harris, and myself clearly believe that if it was a failure, it was deservedly one, because the premises on which it was built—the "reconstruction of the old regime," and the attempt to consolidate the power of the king and the Anglican church—were reactionary, and revealed as such in the period 1681–88. At the other extreme, there may be (and why should there not be?) historians who themselves are Anglican royalists.

The point at which the historiographical and the ideological converge is over the issue of party. Witcombe found himself constantly having to deploy the terms "Court" and "Country" despite not believing in them as party identifiers. One reason for this is that those who reported on the doings of the Long Parliament constantly mentioned the existence, or reappearance, of parties, though the nomenclature of Whig and Tory was an invention of the 1680s. For Andrew Marvell they were clearly divided into Court and Country in 1667 in the debate over the excise. For Gilbert Burnet, those distinctions surged in 1671 as a result of the attack on Sir John Coventry. For Sir John Reresby they were equally in evidence in February 1677, and he had to be tutored by Danby and the king himself as to what he should think of them.

And then there are the facts. The fact that Shaftesbury and Buckingham deserted the king in 1675 and began to work against him; the fact that some of the most notable leaders of the Opposition in the Commons, Sir Richard Temple, Sir Robert Howard, Edward Seymour, Sir Robert Carr, and Sir Frescheville Holles, went over to the Court side in 1670, a conversion or desertion widely reported; the fact that Sir Thomas Littleton was temporarily bought out of opposition by being made treasurer of the navy, returning even more strongly to the offensive when he lost that post—all these facts demonstrate both the power of self-interest and that there were two well-defined interest groups. That men changed sides proves that there were sides to be changed.[6] Even the rectangular geography of St. Stephen's Chapel encouraged the practice of referring to "sides" of the House, and later the assumption that government supporters would sit on the Speaker's right, their opponents on the left. That this was frowned on proves that it happened.

We might also need to reconsider how the story of this Long Parliament has been told. Modern historiography favors a chronological narrative, at least for political and institutional history. Proper historians take for granted that their task is to produce such a narrative by way of effective summary, with the sources, for the sake of efficiency and clarity, relegated to footnote references, which they prefer procedurally curt and sometimes bundled. They are trained to believe that the more shorthand references to archival sources they can list, the more reliable their histories will be; the range of acquaintance is dazzling, but sometimes has the effect of a large cocktail party. No sooner have these witnesses been introduced than we forget their names.

A different strategy, which has certain affiliations with cultural history, is to make the sources themselves the center of the story: that is, to focus on how the history of the parliament was recorded at the time, who said and wrote what, and how much of what they said and wrote was made public, as distinct from being accessible only in major research libraries or local archives. I call this "how we got parliamentary history," the title of my last chapter, which shows that eighteenth-century historians played a crucial role in that process. Using fewer sources, and getting to know them better, may help us to answer the questions posed above. We need to hear the *voices* of those who observed the Long Parliament, and to recognize a voice requires that we hear it often— and sometimes at some length. Proper historians distrust long quotations. Someone with my training cannot do without them.

But in choosing one's sources for such special attention one must be extra-careful not to privilege those whose sympathies one happens to share. Here is one contemporary account of the history of the Long Parliament, which starts only at 1672, but is otherwise wide-ranging:

[After the Restoration] and then for 12 yeare more, we lived in peace plenty and happinesse above all nacions of the world.

But this blessing was too great to be continued long to those who deserved it so ill as we, and then the nacion began to thinke that the court enclined to favour poperie and France, grounding their suspicion upon:

1. The declaracion coming out about this time for laying aside all the penal lawes in matters of religion.[7]
2. The second warr made with the Dutch in conjunction with France, there being no sufficient visible cause to provoke us to it.[8]
3. The departing from the Triple League, which seemed so honourable and so advantageous to England.[9]
4. The connivance at the Jesuits and priests, who did abundantly swarme in the Kingdome, and even about the Court.
5. The conference between the King and his sister, Madam, the Dutchess of Orleanse, at Dover, the cause of meeting and the matter there debated and resolved on being kept very secret.[10]
6. The imploying of severall known or suspected papists in great places of trust, especially Lord Clifford made High Treasurer.[11]
7. Lastly to these and much more than all these together was the Duke of York's being first suspected and afterward universally believed to be a papist, which gave no unreasonable foundacion to feare that the King

> having no children, when the Duke should come to the crowne the protestant religion would be at least opprest, if not extirpated.
>
> [8] . . . the falling of almost all gentlemen's rents since [the] Dutch war (whatsoever the occasion of that . . .) put very many men out of humour.

Contrary to what one might immediately conclude, this summary was *not* written by a member of the Opposition group in the Commons. It *could* have been written by Andrew Marvell, whose *Account of the Growth of Popery and Arbitrary Government,* published illegally in 1678, it resembles in its hints of conspiracy, especially in its reference to the secret clauses in the Treaty of Dover. Its anti-Catholic bias is even stronger than Marvell's in the *Account,* already shocking to Marvell's modern admirers. This overview was, however, written by a loyal servant of the administration, Sir Edward Dering, who was elected to parliament in 1670 and from 1673 was part of the inner circle of Treasurer Danby. Dering entered this damning retrospect not in his parliamentary diary, which he kept from the beginning of his service in the House but abandoned in 1675, but rather in his personal "account book," which is part autobiography.[12] It is dated Tuesday, April 5, 1681, and thus extends beyond the Long Parliament's dissolution, which is noted in the account book on the day it happened, Friday, January 23, 1679.

An entry made three days later, but presented as a continuation of the overview, summarizes the "discovery" of the Popish Plot and what followed, the efforts of the Whigs in the Commons to exclude the duke of York from the succession. Referring to the spate of anti-Catholic legislation that was motivated by the so-called Plot, Dering wrote:

> And some of these lawes came to be enacted, others were lost by the frequent prorogacions and dissolucions which we have lately seen. And since Christmass 1680 to this day, which is but a yeare and a quarter, we have seen fower parliaments dissolved. And the last three plainly upon the single point of having a bill to exclude the Duke of Yorke from succeeding to the crowne, which the Commons have 3 times insisted upon, but the Lords once rejected, and the other times we were dissolved before it came up to them. In the meane time the King of France increaseth dayly at sea and on land. (p. 127)

Although he was here speaking of the history of the short parliaments that rapidly succeeded it, Dering put his finger on the feature that most characterized the Long Parliament, the frequent prorogations by means of which Charles II manacled it whenever it seemed intransigent. In Chapter 2 we will see, step by step and blow by blow, how this manipulation occurred.

One does not to have add much to Dering's overview to get a summary view of the Long Parliament's trajectory. It began in national euphoria at the Restoration and, literally, with the restoration of almost all the features of the earlier Stuart governments: a bicameral parliament with a full block of bishops, and a powerful established Protestant church with its original prayer-book and liturgy. Money for the king's lavish maintenance and to pay his debts was granted generously, with a substantial majority of cavaliers in the Commons, and parliament carefully managed by the earl of Clarendon, the king's old advisor from the days of exile. The first big mistake was the Second Dutch War, embarked on with a good deal of flag-waving, supposedly to improve trade, though the costs far exceeded any gains. That mistake cost Clarendon his chancellorship, and so ended the first period of the Long Parliament as covered by Seaward.

Between the Second and the Third Dutch Wars, the Third being that for which Dering could see "no visible cause," management of parliament fell to the group nicknamed the "Cabal," the five Privy Councilors whose initials spelled that word: Clifford, Ashley (later earl of Shaftesbury), Buckingham, Henry Bennet, earl of Arlington, and John Maitland, duke of Lauderdale, the Scottish minister with mysterious influence in England. The era of the Cabal was made incoherent by internal disagreements between these men, and parliament had already been rendered suspicious by the mismanagement of the war. Two topics dominated debates in the Commons: control of religious dissent, and financial Supply, the technical term for revenue granted to the crown by parliament. How much of either was really necessary? By 1672, when Sir Edward Dering began his overview, a third major topic had arisen to create tensions between the king and his parliament: fear of France as an aggressive military power, and suspicion of Charles's Francophilia. The new war, with England as an ally of France against Holland, was an even bigger mistake and another financial catastrophe. When England withdrew from it in 1674, France remained a serious threat, and England was still supplying Louis XIV with troops, against the will of the Commons.

By 1673 the third major cause outlined by Dering for the growth of suspi-cion of royal policy—the problem of the succession—was on most people's minds, not least because the duke of York had remarried, with the Catholic duchess of Modena. The Commons vehemently protested this marriage, of course to no avail. By 1677 the concern about how to deal with Protestant Dissenters had, in the view of the Commons, been surpassed by concern about what they called "the growth of popery," which really meant the duke's status as heir apparent and suspicion of the king's deals with Louis XIV. The only leverage the Commons had was their control over the country's purse strings, and, as Dering indicated in his last item, country gentlemen like

himself were feeling those purse strings tightening. But the king held the ultimate weapon—his power to prorogue or adjourn parliament at will, a power
he used both for strategic and disciplinary purposes.

In the chapters that follow, we will watch how these tensions emerge and play
out, not, as I have said, by summary of events from 1661 to 1679, though
Chapter 2, "Why Did the Long Parliament Last So Long?" will provide a
working chronology. Chapter 1 will explain in detail what are the best sources
for the kind of history here attempted. These range from the royal speeches
delivered at the opening and closing of sessions, through diaries and journals,
memoirs, newsletters, manuscript satires, and what I call "scofflaw" pamphlets
retailing a section of parliamentary proceedings. Chapters 3 ("The King's
Speeches"), 4 ("The Memoirists"), and 5 ("Scofflaw Pamphlets") will show how
lively parliamentary history looks when different voices are played off against
each other. In Part Three, we will turn to narratives of the most important
sessions. Chapter 6, "Parliament and the Control of Religion," will cover the
first section of the Long Parliament, the part that preceded Dering's overview
and culminated in the king's notorious Declaration of Indulgence in 1672 and
its consequences. Chapter 7 will reintroduce two names featured in this
Introduction, Sir Edward Dering and Andrew Marvell, taking a much closer
look at how differently they recorded the fourteenth session of spring 1675,
when things were going rather more rapidly downhill as a result of the Third
Dutch War. This brings us chronologically to the last downward sweep of the
Long Parliament, which accelerated in 1677 after the notorious Long
Prorogation, and will be described at considerable length in Chapter 8,
"Foreign Policy." Chapter 9 will deal with the events that led to the dissolution
of the Long Parliament, including the Popish Plot.

Finally, Part Four and Chapter 10 will turn to the question of "How We
Got Parliamentary History," a process that involves the role of eighteenth-
century historians. Here we will pay special attention to a source I use
throughout, the debates recorded in shorthand by Anchitell Grey from 1667
onwards, and which were fortuitously published in 1763, with important
annotations. This chapter will argue that the editing and publishing of Grey's
Debates is connected to the production of Richard Chandler's *History and
Proceedings of the House of Commons*, which appeared in multiple volumes from
1741 to 1744, and which we now treat, especially since its appearance online,
as an authoritative document. In fact, the first section of *History and Proceedings*,
chronologically speaking (though it was not the first published), was the work
of James Ralph, whose *History of England* was evolving concurrently, and
whom Chandler enrolled to handle the reigns of the last two Stuarts. It was
Ralph, I shall argue, who edited Grey's *Debates*, and annotated it in such a way
as to bring it into the terrain of Whig historiography, as represented by Wilbur

Abbott's benign and hopeful account of the Long Parliament's long-term significance.

Nothing has been said so far about the House of Lords, and indeed, except for one or two very dramatic moments, the history of the Long Parliament of Charles II, as told here, is a history of the Commons. This book should be read side by side with Andrew Swatland's *The House of Lords in the Reign of Charles II* (Cambridge, 1996), essential information for understanding the process by which that House reconstituted itself after its years of nonexistence from 1649 to 1660. But those dramatic moments—the battle against Danby's Non-Resisting Bill in 1675, and the protests against the Long Prorogation in 1677—will also have their representation here, through the voices of those who insisted we should remember them. The era was also marked by a series of unproductive quarrels between the two Houses over their privileges and jurisdictions, technically well explained by Swatland. And there were other signs of governmental malaise: fractiousness, personal attacks, libels distributed, members of both Houses imprisoned, scuffles on the floor or the steps of parliament—we have heard of such things, haven't we? The official Journals tried to delete them, but thanks to our human recorders they were not entirely successful. They are as valuable as the votes in giving us a sense of group psychology, which is what, along with a reliable narrative, a history of parliament ought to be able to deliver.

❖

CHAPTER 1

Recorders

Sir John Coventry's Nose

Towards the end of December 1670 the House of Commons were debating how to raise a subsidy, at the king's request, of about £800,000. Among the somewhat desperate suggestions as to where this money might be found was one by Sir John Coventry, at this stage a royalist, but young and politically unschooled. Coventry suggested a tax on the theaters, at which a member of the Court party, Sir John Berkenhead, demurred, on the grounds that the king got much pleasure from the players. Coventry then asked provocatively whether the king's pleasure came more from the men or the women players. That summer Nell Gwyn, the actress, had given birth to the king's son, christened Charles and later to be made first duke of St. Albans. During the Christmas recess Coventry was attacked in the street by a group of royal guardsmen, who slit his nose and would probably have injured him more seriously had they not been interrupted. From this point onwards, Coventry became an active member of the Opposition.

We owe our knowledge of this dramatic scandal, theatrical in more senses than one, to the several recorders who believed that what went on in parliament needed to be recorded by whatever unofficial means were available, not least because it was, or should be, of national interest. Anchitell Grey, who was busily recording debates at this time, gives a fairly full account of the response by the Commons to this attack on one of their members. Thanks to Grey, we know that when the House reassembled after the Christmas break it postponed all further discussion of subsidies and instead turned, in fury, to what came to be called Sir John Coventry's Bill, aimed at preventing, by threats of severe punishment, any further acts of street violence directed at MPs.[1] Grey, however, did not mention what gave rise to the attack. For this, we must turn, first, to the illegal newsletters of John Starkey, who on December 24 is its first reporter: second, to Sir Edward Dering, whose *Diary* filled in the Commons debates on the incident on January 10–12; third, to the personal letters of Andrew Marvell, who wrote a colorful account to his nephew William Popple on or about January 24; and finally to Gilbert Burnet's *History of His Own Time*, a retrospective chronicle of the era which delights in gossip. Eventually, when Grey's *Debates* was published in the mid-eighteenth century, its editor, whose identity will be revealed later in this book, inserted into the footnotes to the debates on Sir John Coventry's Bill the story that makes those debates properly intelligible, which he took from Marvell's personal correspondence, published in 1726 in Thomas Cooke's edition of Marvell's poetry. This act of editorial intervention is one of the later moments in my larger subject: How We Got Parliamentary History, as I put it, somewhat in the facetious manner of Sir John Coventry himself.

Forbidden History

The episode of Sir John Coventry's nose occurred about halfway through the Long Parliament, and, as we shall see later, caused one of several sharp downturns in relations between the two major groups within it, which for convenience, and despite the oversimplification involved, we will call the Opposition and the Court. The way it has come down to us, however, speaks to another major question of historiography than that observed in my Introduction. Apart from the very important business of deciding what interpretations of history on the grand scale we can infer from inspection of only a part of it, the story of the Long Parliament of 1661–79 is one that we need to recover because so much effort was made, by unofficial recorders, to preserve it. They were breaking the rules. There *were* no public accounts of what went on in parliament except the Journals of the two Houses, and anyone who has ever inspected these will have discovered how barren they are (in this period) of interest. There are no debates, or even traces of debates. In the Lords Journal the texts of the speeches given by the king and his premier minister at the opening of a session are almost always recorded. There are, of course, some (but not all) votes recorded, and the names of those who served on committees (which tells us a little about who felt strongly about an issue and *might* have spoken about it), and occasional punishments of members for misspeaking. When something occurred in either House that might have left a trace of disgrace, the Journals averted their eyes. When the Houses quarreled over the 1667 case of Thomas Skinner vs. the East India Company, the king himself commanded the records to be razed. When there was a fight on the floor of the Commons in May 1675 over a tied division, one reported by at least three informal sources, the Journal is silent both about the vote and the scuffle. A benign and slightly comic version of this self-censorship happened to the Lords Journal in the case of the four lords who spoke out against the illegality of the Long Prorogation in February 1677. On a motion by the earl of Huntingdon on November 13, 1680, their formal submissions, and even the names of those who requested permission to visit them in the Tower, were marked as canceled in the margin, and therefore appear in the printed Journal only as a series of asterisks. The motive in this case was to erase the disgrace attached to their imprisonment, now that power and moral authority had, in the light of the Popish Plot, temporarily passed to the Opposition.

Parliamentary history as we know it evolved in defiance of parliament itself. In the reign of Elizabeth I, as also of James I, the institution insisted obsessively on its own privacy, as Oliver Arnold has indisputably shown.[2] It therefore opened up a vast contradiction between its claim to be fully representative of the people of England and its refusal to let those constituents know what it was up to. Arnold insists that the discipline imposed by the Elizabethan parliament on its members was severe, resulting in the famous case of Arthur Hall, who had the temerity to publish speeches, and the theatrical punishment of a non-member who had intruded into the House out of curiosity. The first Long Parliament briefly considered opening its proceedings up to public view. In 1642 a committee was appointed to consider the best way "of divulging, dispersing and publishing the Orders and Votes, and also the Declarations of the House, through the Kingdom, and of the well and true printing of them."[3] But the matter seems to have rested there. Indeed, there is a precious moment in the *Diary of Thomas Burton*, on January 12, 1657, when MP Burton records being reproached by Luke Robinson for taking notes during a committee meeting:

> He told me had much ado to forbear moving against my taking notes, for it was expressly against the orders of the House. I told him how Mr. Davy took notes all the Long Parliament, and that Sir Symons D'ewes wrote great volumes; as well his own speeches as other men's. I said, "How should young men learn arguments without their notes," but I answered civilly. He said Mr. Solicitor Ellis was highly ruffed one time for taking notes, and was commanded to tear them in the face of the House. "It takes away," quoth he, "the freedom and liberty of men's speaking, for fear their arguments be told abroad."

The editor of Burton's *Diary* added in a footnote, "I am not aware of any order against taking notes," but cited orders against members giving information to the press of July 13, 1641 and March 22, 1642.

During the early years of the Restoration the official secrecy of parliamentary proceedings was regularly insisted upon. On June 25, 1660, the Commons voted "That no person whatsoever do presume, at his peril, to print any votes or proceedings of this House, without the special leave and order of this House." This order was published by Henry Muddiman in *Mercurius Publicus* for June 21–28. In 1666, the Commons ordered that only members of parliament should be allowed access to the Journal books, and leave was given to bring in a bill "for punishment of such Members as shall make Misrepresentations abroad of what doth pass in the House."[4] It was, of course, taken for granted that MPs should be able to inform their constituents, in private letters, about important votes, prorogations, and especially new taxes. Andrew Marvell's letters to Hull are indicative of this practice.

If the publication of votes was prohibited, a greater inhibition still prevented the recording and publication of who said what in debate, because both Houses, but especially the Commons, were so jealous of their privilege of free speech. Technically, this was for their protection. They did not wish to be held accountable outside the walls of Westminster for what they had said inside. In practice, the ears that they most feared belonged to the king, though everything that was said was readily carried to those ears by eager courtiers anyway. When Charles II himself broke the rules by attending debates in the Lords in April 1670, some were horrified, but Gilbert Burnet reported that members came not only to accept but also to welcome his presence:

> At first the king sat decently on the throne, though even that was a great restraint on the freedom of debate; which had some effect for a while: though afterwards many of the lords seemed to speak with the more bold-ness, because, they said, one heard it to whom they had no other access but in that place; and they took the more liberty, because what they had said could not be reported wrong.[5]

Despite a brief flurry of publishing both votes and debates at the time of the Exclusion Crisis in 1680, the prohibition quietly came back into force in the reign of James II, and persisted till the middle of the eighteenth century, when it was firmly upheld by the great Speaker of the Commons, Arthur Onslow. It was finally removed in 1771, as a result of an overt challenge by John Wilkes and John Almon. But a prohibition is not a taboo. On the contrary, it asks to be defied, and it was so defied at the time. Technically, the prohibition extended only to parliaments that were still sitting. Once dissolved, their proceedings were fair game. But a parliament that remained sitting, however sporadically, for eighteen years represented an extreme form of provocation. The Long Parliament of Charles II was increasingly well reported as its longevity became more and more of an issue. Here are some of the main sources for its history to which we can now turn.

Newsletters

We know that there was an insatiable desire for news in this period. In small part this was met by the official printed newsletters, especially the *London Gazette*, which was controlled by the office of Secretary of State Joseph Williamson and produced by his clerks. Beginning its existence in 1665 as the *Oxford Gazette*, when the king and parliament moved to that city on account of the plague and it was thought dangerous physically to handle newsprint from London, the paper soon returned to the capital and changed its name accordingly. It is a commonplace that the *Gazette* offered very little domestic news, and only such as would be acceptable to the king and his council. It restricted itself to military campaigns, the arrivals and departures of diplomatic figures, notifications of treaties, state funerals, royal hunting trips, etc. Its mission was to make the king look good.[6]

Actually its remit was a little more complicated than that, especially with regard to parliamentary proceedings, in which area it was constrained not only by parliament's own embargoes, but also by the king and Privy Council. In the first few years of the reign it would, in a final brief section marked "Whitehall," report prorogations and resumed sittings, and lists of public bills that Charles signed off. In 1667, it evidently overstepped its bounds. After a brilliant account of the Dutch attack on the Medway it reported on July 29 the king's sudden proroguing of the emergency session called for July 25. The recall was a tactical mistake, made against Clarendon's advice, as was the decision to postpone the king's appearance until the 29th, which gave time for leaders of the Opposition to pass a motion, *nemine contradicente* (unanimously), demanding that the troops be disbanded now that peace seemed imminent. When Charles appeared on that Monday he delivered an extremely curt speech that was ill-received.[7] The *Gazette* (No. 178), however, reported that "he was pleased after a Gracious Speech to prorogue them till the tenth of October." When parliament then met, the *Gazette* also, amazingly, reported on October 15 the text of the Commons' Address thanking him for that disbanding, as well as for removing Clarendon from office! Thus mistakes at the top were too well publicized. Never again (with one tiny exception)[8] did the *Gazette* report an Address by the Commons, though it made space for several of the king's speeches or messages (Nos. 234, 410, 1269, 1273, and, never to be forgotten, 1203—the full text of his furious reproach to the Commons on May 28, 1677). On March 23, 1678, it published, up front, rather than at the end, the king's proclamation for recalling English men from foreign military service (No. 1290), a late salvo in the long-lasting disbanding dispute. Soon after that it would be drawn in to fight the king's battles against the Whig leadership on the issue of the duke of York's exclusion from the succession, publishing the full texts of the loyalty statements (also called Addresses) that came in from across the country to congratulate Charles on having disposed not only of the Long Parliament, but also of the three short Whig parliaments that followed it.

If the official newspaper of the reign was prevented from discussing parliamentary business, how else could the nation satisfy its legitimate curiosity on this subject? The answer was the scribal newsletter. This could take many forms, ranging from newsletters sent regularly from government offices to a list of subscribers,[9] to private newsletters sent to family members or friends abroad, at which point they overlap with the category of private correspondence. One distinguishing feature is whether the subscribers paid for this service. The most famous purveyor of scribal newsletters was Henry Muddiman, who for a brief period was employed by Williamson and Arlington to write the *Oxford Gazette*. Internecine struggles in the newsworld, however, caused him first to transfer his skills to Sir William Morice, the other secretary of state, and then to focus entirely on the scribal newsletter business, which made his fortune. An entire set of his newsletters is preserved at Longleat House. According to his descendant J.G. Muddiman, the earlier Muddiman had, at the Restoration and thanks to his tactical support of General Monck in his *Parliamentary Intelligencer*, been able to transfer his role as official journalist under the Council of State into that of the king's journalist. Significantly, in 1661 he changed the title of the *Parliamentary Intelligencer* to the *Kingdom's Intelligencer*. He acquired the privilege of free postage, and was allowed to announce his newsletters as being "From Whitehall." In exchange for this privilege he avoided "making comments in the letters which might be unacceptable to the Government, and he did not correspond with disloyal subscribers."[10] J.G. Muddiman claimed that in his scribal newsletters Henry Muddiman supplied the parliamentary news that the *Gazette* quickly learned to avoid; in any case, the general ban on reporting parliamentary material was impossible to enforce on scribal newsletters. But Muddiman's newsletters, sent to about 130 people, in fact gave only the baldest information about what went on in parliament.[11] It is probably significant that, while most of his subscribers were members of the nobility and gentry, and included several bishops, only one was a coffee-house.

At the other end of the scale of purveyors of newsletters was John Starkey, bookseller and publisher, who from 1667 to 1671 wrote weekly newsletters to Sir Willoughby Aston in Staffordshire, newsletters that, though not actually seditious, were certainly not interested in putting the government in the best possible light. Perhaps for that reason they have never been published.[12] There was a connection between Starkey and Grey (who happened also to be related to Aston by marriage)[13] that is worth noting here. It is thought that

Starkey got some of his information from Grey. On December 5, 1667, Starkey wrote to Aston a remarkable response to a request for back copies of the Commons Journal:

> Mr. Grey desired me to acquaint you that as for the Copy of the Journall books for these 30 last years it is not to be had for 100 ll. But for the present he recommends to you Mr. Rushworth's Collections, which he hath in manuscript continued downe to this time, and which in time will be printed. That volume that is already out is from 15 li. risen to be now worth 40. He sends you his service. (fol. 34)[14]

Such was the market for parliamentary history, especially, no doubt, in the country.

But the Starkey/Aston letters, which might have claimed the immunity of private correspondence, though Starkey was surely paid for them, are only the tip of an iceberg. The *Calendar of State Papers* for 1673–75 (p. 46) reports that a "Mr. Starky" was taken into custody for selling "certain votes of the last session of Parliament without license or authority" (p. 46). Selling votes does not mean bribery, but rather the unauthorized scribal publication of resolutions and the votes by which they passed or failed in the House of Commons. More precisely, Starkey's name is here linked with that of Francis "Elephant" Smith, a notorious scofflaw publisher. Coventry writes to one W. Bridgeman "requesting him to inform Lord Arlington that his Majesty is pleased that bail be taken for Smith but not for Starky." On December 18, 1673 Henry Ball wrote to Joseph Williamson that "Starkey the bookseller has again petitioned his Majesty, so that it's ordered he first give in bayle and then be sett at liberty, but the Attorney-General ordered to prosecute him."[15]

There is, however, a now famous memorandum by Thomas Osborne (soon to become Charles's chief minister and earl of Danby), written we know not to whom, but perhaps Lord Arlington, perhaps the king himself. This memorandum, published by Andrew Browning in his biography of Danby,[16] is really an extraordinary document of the book trade and the practice of scribal publishing, but its relation to the history of parliament has not yet been fully acknowledged:

> There are two booksellers shops (viz. John Sterkey's and Thomas Collen's, living neer Temple Bar) that poison both City and country with false newes.
> To these shops are sent every afternoon
>
> 1. All novells and accurrents so penned as to make for the disadvantage of the King and his affairs.

2. All resolutions of Parliament that are either voted or a[re] preparing for vote in either House, perfect true, or artificially corrupted, or penned by halves on purpose as may make most for the Faction.
3. All speeches of the most eminent members of each House that were affected, upon every business, are also sent them.
4. Addresses also intended and at any time preparing by either House are here to be had in copies.

All these are thus disposed as followeth.

To these shops, for those things, every afternoon do repair severall sorts of people.

1. Young lawyers of both the Temples and other Inns of Court, who here generally receive their tincture and corruption.
2. Ill-affected citizens of all sorts.
3. Ill-affected gentry.
4. The emissaries and agents of the several parties and factions about town.

Against the time of their coming the masters of those shops have a grand book or books, wherein are registred ready for them all or most of the forenamed particulars, which they dayly produce to those sorts of people to be read, and then, if they please, they either carry away copies or bespeak them against another day.

These take care to communicate them by letter all over the kingdome, and by conversation throughout the City and suburbs.

The like industry is used by the masters of those shops, who together with their servants are every afternoon and night busied in transcribing copies, with which they drive a trade all over the kingdom.

You may at present there have a copy of the intended address to his Majesty which the Houses have not yet agreed to.

Apparently Starkey and Collins were running a news factory with a strongly Oppositional bias. The last item in Danby's memorandum is particularly significant, indicating that Starkey and Collins were circulating the text of an "intended address" to the king still being negotiated between Lords and Commons. Browning tentatively dated this memorandum 1675, but there were no such bicameral Addresses in 1675. It is most likely to be from January 1674, soon after Danby became treasurer, and when both Houses were tensely debating the terms of a peace with Holland, one of the few occasions on which they sent up, eventually, a joint Address. As Lord Aungier wrote to the earl of Essex on January 31: "I suppose on Tuesday both Howses will agree on the manner of their Addresse, there having beene already inter-changeable messages sent to one another."[17] If Starkey had been let out on bail at the end of December, just in time for the new (thirteenth) session which convened on January 7, there would have been an especial bitterness in the last item in Danby's catalogue of mischiefs.

It is worth noting here that, as documents, the Addresses of the Commons to the king, and his answers, were always loaded. Every word mattered. The texts of Addresses were labored and fought over. The king's answers, enigmatic, reproachful, or downright scolding, were equally significant. But the king had the advantage that he could, if he wished (and he usually did), have his statements published. The Addresses of the Commons were supposed to remain confidential—a fact that the *Gazette* misunderstood in October 1667. Towards the end of the Long Parliament this had become a grievance. In his *Account of the Growth of Popery and Arbitrary Government*, which illegally reported the doings of the 1677 session, Andrew Marvell complained about the *Gazette*'s publication of the king's speech of reproof to the Commons, particularly since "none of their own transactions or addresses for the Publick Good are suffered to be Printed, but even all Written Copies of them with the same care as Libels suppressed" (p. 369).

Correspondence

Between Muddiman and Starkey there is, obviously, a huge motivational gap. That gap is filled in a most interesting way by a long series of newsletters (but in different hands) sent regularly to Sir Richard Newdigate in Warwickshire from the office of the secretary of state, beginning in January 1674 and contin-uing past Sir Richard's death in 1710. Sir Richard did not himself enter parlia-ment until 1681. He had difficulty getting elected, and his disappearance after the Oxford parliament and reappearance in 1689 indicate that his sympathies were Whig. He was therefore highly motivated in subscribing to a political newsletter, which he did from the age of thirty, and perhaps his wishes dictated the character of what he received. The Newdigate letters are preserved en masse at the Folger Shakespeare Library, and were helpfully transcribed online by Philip Hines, Jr. in 1994. Much of their content concerns foreign news and social events, such as the royal visits to the races at Newmarket, such as the race run on October 13, 1674, "between Black Buttocks the Duke of Albemarles Horse, & Nuttmeg a Horse of Mr. Framptons," which one might treasure for non-parliamentary reasons. But when parliament was in session, the letters contain remarkably full reports of proceedings in the Commons, evidently taken from the Journal, and *including* the texts of Addresses. Occasionally, the Newdigate letters report "extraordinary" events presumed to be of special interest to the recipient, and hence also to a modern reader who may tire of following the progress of ordinary bills. Thus an early item from the Lords (these are rare) reported that "At the takeing the Oath of allegiance [on January 15, 1673] . . . a question was started by the Earle of Shaftsbury whether or noe the D of Yorke ought to sit in the Prince of Wales's chaire which occasioned a Hot dispute, the Resolution whereof was referred to a farther debate" (L.c.3), a shocking glimpse of early exclusionist feeling. In terms of discretion, therefore, the Newdigate letters stand somewhere between Muddiman's (some of which are interspersed in this archive, because Newdigate subscribed to them as well) and those of the political gossip John Starkey. The most striking individual entry, however, is a hitherto-unnoticed copy of the Mock-King's speech of 1675, widely circulated at the time and later attributed to Andrew Marvell. We will return to this parody of the royal style in Chapter 3, but its inclusion in the Newdigate letters is a clue to the recipient's political sympathies.

There survive literally dozens of unofficial newsletters that *mention* parliament, usually, like the *Gazette*, because of its openings and closings, though the writers of such newsletters often express a view, optimistic or pessimistic, of such junctures. But there is an indistinct boundary between newsletters, written as such, and correspondence that happens to contain news. Modern historians make great use of letters written by or to members of the court or administration. And, indeed, for a history of the Long Parliament such letters are essential. They vary enormously, however, in pertinence and character, and the most valuable for this study are those that verge on the newsletter in purpose (sequentiality) and focus (parliamentary business), but with the bonus of evaluative commentary. Important examples of such that will be used in this study are, in ascending order of value:

1. A set of letters (BL Egerton 2539) by John Nicholas to his father, Sir Edward Nicholas, secretary of state, now retired to the country, but obviously keen to be kept informed. Nicholas wrote frequently from 1666 to 1669, when his father died, most frequently during the impeachment proceedings of Clarendon, which appalled him. Self-evidently private and personal, the Nicholas letters have a special kind of candor.
2. An extremely long letter by Daniel Finch, eldest son of Heneage Finch, the chancellor, to Sir John Finch, his uncle, giving an account of the proceedings of the Commons in the 1677 session after the Long Prorogation; partly, it seems, for his uncle's entertainment. This letter is valuable not only for the information it contains, but also for its speculations. Though he must have already identified with the Court party, Finch was detached enough at this stage to enjoy conspiracy theories.[18]

3. A slew of letters written by his employees to Sir Joseph Williamson, under-secretary of state under Henry Bennet, earl of Arlington. Arlington was plenipotentiary at Cologne in 1673–74 and Williamson accompanied him.[19] These are particularly valuable in giving, from multiple points of view, responses to the eleventh, twelfth, and thirteenth sessions of the Long Parliament, when matters began to go badly wrong as a result of the duke of York's remarriage.

4. Letters written to Arthur Capel, earl of Essex, vice-regent in Ireland from 1672 to 1679, keeping him up to date with how his management of that difficult country was being viewed at home, how the various court lords were arrayed for or against him, and particularly what role the English parliament was playing or likely to play. Partly edited (and where necessary deciphered) by Osmond Airy for the Camden Society, these letters give us yet another perspective on the history of the English parliament, since Essex's correspondents were not all of one mind.[20] When Essex was recalled in 1677, and the duke of Ormond took back his governorship, the letters, sometimes from the same people, continue. Thank goodness for Ireland, the third of the three kingdoms, would-be parliamentary historians might say, since its government necessitated a large and continuous flow of news in both directions.

5. Two very different sets of letters by Andrew Marvell, now both in print. The first, his almost daily reports to his constituents in Hull, with two significant gaps covers the period from the beginning of the first session in May 1661 to early July 1678, a month before he died; these letters function as would a political diary, but give only the results of debates and leave the writer's personal views unspoken. The second set, to friends and especially to his nephew William Popple, lacks strict sequentiality, though several are condensed newsletters in themselves. They are outspoken in their criticism of the king, the court, and also the House of Commons for what Marvell regarded as its spinelessness. The contrast between the two sets of letters, and the different motives that produced them, is part of what makes them so informative.[21]

Diarists and Parliamentary Reporters

"Diary" is a capacious and inexact term for some of the records that survive from this period. Its most familiar usage is in relation to the daily records of one's own life, no matter how trivial a day one has had. Our most famous example of this is, of course, the *Diary* of Samuel Pepys, who wrote, in cipher, daily accounts of his personal and professional life as clerk of the Navy Board.

These occasionally contain pertinent information about parliamentary matters, partly gathered from conversations with parliamentarians, and partly because Pepys was employed to defend the government's handling of the Second Dutch War and its deployment of the funds voted to support it. Pepys's famous *Diary* began on January 1, 1660, but ceased in 1669 apparently because he was losing his eyesight. He was much closer to parliament than was John Evelyn, another famous diarist of the era, and even became a member of the Commons in 1673, but the *Diary* ended well before that. Thereafter we can judge his views from the interventions he made in the Commons, several of which are well reported by Grey.

We also use the term "diary," however, to cover such disparate records as the "Diary of Colonel Bullen Reymes," a tiny manuscript volume (BL Egerton 2043) that briefly reports the daily business of the Commons from May 8, 1661 to February 4, 1662. There it stops, though Reymes remained in the Commons until his death, in 1672. He must have quickly tired of the meticulous, uninspired record he had created; as indeed he might, because those were uneventful months. Then there is the Commons *Diary* of John Milward, which he kept on a daily basis from September 1666 through early May 1668. Milward died in 1670, a year after his eldest son; old age and family tragedy rather than ennui were surely the cause of the diary's cessation. It remained in manuscript until it was published by Caroline Robbins in 1938. The Commons diary of Sir Edward Dering begins in November 1670, thereby taking over, as it were, from Milward, and runs to June 5, 1675, though Dering continued in parliament beyond the demise of the Long Parliament. His *Diary* was edited in two parts, the first by Basil Henning in 1940, the second by M.F. Bond in 1976.[22]

Both Milward and Dering were supporters of the court. Both evidently took ample notes of speeches in the House, but worked them over at the end of the day. Each named the speakers in a debate, and each occasionally gives a sense of what they "really" said. The impression created by these two "diaries" is markedly different from that of the work we now know as Grey's *Debates*, although Henning, in his preface to Dering's *Diary* (p. ix), refers to the *Debates* too as a political diary.

Anchitell Grey, as we know from Stuart Handley's article in the new *Dictionary of National Biography*, and from Edward Rowlands's in *The House of Commons 1660–1690*, was a Derbyshire gentleman elected as an MP for Derby in 1665. In 1667, he began to take shorthand notes of the debates in the Commons, probably because of the drama of Clarendon's impeachment over the handling of the Second Dutch War. Sketchy for the first few years—when published, the first volume could contain all of 1667 through 1672—by the time of the crucial sessions of 1677 and 1678–80, a year could fill an entire

volume. Perhaps Grey's shorthand skills improved. Perhaps his commitment
to the project intensified. The fact that he was taking notes was remarked on
at least once, by Sir Thomas Meres, who passed the information to Samuel
Pepys; and Grey may have contributed information to John Starkey for his
illegal newsletters, wherein he is twice mentioned; but nobody seems to have
interfered with his practice. He must have transcribed his notes into a continuous longhand record, almost certainly shortly after taking them.

Rowlands's analysis of Grey's parliamentary career in *The House of
Commons* shows modest committee activity, only a single recorded speech, and
certainly nothing one could describe as leadership. The chief value of his
service seems to have been its longevity, since this allowed him, and us, to have
a consistent view of the parliaments from Charles II, through James II, to
William III. The same speakers reappear over the long haul, speaking in ways
we have come to expect, or sometimes demonstrating remarkable changes of
position. The demise of major Court party figures—Clarendon, Danby,
Seymour—is played out as a story with all the features we associate with literature (hubris, surprise, choric assessment). The other value of Grey's record
as an MP is that he was, until after the Glorious Revolution, very seldom
absent. According to Rowlands, Grey "lacked the trained analytical mind of
[Lord] Somers and the access to the court caucus of Sir Edward Dering and
Daniel Finch," whom Rowlands saw as superior reporters of the era. But this
is to have decided in advance what one wants from a parliamentary historian.
What Grey was interested in was the verbal texture of debate and what it
revealed about character, both personal and political. Though Grey does not
reveal his partisanship explicitly, he is valuable to us as recording the interests,
in both senses of the word, of a Country party Whig, both in what speeches
he chooses to report in detail, and in what he decides to omit. It is precisely
that protocol that Rowlands disapproved of—recording speeches separately,
rather than combining them, as did Dering, into a rational and coherent
narrative of the day's events—that gives us today the true flavor of an early
modern parliament.

It is hard to determine at this distance the motives of these recorders.
Were they really just keeping a record for themselves, or were they supplying
others outside the House with crucial information? This question was raised
in relation to the diarists of the first Long Parliament, especially Sir Simonds
D'Ewes, by John Morrill when reviewing *The Private Journals of the Long
Parliament* published by Yale University Press in 1992. Morrill remarked
on both the brevity of Framlingham Gawdy's journal ("simply a degraded
version" of the official Journal of the House), and the uneven amplitude of
D'Ewes's. Morrill concluded that D'Ewes was "clearly writing for posterity,
not for his dotage or his kindred," and that his primary motive was to preserve

his own speeches, whether or not actually delivered.[23] This is damaging testimony about D'Ewes, but it chimes with the Restoration journal that has recently surfaced in the British Library, in two different manuscripts, created by Thomas Neale, a follower of Danby. Neale, it is said, created this record of the 1677 sessions as intelligence for his patron; but he undoubtedly also used it to showcase his own speeches, which are presented verbatim, whereas those of his colleagues in the Commons are only reported in brief.[24] It has been claimed by Caroline Robbins (though without evidence) that Milward was reporting to the earl of Devonshire, in which case the diary would have been the basis for a private newsletter. By 1674, Dering was reporting directly to Danby, with whom he became familiar. When Grey's *Debates* was published in 1763, the editor claimed that Grey had taken his notes "only for his own Use or Amusement." This might conceivably have been true.[25]

Towards the end of the Long Parliament's weary life another parliamentary reporter enters the scene, with a flourish now freshly created by a magnificent Oxford edition. Roger Morrice's *Entring Book* begins only on March 5, 1677, but continues until April 1691. It is therefore of vital interest to scholars of the reigns of James II and William III. Preserved at Dr. Williams's Library in London, the *Entring Book* was something of a lifework by a man who never himself sat in parliament, but became instead, as Mark Goldie has designated him, "the chaplain-journalist" successively to two important parliamentary figures, Denzil, Lord Holles, and Sir John Maynard. As one of the Nonconformist ministers ejected from the pulpits by the Act of Uniformity, Morrice naturally had strong sympathies, which included a rabid anti-Catholicism. Goldie devoted several pages of the introductory volume to discussion of the genre of the *Entring Book*, and hence Morrice's motives in creating it (and having it transcribed into prebound stationery volumes). While it seems to be addressed to someone else, rather than compiled for personal reference only, there would have been little point in Morrice informing Holles or Maynard of what went on in parliament, and Goldie finally leaves its purpose a mystery. Its value for this study is in showing how much of parliament's business could, by the last quarter of the century, in fact be accessed by a non-member who gathered his information in large part from conversations in Westminster Hall. Compared to the 1580s, parliamentary business was by this time proving impossible to seal off from public curiosity.

Memoirs

Different again are the writers for whom we have coined the term "memoirists," although sometimes the boundary between diary and memoir blurs. What the forms share, obviously, is a one-person view, usually expressed in the first person. A memoir, however, need not advance day by day. There were three men whose careers together spanned the entire Restoration era (and beyond) who deliberately set out to write memoir accounts of those careers, producing something larger than themselves. Those accounts, embarked on for other reasons, make important contributions to the history of the Long Parliament, provided we take into account the distorting effect of reminiscence, because personal evaluation is central to their tone and principles of selection. The first was, of course, by Clarendon: his *Life*, once separated out from his *History of the Rebellion*, contains fascinating material about the first seven years of our Long Parliament. The second was by Gilbert Burnet, later to be made bishop of Salisbury under William, whose *History of his own Time* is full of information about parliament that, since he was never a member, was somewhat mysteriously acquired. The third was by Sir William Temple, whose *Memoirs of what passed in Christendom from the War Begun in 1672 to the Peace Concluded 1679* became a major source for eighteenth-century historians. The war in question was that conducted by France against Holland, in which England was intermittently involved, on both sides, but Temple includes a number of useful remarks about the role of the House of Commons therein. These three memoirs, along with the frequently cited *Memoirs of Sir John Reresby*, who was a member of parliament from 1673 until 1688, were published in the early eighteenth century or, in the case of Temple's, the late seventeenth (1691). They are therefore in two respects—their content and the reason for their publication—part of the larger story of how we got parliamentary history, and they too will be the subject of a separate chapter.

The Scofflaw Pamphlets

If it was illegal to publish parliamentary votes, debates, and speeches (except, of course, those of the king and his chief minister at the opening or closing of sessions), it was by no means impossible. We now know a great deal about the machinery of illegal printing and marketing, ironically because Sir Roger L'Estrange, appointed surveyor of the press in 1662, was so indefatigable in trying to prevent the practice. We know the names of the equally indefatigable scofflaw printers and publishers—John Twyn, Simon Dover, Francis "Elephant" Smith, Thomas and Anne Brewster, Giles and Elizabeth Calvert, Thomas Ratcliffe, Nathaniel Ponder, John and Joan Darby, Nathaniel Thompson, Langley Curtis, Richard and Abigail Baldwin—in part from records of the searches of their presses conducted by members of the Stationers' Company, or from their examinations by L'Estrange or members of the Privy Council. These examinations seldom produced decisive results because the printers, distributors, and booksellers denied everything and were rarely caught red-handed. Successful trials (resulting in proven guilt) and imprisonment were unusual, still more so executions. On February 16, 1677, the House of Lords established a committee "to make enquiries as to the authors and printers of certain libellous pamphlets"; this sat till April 9, and heard a great deal of dead-end testimony, including complaints about inveterate night printing, and (from L'Estrange) information about a "factious majority" of the Stationers' Company "whose interest it is to free the press and hinder its regulation."[26] L'Estrange's 1663 *Considerations and Proposals in Order to the regulation of the Press* hopefully listed among the possible punishments "Death, Mutilation, Imprisonment, Banishment, Corporal Payns, Disgrace, Pecuniary Mulcts," to be meted out in proportion to the malice of the offense. He remarked that "for the Authors, nothing can be too Severe, that stands with Humanity, and Conscience. . . . There are not many of them in an Age, and so the less work to do." But for printers and stationers, he preferred fines or some "Marque of Ignominy . . . as one Stocking Blew, and another Red, a Blew Bonnet with a Red T or S. upon it, to Denote the Crime to be Either Treason, or Sedition" (pp. 32–33); an unintentionally carnival thought.

Most of this printing "in corners" was focused on the problems caused by the Dissenters. But during this Long Parliament there were several spates of scofflaw pamphlets specifically focused on proceedings in parliament. Darby in particular might be seen as *the* parliamentary printer of the 1670s, and his output can usually be recognized by its phony claims to have been printed in "Amsterdam." In the 1680s, he was joined as a Whig publicist by Richard Baldwin, who was responsible for publishing the Commons' debates at that critical moment.

The first four sessions were quiet on this front. When the Second Dutch War began to go badly, several satires appeared in the streets, reflecting, but only in passing, on how it had been financed. The most important of these, though we have no proof it was actually published, was the *Last Instructions to a Painter* by Andrew Marvell, written at the end of 1667 and containing a detailed account of the debates in the Commons on whether to rescue the war's financing by creating an excise tax. This poem named names and identified parties, and was one of the first documents to indicate that Court and Country parties had already come into existence, their members identifiable by name. At the same time someone put together, obviously for publication, *The Proceedings in the House of Commons, touching the impeachment of Edward, late earl of Clarendon . . . anno 1667. With the many debates and speeches in the House.* The names of speakers were partially concealed by abbreviation. So far as we can tell, this did not actually appear in print until 1700, by which time it had acquired a new and different pertinence.

The next scofflaw pamphlet consisted of a printed text of the famous speech by Lord John Lucas in the Lords, when the king was present, which argued against being too generous to him with Supply. The speech was delivered on February 22, 1671, a month after the Sir John Coventry fracas. But as Marvell wrote to William Popple, there were "[scribal] Copys going about every where" (*P&L*, 2:323), and the Lords voted it a libel, to be burned by the public hangman. In 1673, it appeared as a pamphlet, giving simply "London" as its place of origin, and featuring on its title-page a quotation from Juvenal's First Satire: "*Aude aliquid brevibus, Gyaris & Carcere dignum / Si vis esse aliquid / Probitas Laudatur & alget*" "If you wish to *be* anybody nowadays, you must dare some crime that merits narrow Gyara or a gaol; honesty is praised and left to shiver," ll. 73–74). A prefatory note to the reader explained the point of publication and praised the heroism of Lucas, who had died on July 2, 1671. The publisher added at the end "a short though not a full Account of the Mischief happened since this Speech," including the Stop of the Exchequer, the breaking of the Triple League, and the duke of York's marriage to the Catholic duchess of Modena. Thus Lucas's speech was not only preserved and publicized, but was meant to be seen as symbolic of the breakdown of both domestic and foreign policy; while the quotation from Juvenal made a generic suggestion about why certain eras produce satire.

It is important to distinguish between scofflaw pamphlets that merely protested at recent events and/or tried to influence future ones, and those that provided detailed information on parliamentary procedures that we otherwise would not have today. In the spring of 1673, for example, there was published in Holland and distributed in England a clever pamphlet by Peter du Moulin, *England's Appeale*, probably approved by William of Orange himself, and intended to let the English parliament know how the money it had granted was actually being deployed in the king's foreign affairs, and the dangers of the current alliance between England and France. Its contents were completely different, therefore, from those of two other pamphlets published in 1673, the brief *Votes and Addresses of the Honourable House of Commons . . . made this present year 1673, concerning Popery and other Grievances*, which reported the texts of the Commons' protests to the king about the Modena marriage and the upshot, the unruly prorogation of November 3; and the much longer *Relation of the most Material Matters handled in Parliament: relating to Religion, Property, and the Liberty of the Subject, With the answers unto such Addresses as were made unto his Majesty*. With their publicization of the Addresses, these pamphlets broke one rule. But the *Relation* also placed the parliamentary Addresses and the king's replies in a sardonic framework of analysis, culminating in an imaginary breakdown of how the moneys voted to the king had actually been spent, including the sums paid to individual courtiers or ladies of pleasure. This was not just a glance back at Roman satire, but the thing itself, with the offenders appearing under their real names.

In lieu of official "proceedings," scofflaw pamphlets returned with a vengeance in 1675 and 1677–78, and became so important that they deserve a chapter to themselves. Not the least part of their importance is that they provided crucial information for the eighteenth-century historians of parliament, notably Archdeacon Echard, who lacked access to the manuscript diaries available to modern scholars yet still managed to produce a reasonably accurate account of the trajectory of the Long Parliament.

The King's Speeches

There is to my knowledge no study of the role of the royal speech in the history of the second Long Parliament. Arthur Bryant's *Letters, Speeches and Declarations of King Charles II*[27] is essentially an anthology, placing selected speeches in context but in no way otherwise explaining or interpreting them. Bryant was more interested in the letters, as expressing the king's personality and unexpectedly fine literary style. But in this reign the royal speech that opened each session was an important statement of would-be royal policy, usually elaborated by a longer speech by the then chief minister, whether Clarendon, Bridgeman, Shaftesbury, or Heneage Finch. Almost inevitably it asked for money. When such a request was not included, there was policy behind its omission. The king's opening speeches and those of his ministers were often, though not always, printed. When they were not, there was usually some reason to wish them not widely disseminated. When delivered to both Houses, they were always recorded in the Lords Journal, where they stood in splendid isolation as the only matter of substance. Sometimes a copy was given to the Speaker of the Commons, so that members could debate the king's wishes and remarks with a text in front of them, so to speak. This was particularly important in 1668, when the king's speech was perceived to have two parts, one requiring a Supply, the other requesting some indulgence for Nonconformists. Thus the king's fiscal needs and his desire for some degree of toleration were formally recognized as being in conflict with each other in the view of the majority of the members of the Commons.

This whole matter is of such unexplored importance that it deserves a chapter of its own. But to give a foretaste, let us consider the speeches at the session in which Sir John Coventry made the dangerous remark that led to the attack on his nose. Parliament met according to the adjournment on October 24, 1670. The king made an extremely short speech asking for members' "kindness" and expressing his "value and love" for them. It was left to Orlando Bridgeman, the lord keeper, to explain what forms that kindness should take, including the funds for setting out a fleet that, "by estimate thereof, cannot cost less than eight hundred thousand pounds." However, he also enumerated the various leagues and treaties the king had recently entered into, including not only the Triple League but also "those Treaties now depending between His Majesty and France." It so happened that in the interval of the adjournment, in June, Charles had arranged with his sister, the duchess of Orleans, the secret terms of the Treaty of Dover, which would undermine the Triple League.

Both speeches were duly recorded in the Lords Journal. Andrew Marvell, writing to his Hull constituents on October 25, took the trouble to give them a very long summary of Bridgeman's speech, which he promises to send in full "if it be printed (there is some doubt of it)" (*P&L*, 2:110). On November 1, he wrote again: "The Kings & Keepers speeches were by order from the L. Arlington prohibited printing but you will nevertheless receive a written copy," i.e. a scribal copy. This was possible because Bridgeman's speech was "red again in the house," so that members could have acquired a copy from the Speaker. In a private letter to his nephew William Popple on November 28, Marvell told the story slightly differently: "Both Speeches forbid to be printed, for the King said very little, and the Keeper, it was thought, too much in his politic simple Discourse of foreign Affairs" (*P&L*, 2:318). Unaccountably, Witcombe states that Arlington's attempt to prevent the printing of this speech failed.[28] There is no trace of it among the separately *published* speeches of Charles during this period, though Marvell, in his *Account of the Growth of Popery and Arbitrary Government*, would see to it that posterity should be able to read it.

The Talk of the Town: The Nose Bill

The king's speeches, sometimes cajoling, sometimes castigating, sometimes ludicrously disingenuous, must be read extremely closely: not only so as to follow what he thought of as policy and the Opposition called "designs," but also as an extreme and central case of the importance of *voice* in a modern historiography of parliament. This is equally true, evidently, of the correspondence that has survived and of the detailed reports of debates, especially those by Anchitell Grey. Without taking account of voice, all we have are facts. And we may not have the facts straight. Voice, if we can catch it at this distance, is a key to political opinion. To conclude this Introduction, let us return to the event with which we began, the attack on Sir John Coventry's nose, which took place very early in the morning on December 21, 1670, the morning after parliament had adjourned for the Christmas recess.

The first report of this event came, as I have said, in one of John Starkey's newsletters to Sir Willoughby Aston. On December 24, 1670, Starkey wrote Aston a letter entirely devoted to the Coventry affair:

Since my last an accident hath hapned which is all the talke of the towne, and of which I had given you an account the last post but that I forbore in hopes of a perfect discovery by this.

Sir John Coventry an eminent member of the house of Commons and of the Country party, being on Tuesday night at supper att the Cock in Suffolke Street with some other members, where they stayed till near 2 a clock. And at the dore parted, he going on foot to his owne house in the same street, was set upon by a party of horse and foot about 16 in number who first knockt him downe and then 2 of those on foot held him whilst another endeavourd to cutt of his nose, but did only give it a cutt cross as deepe as could be, others wounded him else where, he hath a wounde in the head 2 in the belly and 3 across the hands besides bruises, upon his footman crying out (who at first they had seised on and stopt his mouth with a napkin) company came in to his rescue, upon which the party that had assaulted him drew of, and he was taken up almost for dead, and carryed home. His nose is bound up, and he in a hopefull way of recovery, none of his wounds being dangerous. All the attackers got away undiscovered. They had waited in the street for him near 3 hours and being asked by the Belman what they did there, said they were ordered to seize two gentlemen that were to fight a duel the next morning, upon which he left them, he sayes the footmen had red coates on like souldiers, and the horsemen with halberds like troopers. Various are the Conjectures what the occasion should be, some remember that at the last meeting of the parliament in the spring he was very earnest in bringing in a new bill for the more speedy conviction of papists, upon which he had a letter then sent him from an unknowne that if he proceeded any further in that affaire he must expect to be pistolled, which he did not then reguard. Others imagind it may be for something he said in the house of Commons when they were debating about taxing the playhouses, Sr. Jo. Birkenhead in their defense said that the players had been very serviceable to his majesty upon which Sr. J. Coventry desird he might explaine himselfe whether he meant the men players or women players. This was lookt upon as too offensive, and ought not to have been spoken there. Tis now reported that the busines is discoverd, but [four words heavily inked out.] (f. 202)

It is impossible not to sympathize with the victim in this account, being surprised and so greatly outnumbered, while words and phrases like, "his owne house" and "a hopefull way of recovery" tell the reader where the newsletter writer stands. The self-censorship (the four words heavily inked out) connects to "ought not to have been spoken there".

On December 31, Starkey returned to the topic: "The Attempt on Sr. John Coventry being still the only talke of the towne, and like to prove of great consequence I suppose you are as desirous in the Country to hear of the discovery as we are" (f. 203). Starkey then proceeded to summarize what the justices of the peace had been able to discover about the identity of the assailants: "Sir John hath a list of the Actors." But he also detailed the confrontation between Charles himself and the justice system, with the king attempting to protect his guardsmen from arrest, or arranging for their bail. By February 7, Starkey starts to refer to the Coventry bill as "the Nose bill," a joke repeated three times in the letter of February 14.

On January 5, Andrew Marvell wrote to his Hull constituents that no mention had yet been made in the Commons "of Sir John Coventryes misfortune but will be shortly," implying, since he himself had not previously told them about the incident that all the country had heard about it. Five days later he informed them that, after Sir Thomas Clarges "having been one of the justices of the Peace who examined the fact made a perfect narrative of the matter," the Commons voted to prepare what came to be known as "Sir John Coventry's Bill" (*P&L*, 2:124–25). But writing to his nephew privately, Marvell gave a much more colorful account, which is close to Starkey's but somewhat complicates matters: "Sir John Coventry having moved for an Imposition on the Playhouses, Sir John Berkenhead, to excuse them, sayed they had been of great service to the King. Upon which Sir John Coventry desired that Gentleman to explain, whether he meant the Men or Women Players" (*P&L*, 2:321). Marvell then proceeded to fill in what had been learned subsequently. "On the very Tuesday Night of the Adjournment twenty five of the Duke of Monmouth's Troop, and some few foot . . . Sir Thomas Sands, Lieutenant of the Troop, commanded the Party; and Obrian, the Earl of Inchequin's Son, was a principal Actor" (*P&L*, 2:321–22). Marvell's use of "Actor" may be casual, but he repeats it. The size of the attacking band has increased, but, more important, Marvell here attributes to Coventry himself the original motion to tax the playhouses, which gives point to his retort to Berkenhead. Presumably Marvell was present; there is no record in Grey's *Debates* of such a motion, only a report that when the committee on Supply proposed such a tax "the House disagreed."[29]

Both of these reports, that of the parliamentarian and that of the scofflaw bookseller, make much of the details. Starkey dwells on the wounds, Marvell increases the number of the assailants. Starkey sees the event primarily as great news, the talk of the town, a bit of a joke. Marvell sees it as court business-as-usual. "For considering that . . . O'Brian was concealed in the Duke of Momouth's lodgings . . . that Wroth and Lake were bayled at the Sessions by Order from Mr. Attorney . . . this Act will not be passed without great Consequence." "Great Consequence." This last phrase echoes Starkey's letter of December 31; and in general Marvell and Starkey share the same level of information, and the same slightly salacious interest in it.

By contrast, Sir Edward Dering wrote decorously in his *Diary* for January 9 that the House would "proceed tomorrow upon consideration of the horrid act committed upon the person of Sir John Coventry . . . who the day of our recess . . . was set upon by about 16 men, horse and foot, wounded, and his nose barbarously and villainously cut with a knife" (Dering 1, p. 44). The following day he reported what Clarges had learned as to the names of those involved; but what interested Dering, and what he reported in detail, was the division over the proposal by Sir Robert Atkyns that the House should do no more business till the Coventry bill were passed. Dering carefully listed those who were for stopping all business, and those who were not—they divided along almost strictly party lines. The list of names is itself an interesting record, showing as it does that Littleton, Seymour, Sir Richard Temple, Sir Robert Howard, and Sir Frescheville Holles chose this procedural though highly symbolic vote to publicly cross the floor and vote with the Court party. Dering continued to report the details of the debate at considerable length, eventually stating that it was resolved "that no other business be proceeded in while this bill is passing *this* House": that is to say, sidestepping the question of what would happen should it be held up in the Lords (Dering 1, p. 47).

Dering was interested in procedure; Starkey and Marvell were obviously interested in the court's protection of those who had committed the assault. But Grey makes it clear that at issue was not just one nose, but the principle of freedom of speech for parliamentarians, and fear of the military. Early on Thursday, January 10, Sir John Monson reported that he "has been lately in the country, and never saw a greater concern for a business—They fear we shall come under the government of France, to be governed by an army." William Hale protested that, if such outrages went unpunished, "we must go to bed by sun-set, like the birds," and hoped that the offenders would be hanged. Sir Nicholas Carew, to whom Grey attributes the proposal of stopping all other business, explained "Carew's reason, 'that we may have freedom of speech' till this Bill be done—Without a better guard than Coventry had, he cannot speak freely to any thing else—Perhaps this may be a new way of frightening people." And Colonel Birch, responding to the rumors of obstruction of justice from above, added interestingly that he could not "believe that any in the Government had a share in this business, because they would have timed it better." Birch realized, as did everyone else, that the scandal had seriously altered the mood of the Commons, which until then had been more than willing to supply the king. Dering, however, neither interprets the event nor explains its historical significance. Although the Supply did finally, lavishly, go through the Commons, and was sent up to the Lords on February 21, the following day Lord Lucas delivered his speech in the Lords against, as Marvell put it, "our Prodigality in giving" (*P&L*, 2:322), which rapidly circulated in scribal copies with something of the same effect as had the news of the nose.[30] Turned into a scofflaw pamphlet in 1673, it became part of the arsenal of the Opposition in what was now a different political climate.

There is, however, one more account of the Sir John Coventry affair. This derives not from a diary or a newsletter but from a memoir, and hence is not contemporary in the sense of having been recorded at the time. How much authority it has must remain a historiographical question. The account appears in Gilbert Burnet's *History of His own Time*, whose evolution, revision, and posthumous publication are explained in Chapter 4. Burnet, who died in 1713, did not have access to any written version of the Sir John Coventry affair. When Archdeacon Echard reported on it in his 1718 *History of England* he remarked that "the cause of this Barbarity is not known."[31] But, as was usual with him, Burnet seems to have known all about it, partly from "the talk of the town" at the time, partly from his friends in the Commons, partly from his then friendship with the duke of York. The length of the following quotation is justified by its difference, though not deviance, from what we have already heard, and from the broader interpretive context in which Burnet places the incident:

> [The king] resolved to keep all things close within himself . . . and by doing popular things to get money of his parliament, under the pretence of supporting the triple alliance. So money-bills passed easily in the house of commons: which by a strange reverse came to be opposed in the house of lords; who began to complain, that the money-bills came up so thick, that it was said, there was no end of their giving. *End* signifying purpose, as well as a measure, this passed as a severe jest at this time. (1:468)

Having noted one "severe jest," Burnet moves on to another:

> Sir John Coventry made a gross reflection on the king's amours. He was one of those who struggled much against the giving money. The common method is: after those who oppose such bills fail in the main vote, the next thing they endeavour is, to lay the money on funds that will be unacceptable, and will prove deficient. So these men proposed the laying a

tax on the playhouses, which, in so dissolute a time, were become nests of prostitution.

This adds an ulterior motive to Coventry's choice of the playhouses as taxable, though he probably did not share Burnet's moral disapprobation:

> This was opposed by the court: it was said, the players were the king's servants, and a part of his pleasure. Coventry asked, whether did the king's pleasure lie among the men or the women that acted? This was carried with great indignation to the court. It was said, this was the first time that the king was personally reflected on: . . . it was therefore fit to take such severe notice of this, that nobody should dare to talk at that rate for the future. *The duke of York told me*, he said all he could to the king to divert him from the resolution he took; which was to send some of the guards, and watch in the streets where Sir John lodged, and leave a mark upon him. (1:468–69; italics added)

Note that Burnet both confirms that control of speech was the issue, and adds rather direct evidence that Charles himself ordered the attack.[32] Burnet follows this important information with a vivid and heroic account of Coventry's self-defense, by which "he got more credit . . . than by all the actions of his life" (1:469). And having remarked on the excellence of the cosmetic surgery that Coventry received, Burnet expanded on the consequences of the scandal: "This gave great advantage to all those that opposed the court: and was often remembered, and much improved, by all the angry men of this time. *The names of the court and country party, which till now had seemed to be forgotten, were again revived*" (1:469; italics added). This is important information for those who still dispute whether there were political parties prior to the Exclusion Crisis, and suggests that what Marvell took for granted in 1667 in the *Last Instructions* had been refocused, not least because of the defections from the Opposition of Littleton, Seymour, Temple, Howard, and Holles.

Thus what might have seemed at the beginning of this chapter just another disreputable anecdote from the reign not only comes vividly alive in its various tellings but is revealed as a turning-point, a causal moment in the parliamentary trajectory. To the extent that the Long Parliament had an overall attitude or a mood, from this moment it never recovered its benevolence.

Preliminary Conclusions

Newsletters, printed and scribal; correspondence, semi-public or strictly confidential; diaries, memoirs, scofflaw pamphlets, royal speeches—to separate these sources into categories, or, as a literary historian would say, genres, brings us face to face with the fact that not all sources are equal. Of course historians know this, but normal historical practice—the search for the fact as distinguishable from opinion, or as the collation of divergent opinions—does not revel in such disparities. I do. A generic approach to sources allows me to consider as pertinent to a particular writer's testimony the formal conventions of the genre, his personal allegiances and how they are displayed, the ego quotient of his writing, and whether he has a sense of humor. And the variety of forms in which parliamentary matters were recorded is itself an historical fact, showing the intense level of public interest. There was nothing like this range of comment on parliamentary sessions in the reigns of James I and Charles I, not least because there were eleven years during the latter when parliament never sat. No bishops, no king, warned James I: no parliament, no news, his son might have observed with complacency, at least until 1640. Apparently his grandson attempted to have both a tame parliament and control of the media. Both eluded him, and the result is an unusually rich political culture.

In later chapters I will demonstrate the formal features of the speeches of Charles II—a particularly demanding exercise in our ability to hear tone; of the scofflaw pamphlets, which were increasingly written as a genre, with allusions to predecessors; and the most important Restoration memoirs, in which the writer's omnipresence as protagonist gives him both precious access to information and imperils its value as objective testimony. But let it be said that none of the sources identified here can count as objective. Therefore we need to listen to them all.

CHAPTER 2

❖

Chronology
Why Did the Long Parliament Last So Long?

The Long Parliament of Charles II sat from May 8, 1661 to December 30, 1678, though there were sometimes long gaps between sessions, as the king adjourned or prorogued parliament at will. Eighteen years between general elections is, was, an unprecedentedly long time. How and why did this come about? The reason most often given at the time, or at least by 1675, is that the members of the House of Commons were reluctant to lose their jobs, and therefore avoided action that would have brought about dissolution. Andrew Marvell was a strong purveyor of that theory in his *Account of the Growth of Popery and Arbitrary Government*, and he was by no means alone. But in fact from 1675 onwards, when the parliament's longevity increasingly became a topic, the Opposition group in the Commons began to flex their muscles and openly challenge the king. This chapter will argue that the main reason Charles kept them on hand, if not in line, was that he believed he could manage them, whereas a new parliament might be even more refractory, and to govern without a parliament at all might bring down on his head the fate of his father.

He had partly protected himself against that outcome by his urgent request, early in the reign, that the Commons repeal the Triennial Act which had been one of the major constitutional achievements of the first Long Parliament. The Commons leaped to do his bidding. Another cause that militated against dissolution was the influence of Danby, who became treasurer on June 19, 1673, and desperately needed the taxes only the Commons could authorize. But all the evidence suggests that Charles himself learned, and ultimately preferred, to treat the Commons like a peculiarly large group of servants who could be ordered about at his will or whim. This psychostrategical behavior will take some time to lay out. Towards the end of the parliament's life, however, the use of prorogations instead of dissolution had another strategy behind it—that of keeping in the Tower the four lords who had protested the illegality of the longest prorogation of all.

The following schedule of sessions and intersessions (and what happened during those recesses) should make the narrative easier to follow; but the chronology is complex enough to mean that small disagreements about dates (between historians) are almost unavoidable.

One problem concerns the number of sessions. Since the publication of Richard Chandler's *History and Proceedings of the House of Commons*, it has become traditional to record the Long Parliament as having had eighteen sessions, plus one "intermediate session" of one day's duration that was not entirely legal. A session is deemed ended when it is formally prorogued by the king, which means that all public bills not yet completed and signed off by the king lapse, and must be reintroduced from scratch in the next session. When a session is merely adjourned, discussions of bills pending can continue where they left off when parliament resumes. With respect to the Long Parliament, it is clear that what Chandler's *Proceedings* regarded as the first and second sessions were really only one long session, divided by an adjournment. That was the position of both Abbott and Witcombe, working from the Commons Journal, and Charles II made it clear that it was to be only an adjournment, so that work could continue on unfinished legislation. This is supported by a manuscript in the Leeds Papers, dated March 12, 1675, and signed by John Browne, clerk of the parliament, which appears to have been prepared precisely in order to clarify the situation for Danby.[1] Archdeacon Echard, however, who was intensely interested in the lengths of sessions and intermissions, believed that there were eighteen sessions in all, not counting the extraordinary two-day meeting in July 1667. Their beginnings and endings are marked not only in the text but also in the margins of his *History*. And since the first part of *Proceedings*, which was compiled by James Ralph, relied heavily on Echard, this understanding became written, if not in stone, then at least in the first official-looking history of parliament we possess. Since then it has been endorsed in the online version of *Proceedings*, becoming virtually undislodgable. No doubt Echard was influenced by the fact that, after the long adjournment from July 30 to November 20, 1661, Charles II greeted his reseated parliament with a powerful new speech, even though, as he admitted, it was not formally necessary.

The following chronology accepts the *Proceedings'* version of eighteen sessions. As a necessary evil, it reduces eighteen years of complex political history to tabular form. Beyond convenings, adjournments, and prorogations, it includes only those events that help to explain *why* Charles II convened and dismissed his Long Parliament so many times, and chose not to hazard a new election—until, at last, the Commons' interference with the question of the succession seemed to make it worth the risk.

It is conventional to divide the Long Parliament into three sections, according to which of the king's ministers were or seemed to be in control:

Era of Clarendon

First Session (sixty-three days)[2]

May 8, 1661	Parliament convenes
June 30	Bishops restored to House of Lords
July 16	Control over militia restored to king
July 30	Adjournment to November 20

Second Session (123 days)

November 20, 1661	Parliament convenes; king's speech
December 16	Supply of £1,200,000 voted
December 19	Corporation Act
January 1662	Proceedings against regicides
March 1	King's speech
March 12	Hearth tax voted
March 23	Adjournment to April 3
April	Act of Uniformity debated
May 19, 1662	Prorogued to February 18, 1663

Nine months' recess

August 24	Act of Uniformity comes into effect. Dissenting ministers expelled from their pulpits
December 26	Proclamation announces the king's desire for some indulgence of Dissenters, including Catholics (first Declaration of Indulgence)[3]

Third Session (109 days)

February 18, 1663	Parliament convenes
February 27	Commons Address against Declaration of Indulgence
April 1	King's speech, still ambiguous about Declaration
April 14–29	Whitsun recess
June 23	Supply of £120,000 voted
July 15	Supply Bill finally sent up to Lords
July 27	Prorogation until March 16, 1664

Recess of about eight months.

Fourth Session (thirty-nine days)

March 16, 1664	Parliament convenes
March 21	King's speech asks for repeal of Triennial Act
March 28	Commons votes to repeal Triennial Act (made law on April 5)
April	First Conventicles Act debated in Commons (made law on May 17)
May 17	Parliament prorogued to August 20
August 20	Parliament convenes, only to be prorogued again until November 24

Recess of six months plus, during which the ministers, led by Clarendon, plan for war with Dutch, and scheme to arrange for its financing. The postponement to November 24 allows the court to mount evidence as to the sums needed.

Fifth Session (sixty-three days)

November 24, 1664	Parliament convenes
November 25	Paston's motion for Supply of £2,500,000
February 22, 1665	Declaration of war against Dutch
March 2	Prorogation to June 21
April	Beginning of Great Plague
June 21	Parliament meets, only to be prorogued to August 1
August 1	Parliament meets, only to be prorogued to October 9

Recess of nearly four months, caused by plague.

Sixth Session (twenty days)

October 9, 1665	Parliament convenes at Oxford; king asks for more money to support war
October 19	Five-Mile Bill introduced (passed in seven days)
October 21	Commons vote £1,250,000 for the war
October 26	Non-Resisting Bill introduced; defeated by three votes
October 31	Prorogation to February 20, 1666
February 20, 1666	Parliament meets, only to be prorogued to April 23
April 23	Parliament meets, only to be prorogued to September 18

Recess of 11 months:

| June 1–4, 1666 | Four Days' Battle with Dutch |
| September 2–6 | Great Fire of London |

Seventh Session (105 days)

September 18, 1666	Parliament convenes
September 21	King delivers speech asking for money
September 22	Debates on Irish Cattle Bill begin
October 12	Supply of £1,800,000 voted
	Battle over excise tax, which was defeated
December 7	Garroway proposes a proviso to Poll Bill calling for commissioners of accounts
January 18, 1667	King addresses Commons
January 25	Supply Bill passes Commons
February 8	Prorogation to October 10, 1667

The recess would have been seven months; but on June 10–13 the Dutch fleet sailed up the Thames and Medway and attacked the British fleet at Chatham. The court, in panic, debated whether to recall parliament despite the prorogation. Clarendon advised that this was illegal, and instead that parliament should be dissolved and new elections called. His advice was ignored.

Intermediate Session (one day)

July 25, 1667	Parliament recalled by proclamation; Speaker tries to adjourn until the 29th, but Commons manage to pass unanimous resolution demanding the disbanding of the army
July 29	King's brief speech immediately prorogues parliament to October 10

Recess of about two months.

August 31	Clarendon surrenders the Seals

Eighth Session (127 days)

October 10, 1667	Parliament convenes; Commons thank king for removing Clarendon from chancellorship
October 24	Beginnings of debate on miscarriages of war
October 26	Impeachment proceedings against Clarendon begin
November 29	Clarendon flees
December 19	Parliament adjourns until February 6, 1668, for Christmas recess
February 6, 1668	Parliament reconvenes; king's speech in two parts, asks for money and some indulgence
March 13	Commons introduce new bill against conventicles
May 2	Controversy between Houses over Skinner vs. East India Company
May 9	Parliament adjourned to August 11
August 11	Adjournment extended to November 10
November 10	Adjournment extended to March 1, 1669
March 1, 1669	Parliament convenes, only to be prorogued until October 19

Recess of nearly eighteen months; king issues proclamation against Dissenters. This concludes the first phase of the Long Parliament, the phase covered by Paul Seaward's *Cavalier Parliament*. After Clarendon's eviction, the government is "run" by Clifford, Arlington, and Buckingham, while Shaftesbury gradually moves to the forefront.

Era of the Cabal

Ninth Session (thirty-seven days)

October 19, 1669	Parliament convenes; king's conciliatory speech mentions only his debts and a proposed union with Scotland
November 2	Conventicles Act (lapsed by prorogation) reintroduced
November 26	Supply of only £400,000 voted
	More conflict between the Houses

December 11   Prorogation until February 14, 1670

Recess of two months and three days; Charles deals effectively with the commissioners of accounts; rallies the cavaliers.

Tenth Session (172 days)

February 14, 1670   Parliament convenes; king opens session in state
February 18   Supply voted; wine tax extended for eight years; eighty members of Country party walk out in disgust
March 9   New Conventicles Bill sent up to the Lords
April 11   King orders an adjournment until October 24

Recess of more than six months.

May 15   King meets his sister at Dover to negotiate secret treaty with France
May 21   Treaty signed by Clifford and Arlington
October 24   Parliament reconvenes; new speech by king about power of France; Bridgeman's speech about alliances
December 10   King reads message from Louis XIV to Commons
December 20   Christmas recess for nine days
January 1671   Sir John Coventry's case, severely interrupting subsidy debates
February 22   Speech of Lord Lucas in Lords against prodigality of Commons
February 28   Subsidy bill engrossed (£300,000 for eight years)
March 11   Commons pass a Test Act against Catholics (lapsed by prorogation)
April 22   Prorogation to October 30, 1671
October 30   Parliament meets, only to be prorogued again to April 16, 1672
April 16, 1672   Parliament meets, only to be prorogued again until February 4, 1673

Recess of twenty-one months.

January 1, 1672   Stop of the Exchequer
March 15   Second Declaration of Indulgence
March 17   Third Dutch War declared
November 17   Shaftesbury made lord chancellor

Eleventh Session (forty-five days)

February 4, 1673   Parliament convenes; Shaftesbury's *Delendo est Carthago* speech
                       Supply requested to support war
                       Commons' rejected new members elected on Shaftesbury's writs

	Commons vote an Address against Declaration of Indulgence
March 8	King withdraws Declaration
March 21	Test Act against Catholics in office, leading to Clifford's resignation
March 26	Supply bill for £1,180,000 voted
March 27	Commons resolve to accept no more motions for Supply this session
March 29	King adjourns parliament until October 20

Recess of six months and three weeks, during which Charles determines on an immediate prorogation of the session after adjournment is over, and news breaks of the duke of York's marriage contract to the duchess of Modena September 30. On Clifford's resignation, driven out of office by the Test Act, Danby is made Lord Treasurer (June).

| October 20 | Parliament reconvenes; immediately protests Modena marriage; immediately prorogued to October 27 |

Twelfth Session (six days)

October 27, 1673	Parliament convenes; Commons refuse to give thanks for king's speech
October 28	King's answer to Address re. Modena marriage read; Commons vote new and stronger Address to same effect
	Commons refuse Supply for war
November 3	Standing army voted a grievance
November 4	Prorogation till January 7, 1674

Here occurs a strategic recess of two months, during which Mary of Modena arrives in England, on November 21, and the royal marriage is consummated. Shaftesbury loses the chancellorship, to be replaced by Finch as lord keeper, and soon joins the Opposition. Debates in Privy Council as to whether to dissolve parliament are resolved in favor of Danby's argument that a session is needed to provide money.

Era of Danby

Thirteenth Session (thirty-seven days)

January 7, 1674	Parliament convenes; immediately adjourns itself to January 12
	Attacks by Commons on Lauderdale, Buckingham, and Arlington, marking the end of the Cabal as a force
January 20	Habeas Corpus Bill introduced
February 7	Commons call to disband the army
February 11	King tells parliament of peace with Dutch

| February 24 | Prorogation to November 10 |
| November 10 | Parliament convenes, only to be prorogued to April 13, 1675 |

Recess of fourteen months.

Fourteenth Session (forty-four days)

March 1675	Mock-King's speech circulates
April 13	Parliament convenes
April 15	Danby's Non-Resisting Bill introduced in Lords
April 20	Commons' Address for recalling soldiers from French service
	New Address against Lauderdale
May	Attempts to impeach Danby
May 13	Procedural dispute (Shirley/Fagg) between Houses
	Opposition lords argue for dissolution
June 9	Prorogation to October 13, 1675

Recess of four months.

Fifteenth Session (twenty-eight days)

October 12, 1675	Commons decline to remove anticipations on king's budget
	Vote £300,000 for ships only
	Vote against any more money bills that session
Early November	*Letter from a Person of Quality* and other pamphlets argue for dissolution
November 16	Recurrence of Shirley/Fagg dispute[4]
November 22	Prorogation to February 15, 1677

Long Prorogation: fifteen months, during which Charles receives further supplies from Louis XIV.

December 29	Coffee-houses closed by proclamation
January 8, 1676	Coffee-houses reopen
August–February	Danby's plan to farm the excise

Sixteenth Session (119 days)

February 15, 1677	Parliament reconvenes; Opposition lords challenge the legality of Long Prorogation
February 16	Shaftesbury, Buckingham, Salisbury, and Wharton sent to the Tower
March 2	Commons vote £600,000 for ships
March 6	Commons vote Address to king against growing power of France
March 12	Commons vote to continue excise tax for three years
March 17	Louis XIV takes Valenciennes

March 20	Lords send down "Act for Securing the Protestant Religion"; Series of Addresses to king about alliances desired by Commons
April 16	Parliament adjourned to May 21
May 21	Parliament reconvenes for one week
May 28	Adjourned to July 16
July 16	Parliament convenes, only to be further adjourned to December 3

Recess of nearly six months; marriage of William and Mary solemnized on November 4.

December 3, 1677	Parliament ordered by proclamation to adjourn itself to April 4, 1678
January 15, 1678	Parliament reconvenes (recalled by proclamation), only to receive message from king to adjourn to January 28
January 28	Parliament reconvenes; king's message about treaty with Holland; Commons dispute the terms of the treaty
February 21	*Account of the Growth of Popery* appears in London Commons vote £1,000,000 "to enter into actual war against the French king"
February 22	Louis XIV attacks Ghent
March 27	Parliament adjourned to April 11
April 11	Parliament meets, only to have adjournment extended to April 15
April 15	Parliament meets, only to have adjournment extended to April 29
April 29	Parliament meets, chancellor's (Finch's) speech read
May 5–11	Commons addresses king about alliances, against councilors, especially Lauderdale
May 13	Parliament prorogued until May 23

Recess of ten days.

Seventeenth Session (forty-three days)

May 23, 1678	Parliament convenes; king's speech against tacking
May 30	Commons vote that Supply should be granted to disband all forces raised since September 1677
June 18	King addresses both Houses
July 15	Prorogation to August 1
August 29	Parliament convenes, only to be reprorogued to October 1
October 1	Parliament convenes, only to be reprorogued to October 21

Recess of about three months; during which the Peace of Nijmegen is signed in August by Holland and France.

August 13	First rumors of Popish Plot
October 17	Sir Edmund Berry Godfrey found murdered

Eighteenth Session (sixty-two days)

October 21, 1678	Parliament convenes
November 2	First debate in Commons on Address for removing duke of York from king's person and councils
November 9	King's speech to both Houses warns against tampering with the succession
November 12	Address for tendering oaths of allegiance and supremacy to the king's servants
November 18	Commons sends Williamson to the Tower
December 19	Montagu's letters revealed; impeachment of Danby
December 30	Prorogation

On January 24, 1679, the Long Parliament is dissolved by proclamation.

What can a modern reader make of this story, whose abbreviated and hence inelegant form throws into stark relief the arbitrariness with which Charles II and his ministers deployed an institution whose very existence depended to some extent on regularity and predictability, at least from the perspective of its members? Nobody with any sense of institutional decorum could think that all was well when the shortest session of parliament was six days (not counting the irregular session of July 1667) and the longest was 172 days; when the recesses between prorogations varied in length from ten days to fifteen months; and when over and over again the members of the Commons were recalled to their seats only for parliament to be immediately adjourned or prorogued once more. If you lived in Yorkshire, as did Sir John Reresby, it would take nearly a week to travel to London. On January 7, 1674, when parliament convened for the thirteenth session, Reresby arranged to have his still-contested election heard, "but before the day of hearing came the Parlament was proroughed till the 10th of November next, soe that I was at the charge of bringing up witnesses to London to noe purpas" (p. 91). As the reign progressed, it was hardly surprising if country gentlemen waited to see if a session were really to be held before starting on their journey; with the result that, if business were allowed to begin, the House would be seriously "thin."

Just as deleterious was the fact that public bills lapsed on prorogation. On January 18, 1677, as the Long Prorogation ran out, Andrew Marvell wrote to his constituents in Hull to ask if there were any local business he should attend to, but without much optimism:

It is true that by reason of so many Prorogations of late years repeated, the Publick businesse in Parliament hath not attain'd the hoped maturity; so that the weight and multiplicity of those affairs at present will probably much exclude, and retard at lest, any thing of more Private and particular consideration. (*P&L*, 2:177).

Although the fourteenth session, in the spring of 1675, lasted for three months, no public acts were passed. Once again the Habeas Corpus Bill was left dangling.

Another consequence of the longevity of this parliament was the dramatically increased importance of by-elections, by which, as Abbott observed and charted, the groupings within the Commons could be considerably changed over time. But these infusions of new men were small compared to the general sense of decadent continuity. And to run in a heavily contested by-election was costly. Marvell's analysis in his *Account of the Growth of Popery* is so telling (and so pertinent to our own time) that it deserves extended quotation:

the Vice, and the Expence [of elections] are risen to such a prodigious height, that few sober men can indure to stand to be chosen on such conditions ... men therefore care not thus, how they get into the House of Commons, neither can it be expected that they should make any conscience of what they do there, but they are only intent how to reimburse themselves (if their Elections were at their own charge) or how to bargine their Votes for a Place, or a Pension. They list themselves streightways into some Court faction. ... And which is yet worse, by being so thoroughly acquainted, they understand their Number and Party. So that the use of so publick a Counsel is frustrated, there is no place for deliberation, no perswading by reason, but they can see one anothers Votes through both Throats and Cravats before they hear them. (p. 304)

The last point is particularly shrewd, and particularly devastating. Although this undermining of the deliberative tradition was probably not the intention of Charles II, it clearly became an overt aspect of Danby's strategy from the moment he became manager-in-chief.

Repeal of the Triennial Act

What was crucial to the king's strategy was the repeal of the Triennial Act. There had been inconclusive attempts to achieve this in 1662 and 1663. When the fourth session convened on March 16, 1664, the king's speech, postponed for five days, was ingenious. First, he disclaimed any dark inferences to be gathered from the last prorogation, and asked

> what good Meaning those Men could have, who, from the Time of the Prorogation to the day of your Meeting, have continually whispered, and industriously infused into the Minds of the People, that the Parliament should meet no more; that it should be presently dissolved; or *so continued by Prorogation, that they should be kept without a Parliament.* I pray, watch these Whisperers all you can, as Men who use their utmost endeavours to sow Jealousies between you and Me. (*LJ*, 11:582; italics added)

He then raised the anxiety level over the unrest in the North, and stated that some of the rebels, in their examinations, revealed their belief "by some Computation of their own upon some Clause in the Triennial Bill, that this present Parliament was at an End some Months since." Wrong:

> I have often Myself read over that Bill; and though there is no Colour for the Fancy of the Determination of this Parliament, yet I will not deny to you, that I have always expected that you would, and even wondered that you have not considered the wonderful Clauses in the Bill, which passed in a Time very uncareful for the Dignity of the Crown, or the Security of the People.

Next he reassured them of his intentions: "I need not tell you how much I love Parliaments. Never King was so much beholding to Parliaments as I have been; nor do I think the Crown can ever be happy without frequent Parliaments." Then came the challenge: "I would never suffer a Parliament to come together by the Means prescribed by that Bill." Finally, he thanked the Commons for the Supply of the last session, while explaining that it had not yielded nearly as much as intended.

As rhetorical strategy, this was brilliant. And that same day it was moved that the Triennial Act should be brought up for review.

The Triennial Act (16 Ch. I, c. I) had been passed in February 1641 and declared that there should never be a recurrence of the eleven years of personal rule that Charles I had notoriously enjoyed, not having called a parliament since the spring of 1629. As with many acts, the fine print was hard to read, and subject to misunderstanding. And since it was intended to prevent long gaps *between* parliaments, not to limit their length, the provision for new writs every "third year next after the last day of the last meeting and sitting [of the] present parliament" could only dubiously be applied to a parliament that had, though first convened in May 1661, met as recently as July 1663. The *idea* of a new parliament every three years, however, became connected with this, one of the great acts of the first Long Parliament. What Charles II was referring to, defiantly, as the "Means prescribed by that Bill" was the provision that if the king did not call the writs within the time prescribed, parliament should assemble itself in order to do so. Clearly this was a threat under which a strong new monarch was not prepared to live.

The debate on the Triennial Act was one of the better-recorded moments of the earliest phase of the Long Parliament, for which such records are generally scant. Most of the diarists and journal-keepers had not yet entered the field; but Dr. Denton informed Sir Ralph Verney in a letter of May 25 that

> The debate on Tuesday was about the Triennial Bill, for the damning of which [William] Prynne spake most desperately, and Sir R[ichard] T[emple] as desperately to preserve it, and if all be true, made a very coxcom[b]ing of Prynne, confounding him demonstratively, causing several Acts to be read, showing his palpable mistakes in wilful perverting the text, and that the Bill was not an act of grace, but the people's right, and ought not to be denied them; nay, that it was a condescension in the Parliament and a waiving of part of their right, by taking a triennial when an annual Parliament was their due by former Acts of Parliament, which he caused to be read, for which you may be sure he is farther become a Whitehall favorite, the clean contrary way.[5]

Samuel Pepys both noted the king's speech on the 21st and that one of the most important country gentlemen, John Vaughan, who had to travel from Wales, had arrived to participate in the debate only on the 28th—an instance of the "thin house" problem noted above:

> Mr. Vaughn, the great speaker, is this day come to town, and hath declared himself in a speech of an hour and a half, with great reason and eloquence, against the repealing of the bill for Trienniall parliaments—but with no successe; but the House hath carried it that there shall be such Parliaments, but without any coercive power upon the King if he will bring this act. But Lord, to see how the best things are not done without some design; for I perceive all these gentlemen that I was with today were against [the Triennial Act] yet purely, I could perceive, because it was the King's mind to have it; and should he demand anything else, I believe they would give it him.[6]

Between them, Denton (who also reported Vaughan's hour and a half fili-buster) and Pepys, who recorded accurately that the act was not repealed but amended to remove its "coercive power", give us a strong sense of the climate of the Commons in 1664. Dog-like devotion had the majority in sway, with only a few holdouts.

On February 18, 1668, when the same old parliament was still meeting four years later, but when the mood had soured as the upshot of the Second Dutch War became clear, Sir Richard Temple brought in a new bill for triennial parliaments. And here we have a most interesting disparity among the sources. Grey emphasized the fact that Temple made this move without prior permission, that his bill was formally unseemly, "blotched and interlined, which ought not to be when first presented," and that "the gentleman that brought it in did not [thereby] increase his interest in the House." It was this view that became enshrined in Temple's profile in *The House of Commons*. Milward, who was horrified by the proposal, is helpful in spelling it out and identifying its supporters. Calling it a "bill condemned by all moderate men," he explained:

> It was composed of strange and very dangerous heads to take away the King's power and prerogative of calling Parliament, as first if the King did not call a Parliament within three years, that then the Lord Keeper should issue out his writs to call one; secondly, that the Lord Keeper should take an oath to do it; thirdly, that no prorogation should be above eighteen months; fourthly, that if the Lord Keeper did not then issue out writs in his own name it should be treason in him. This bill was seconded and justified by Sir Thomas Littleton, Sir Robert Howard and Sir Robert Carr, Sir Robert Brooke and all that gang, but most generally spoken against with abhorrency in the House. (pp. 189–90)

This was an absurd responsibility to place on the shoulders of the lord keeper, who at this time was Sir Orlando Bridgeman, scarcely a strong independent figure.

But there was still a third account of this debate, though admittedly a secondhand one. Samuel Pepys reported in his *Diary* for that day (February 18, 1668) that

> they are upon a Bill . . . for obliging the King to call Parliaments every three years; or if he fail, for others to be obliged to do it, and to keep him from a power of dissolving any Parliament in less than forty days after their first day of sitting, which is such a Bill as do speak very high proceedings, to the lessening of the King; and this they will carry, and whatever else they desire, before they give any money; and the King must have money, whatever it cost him.

If this were our only account, we would be puzzled to discover that no such bill was passed. Indeed, it was tactfully withdrawn without a division.

With this "coercive power" removed in 1664, and not reinstated in 1668, Charles II had accomplished his goal, which was complete control over when parliament should meet and when it should be dismissed. Was it that sense of control—the exercise of prerogative—that persuaded him to keep that same old parliament? A new one would have been (and, as it turned out, was) equally subject to those limitations. So now let us consider what I called above the psychostrategical causes of the Long Parliament's elongation.

Charles II was far from the indolent, pleasure-loving monarch sometimes imagined by historians, no doubt to protect him from the charge of being, instead, a deceitful crook. He took an intensely focused interest in what was or was not happening in parliament. Several letters to his sister in France apologize for gaps in their correspondence caused by his need to prepare for a parliamentary session.[7] During Clarendon's impeachment he lobbied assiduously against his own chief minister. Before the important fourteenth session, of April 1675, he had Sir Henry Coventry write to Sir Thomas Payton, Sir Francis Windham, Sir Job Charlton, and seven other loyal country gentlemen, asking them to be sure to appear for the opening session.[8] In early April 1670, he took the unprecedented step of sitting in the House of Lords to hear the debates on the Conventicle Bill and the Roos divorce proceedings, and continued that practice throughout the 1670s.

Acting as whip from Whitehall was understandable. Getting pleasure from a sense of his own control over parliament was natural. But what was puzzling was Charles's stubborn attachment to this parliament. On March 2, 1669, Marvell wrote to Hull that the previous day parliament had been prorogued until October 19. It had in fact been adjourned since May 1668 (not long after Temple's aborted attempt at restructuring), so that there had already been a recess of ten months. Marvell's comment is both restrained and highly important:

> This further his Majesty declares on all occasions that he is resolved not to part with this Parlament. Alsoe my Lord Keeper declar'd openly at his house at the sealing of the Commission and gave those present leave to report it, that whereas there was a rumor of a new parliament, his Majesty to his knowledge was resolved to continue this, and that if any necessity of calling a Parliament before that time, his Majesty knew an expedient notwithstanding this prorogation to call us again together for his service. (*P&L*, 2:82)

The new session which began on October 19 did not last long. It was prorogued on December 11, by royal commission. No official explanation was given. John Starkey, however, wrote an unusually long account of the reasons to Sir Willoughby Aston on December 16, 1669:

> First, the mony they gave was too little, and in the way they intended to raise it would signify nothing to his Majesty, for they in effect did take it out of the customes to give it upon wines, and it would be so long before it could be raised that the Interest would rate out the principall, and their pulse being felt as to the adding 200000 li. to it brought an adjournment they would not have enlarged their gift, and that very day they were prorogued, the committee did intend to adjourne, but at their next meeting it may be hoped that a greater sum of mony may be given, possibly before the Country Gentlemen come up. . . . besides it may be they shall be told something to this effect, that if they will not give that Supply that is expected, we must try whether another parliament will be more kind, that word will make the Courtiers and Indebted Members who are thought to be the major part give what ever is desired rather than be dissolved. (f. 59)

Here is an early instance of the corruption or self-interest theory mentioned above. "We must try whether another parliament will be more kind." Starkey here imagines that the next royal speech will contain, a threat of dissolution, and shrewdly interprets that word "kind" as a euphemism for "compliant". Throughout 1668, Starkey had been one distinct source of rumors that a dissolution might be pending.

By 1674, Starkey's newsletters to Aston have stopped. Instead we have the various letters to Essex in Ireland. On February 10, Lord Conway wrote, in cipher: "I see no appearance that *Parliament will give money, and feare of Duke makes them every day fetter the Crowne, so that I think they will be soone prorogued,* and Osborne will make it his business to keep *King within the compass of his revenue.*"[9] On February 17, he wrote; "I believe that when *Peace is ratified with Holland, Parliament will be prorogued, and some months after dissolved by Proclamation*" (p. 175). He was as surprised as anyone, however, when, on February 14, Charles prorogued the parliament to November 10 (p. 179). Conway added: "I never saw such consternation as was among the members of both Houses; every man amased and reproching one another that they had sat so long upon Eggs and could hatch nothing" (p. 180). The metaphor of the Opposition as a batch of frustrated hens is funny, but in the longer story it loses some of its appeal.

On May 2, 1674, Charles issued a proclamation "to Restrain the Spreading of False News and Licentious talking of Matters of State and Government," in which he particularly objected to "that very false Report of an intention to dissolve this present Parliament, which hath not been under deliberation, His

Majesty seeing no cause to change his resolutions taken touching their meeting." However, he had no problem with prorogations—or, more accurately, could use prorogations to do safely what a dissolution would not allow him to do. On September 21, William Harbord informed Essex of an important Privy Council meeting:

> The King the last ffriday in Councell declared his thoughts of proroguing the parliaments till spring, not ascertaining the time, but yesterday his Majesty, Duke, Treasurer & Williamson mett at Mr. Coventry his office, & I believe there it was agreed. . . . Coventry hath stoutly opposed it, but could not prevaile. The french have Labored int, and I am apt to believe that a stratagem was made use off to bring It about, which was the opportune contriving a story of a great victory procured by the frenche, & the Boats stopped 2 or 3 dayes that so It might not Admitt of a suddain Contradiction. . . . You can not Imagine how great a Surprise this Actt of Councell hath made among the people who talk very broad. (p. 260)

In consequence, parliament would convene on the previously specified date, November 10, only to be prorogued to April 1675.

If someone had now quoted to the king his own commitment to parliamentary government in his speech at the opening of the 1664 session, a decade ago, what would he have said? At this stage Danby was in control, and it was in his interest to keep the same men in the Commons whose support he had begun so effectively to enlist, and whose anti-France feelings matched his own (though naturally privately held) views. But Charles's own resolve to keep this same parliament in being was beginning to look like an obsession, not least since Louis XIV was urging him to dissolve it (and not to replace it with another).

Then, to make matters more complicated, towards the end of the fifteenth session, in the autumn of 1675, the Opposition leaders in the Lords began lobbying for a dissolution. Their reason for doing this was ostensibly that the Commons had sat too long and were no longer representative of those who had elected them. This was code for their view that the majority of the Commons had been so corrupted by Danby's bribes and pensions that real opposition was not to be hoped for in that House. They were also furious at the challenge to their privileges that had occurred in the Shirley/Fagg affair, a slight exaggerated by Shaftesbury. Several scofflaw pamphlets spoke to the ostensible rationale. *Two Speeches*, published with a false Amsterdam imprint, included "the Protestation, and Reasons of several Lords for the Dissolution of this Parliament: Entred in the Lords Journal the day the Parliament was Prorogued, Nov. 22, 1675"; and *Two Seasonable Discourses Concerning this Present Parliament* ("Oxford, Printed in the Year, 1675") set out the constitutional and pragmatic arguments for dissolution at considerable length. The second paragraph of *Two Seasonable Discourses* deserves quotation, especially for a modern readership aware of the advantages possessed by long incumbents:

> It is most unreasonable, that any particular number of Men should for many Years ingross so great a Trust of the People, as to be their Representatives in the House of Commons; And all other the Gentry, and Members of Corporations . . . should be so long excluded. . . . How many may there be in future Parliaments, if continued as long as This, that may be Protestants when they are chosen, and yet may come in so many Years justly to be suspected to have changed their Religion? Nay, How many in this present Parliament are there, who were chosen by the People when they were of the same adequate Interest with them, and . . . are become Officers in the Court, and about the Revenue. . . . And if they should say, They are the same Men they were, We may call their Fellow Members that have sate with them to Witness, whether the Proverb be not true, that *Honores mutant mores*, whether they have the same Opinion, and the same Freedom they had before. (pp. 1–2)

"Honors (rewards) alter behavior." It is a telling sociological argument; and the pamphlet also informs us of the extremist positions being urged against dissolution, that a new parliament would endanger the crown and that "the Church and this Parliament [would] fall together." It concluded with a clever and memorable figure, referring back to the printer's device of a two-headed dragon on the frontispiece: "A standing Parliament and a standing Army are like those Twins that have their lower parts united, and are divided only above the Navel" (p. 9).

Honores mutant mores (Honors change manners), a famous Latin adage, was precisely the situation that Danby counted on, and needed more time to achieve. The result of the battle in the Lords was not a dissolution but the Long Prorogation, which smacks of the king's indecision or, given his commitments to Louis XIV, disingenuity. Nevertheless, Charles managed to extract from Ruvigny the full amount of the subsidy Louis XIV had promised him in exchange for an actual dissolution, and Danby had fifteen months to consolidate his votes—the occasion of the famous list of Court party supporters described by Andrew Browning, Danby's biographer.[10] In May 1676, another attempt to produce dissolution was made by Arlington and the duke of York,[11] but the king refused to allow the matter to be debated in council. A spate of tracts protesting the legality of a prorogation of over a year appeared in 1676, setting out the constitutional and legal arguments, a strategy that backfired.[12] For when parliament finally convened, Danby had carefully prepared for the protest of the Opposition lords, and they were easily routed, and quickly imprisoned. The Commons, who unlike the hereditary peers stood to lose their jobs by dissolution, hedged and fudged the question of the session's legality. This allowed Danby to turn his attention to getting a Supply from the Commons, and in this too he was successful. But the long sixteenth session, which was continued by long adjournments, was diverted by foreign policy concerns, so that the Commons began demanding a renegotiation of England's European alliances, and once again parliament was prorogued, on May 13, 1678.

One element not to be overlooked in this strategy was Shaftesbury. As Browning pointed out, throughout 1677 Shaftesbury languished in the Tower. "For a full year, the Government, by its policy of adjourning rather than proroguing Parliament, had made it impossible for Shaftesbury to secure his release from the ordinary courts of law" (p. 267). Browning cites a memorandum by Danby to the effect that he approved the policy of adjournments and hence the lengthening of the sixteenth session because it would force Shaftesbury to remain without legal recourse, and oblige him to make a formal submission to the Lords; even that process Danby vigorously opposed.[13] But he could not have anticipated his own demise in the eighteenth session, when his dangerous letter to Ralph Montagu—the only proof of his participation in the king's double-dealing with France—returned to haunt him. On December 16, 1678, the Commons began proceedings to impeach him of high treason.

Sir John Reresby, who defended Danby in the impeachment debates, reported in his *Memoirs* for January 24, 1679:

> My Lord Treasurer sent for me, and tould me the King had declared that he would desolve that Parlament, and advised me to make an interest as soon as I could in order to a new election, for another Parlament would be speedily called. This Parlament was very loyall and firm for the most part both to the King and Church, which made that part which was otherwise desirous to gett it dissolved; and the way they found out for it (as was credibly reported) was to persuade the Treasurer to obteane it of the King, promissing him if it succeeded ther should be noe further prossecution against him in the next Parlament. But they deceived him, as appeared afterwards. (p. 168)

This was only one of a number of rumors and theories as to what role Danby himself, once the supporter of parliaments, played in the dissolution.

Reading the chronology above, it is impossible not to notice the increasingly close correlation between the completion of Supply bills and prorogations. In the third session, prorogation followed in twelve days; in the sixth session, ten days; in the seventh session, thirteen days; in the ninth session, fifteen days; in the tenth session, a longer space of seven weeks; in the eleventh session, three days before an adjournment which quickly became a prorogation. Although in the spring of 1673 the Commons had voted a Supply of £1,180,000, they also determined to vote no more money that session. This vote occurred on March 27, and on March 29 parliament was adjourned for six months and three weeks, during which time Charles told the Speakers of both Houses that, when the adjournment was over, he wanted an immediate prorogation, so that money could again be demanded. On October 20, parliament reconvened, and was immediately prorogued to October 27.[14]

Although it was conventional to conclude a session upon the grant of Supply, members clearly felt they were being manipulated. As early as November 13, 1666, John Milward reported "a long dispute about some words that were spoken by Mr. Whorwood" during the debate on supplying the king: "When we have raised the King's supply we may go home like fools, as we came" (p. 41). On February 20, 1668, that loyal courtier John Nicholas wrote to his father that the Commons had not "so much said they will supply [the king]: and the deceiving them the last yeare in taking their money & not setting out a Fleete is an objection not to be replyed to."[15] In August 1671, Andrew Marvell wrote privately to his nephew of the cynicism abroad about Supply:

> The King having, upon Pretence of the great Preparations of his Neighbours, demanded three hundred thousand Pounds for his Navy, (tho in Conclusion he hath not set out any,) and that the Parliament should pay his Debts, which the Ministers would never particularize to the House of Commons, our House gave several Bills. You see how far Things were stretched, tho beyond Reason, there being no Satisfaction how those Debts were contracted, and all Men foreseeing that what was given would not be applyed to discharge the Debts . . . but diverted as formerly. (*P&L*, 2:324)

This was written during a recess of twenty-one months that followed a generous subsidy of £300,000 for eight years. Later in the letter Marvell remarked: "They have signed and sealed ten thousand Pounds a year more to the Dutchess of Cleveland," the reigning royal mistress, and at least twice as much from other sources such as the Post Office (2:325).

By citing these responses I do not intend to resurrect the old debate about whether the king was profligate or the Commons parsimonious. As so often, the truth lies somewhere between the two positions. Though the Commons usually overestimated what their grants would actually produce in revenue, they were willing, when given the figures, to provide for proven needs; and, to cite Witcombe, "the grants made before 1664, the war grants of 1664 to 1666, and the final grants of 1670 to 1671 make it difficult to accept the picture of a niggardly Commons starving a patriot King" (p. 174). But the story continues after those dates. With the secret Treaty of Dover in his pocket, Charles could afford not to make Supply so central an issue; but even so, on June 18, 1678, he demanded £300,000 per annum for the rest of his life, and when on July 8 a much more modest and carefully targeted Supply was voted, it was followed a week later by a series of prorogations.

The other startling fact that jumps out of the chronology is that after the first three sessions Charles and his ministers used the recesses *between* sessions to effect measures of which many parliamentarians either disapproved or about which they felt they should have been consulted. Between the fourth and fifth sessions the court started the Second Dutch War and schemed to get the Commons to finance it. Between the tenth and eleventh sessions the king put a stop on the Exchequer, published his Declaration of Indulgence, and again declared war on the Dutch. Between the eleventh and twelfth sessions the duke of York contracted marriage to the duchess of Modena, and her arrival in England was timed to occur between the twelfth and thirteenth sessions. Between the fifteenth and sixteenth sessions the coffee-houses were closed by proclamation, which might seem a trivial matter did one not know of their importance as centers of political discussion and information.[16] Between the seventeenth and eighteenth sessions Charles, instead of embarking on the war against France towards which the Commons were pushing him, signed a peace treaty with both Holland and France, to the considerable advantage of France. When he met the Commons for the opening of the eighteenth session, his speech began with the remarkable statement that he had *not* disbanded the troops, the event the Commons had insisted on and for which they voted £200,000: yet he was "confident no Man here would repine at it, or think the Money raised for their disbanding to have been ill-employed in their Continuance." Had the Commons not been distracted by the news of the Popish Plot, this brazen statement would surely have been challenged.

At stake, of course, was the huge question of what parliament was for. Was it primarily, even exclusively, a fiscal instrument, a machine for raising money and distributing it appropriately? If so, what kind of distributions were appropriate, and how much accountability should there be? Was it, on the other hand, the king's great council, intended to advise him on the most significant issues, such as the marriage of the heir to the throne, or the making of war and peace? Members of the second Long Parliament very seldom asked such questions directly. Sir Thomas Meres did so at the beginning of the Supply debate, on February 7, 1673, not only by wondering why the king had not consulted parliament before declaring the Third Dutch War, but by observing that parliaments had a responsibility to consider what the country could afford to pay. He was promptly squashed by Secretary Coventry citing the royal prerogative. That prerogative would be asserted in its most unqualified form in the king's angriest speech of the reign, delivered on May 28, 1677, which discarded the new Address about alliances as, in effect, making him but "the empty sound of a king."

At the end of his second long article on the Long Parliament, Wilbur C. Abbott gave, as mentioned in the last chapter, a benign and Whiggish summary:

> The parliament thus ended was not merely the longest in all English history: in importance it yields only to that long parliament of the first Charles which had raised so many of the questions this endeavoured to settle. . . . It made good in principle and practice the control of finance by the commons. . . . It made good the doctrine of ministerial responsibility to parliament in so far as the constitutional arrangements then permitted, and began that series of changes which led to the present system. It made an inroad on the royal prerogative in foreign affairs . . . and it not only suggested the exclusion bill but began that connexion with William III which culminated in his accession to the throne. . . . Strange as it may seem, moderate men had won what they desired . . . the king accepted the situation . . . and accepted it so gracefully that many historians, blinded by the fate of the exclusion bill and of the conspirators, award him a victory he never won and assign to him a success he would have been the first to disclaim. (pp. 283–84)

It is almost impossible to reconcile this assessment with the chronology and analysis proffered in this chapter, which seem to show the king close to absolute control. And yet there is a way in which the very shackling of the Commons, the sense of manipulation experienced by moderate men, led not only to more determined resistance, but also to connections between ideas that might not otherwise have been made. Sir Thomas Meres, a moderate man if ever there were one, spoke much more strongly in February 1677 than he had in 1673:

> he will venture to show you that there is no need of giving now. . . . He told you the last Session, "They could live at Whitehall without your money;" And they have done so since, and may do so fourteen months more. But it seems twas much more easy to be without us; for we find faults, and see great spots. . . . But yet ships are not built, and debts not paid, since 1670. . . . And after the Parliament was prorogued, the Dutch war was

made, and the league with France, the Triple League broken. And the reason of all this was plain; they needed not the Parliament. . . . Then the Dutch war was made, and we were called—But did ever any age know such a war made without advice of Parliament?. . . . 'twill be a mighty mischief to give an additional revenue. Your Parliament by it is of no effect nor use; and he shall never expect good, till this additional revenue goes off. It is so great they will need no Parliament, and you will be turned off at least six years. (Grey)

He was not far out in his predictions. Though the immediate cause was the Exclusion Crisis, the fifth and last parliament of Charles II convened on March 21, 1681, and was dissolved on March 28. The last four years of the reign, in defiance of the amended Triennial Act, were parliament-free.

PART TWO

PERSPECTIVES

CHAPTER 3

❖

Top Down
The King's Speeches

Stylo minaci & imperatorio
"I'le speech them againe"

The royal speeches delivered to parliament, usually at the opening of a session, but also occasionally at a prorogation or adjournment, are an underinvestigated source of parliamentary history. To reread them as a series, each in its context, modifies the formulaic role they were assigned in the Journals of both Houses, especially the Lords Journal, where the monopolistic block of royal (and ministerial) rhetoric overwhelms the otherwise frugal record. One must read them, not only with a view to detecting what motivated each speech, and hence the changing royal strategy over the eighteen years in question, but also in relation to what I have called the king's psychostrategical attitude to parliament. The king's speeches set not only the agenda, from his perspective, but the character of his relationship with his parliament. My epigraph subtitle is a quotation from one of Andrew Marvell's personal letters to his nephew, dated March 21, 1670 (*P&L*, 2:314), and it refers to a speech delivered by Charles on February 14, at the opening of the tenth session, which was conducted in unusual state. Had we not the benefit of Marvell's review, we might not have recognized the *stylum minacem* (the menacing style) in Charles's all-too-familiar demands for a Supply and allusions to his great and pressing debts. But Marvell's remark is only one of a large number of contemporary responses to the king's speeches, responses that we can use to test or confirm our own ability to detect tone, nuance, and, in some cases, disingenuity.

It was normal procedure for both Houses immediately to thank the king for his speech, and later to debate its implications. We often need these debates fully to interpret the speeches, whose every word was taken to be weight-bearing. It is striking how much longer—more fulsome—were the speeches at the beginning of the reign than those made after trouble between the king and his parliament had become the norm. But shorter speeches require a different kind of attention. A very short speech by the king could be followed by a very elaborate one by his chief minister, which would set out the complex rationale or background to requests for money, but might also go beyond the explanatory to the hortatory or obfuscatory.

Almost all the royal speeches were promptly—very promptly—published, in London, by the king's printers, John Bill and Christopher Barker, though those that were given in mid-session were not usually accorded that degree of publicity. Some also had an Edinburgh edition and a few were reprinted in Dublin. In their titles the formulaic ruled. The standard formula was *His Majesties gracious* [or sometimes, *most gracious*] *speech to both Houses of Parliament, on . . .* though several inserted *together with the Lord Keeper's* or *the Lord Chancellor's*. It is somewhat surprising that the printed speeches were not collected at the end of the reign or at the Glorious Revolution. Instead, recognition of their importance had to wait until 1772, when there appeared *A Collection of King's Speeches; with the Messages to and from both Houses of Parliament, Addresses by the Lords and Commons, and the Speeches of the Lords Chancellors and Speakers of the House of Commons; From the RESTAURATION, in the Year One thousand six hundred and sixty, to the Year One thousand six hundred and eighty five*. Published by Charles Eyre and William Strahan, printers to George III, the volume was a product of the extraordinary interest that the eighteenth century showed in the Restoration era. It was also remarkable in including the Addresses of the Commons, which were unpublishable legally during the reign of Charles II. Though not quite complete, this collection provides a convenient source for sequential citations, rather than sending the reader in each case to an early imprint or, where that is missing, to the parliamentary Journals.

A veritable flurry of speechifying accompanied the opening of the first session of what was then appropriately called the Cavalier Parliament. The king's speeches were, for him, expansive, and personal in tone; Clarendon's were extremely long; and the general floridness was increased by the Speaker of the House, Sir Edward Turnor, who reveled in the sound of his own voice, in classical quotations and biblical allusions. The king began the first session on May 8, 1661 with these graceful words:

> I will not spend the Time in telling you why I called you hither. I am sure I am very glad to see you here. I doe Valewe Myselfe much upon keeping my Worde, upon making Good whatsoever I do promise to My Subjects; and I well remember, when I was last in this Place, I promised that I would call a Parliament as soone as could be reasonably expected, or desired. (1772, p. 21)

The choice of date is allusively explained as the anniversary of his return (though this actually occurred on May 29, 1660). Charles then promoted the Act of Indemnity, another graceful move which protected those who had rebelled against his father from future punishment; and informed the two Houses that he would share with them some good news: "I have been often put in Minde by My Friendes that it was high Time to marry. . . . I can now tell you not only that I am resolved to marry, but whom I resolve to marry, if God please. . . . It is with the Daughter of Portugal." Stressing that the decision was not reached without full consultation with his Privy Council (a statement contradicted by Clarendon's *Life*), he gave them all something cheerful (and hopefully fruitful) to look forward to. It was left to Clarendon to raise the issue of the deficit, and "to commend the poor Seamen" who had not been paid for months; to fill in the international complications of the marriage treaty; to mention the need for a religious settlement; and to alert members to the security dangers posed by residual rebels. The chancellor's first speech must have taken about an hour to deliver; but after Turnor's speech accepting his mission, a performance virtually idolatrous of the king, Clarendon spoke again, urging on the parliament its duty to see that the country would never again be in danger from commonwealth ideas or "poor mechanick Persons" (1772, p. 32). Thus the new regime established its tone and its agenda. On July 8 the Act of Indemnity was presented (after another nudge), and on July 30 Turner reported parliament's votes to restore the bishops to the House of Lords and to place the control of the militia in the king's hands alone.

The adjournment to November 20 was intended to allow Charles to go on a progress to Worcester, a visit to commemorate his miraculous escape after the battle of Worcester in 1651. When parliament reconvened, the king decided to deliver a new speech, though this was not technically required after merely an adjournment. In this instance, the tone was very different, the rhetoric inflated to crisis level, its long opening sentence, with its Ciceronian complexity, surely written by Clarendon. But this speech also introduces one of the most peculiar features of Charles's communications; his apparent need to mention accusations made against him. This was not smart. It merely rendered those accusations more widespread:

> I do not now importune you to make more Haste in the settling the constant Revenue of the Crown, than is agreeable to the Method you propose to yourselves; to desire you seriously to consider the unsupportable Weight that lies upon it; the Obligations it lies under, to provide for the Interest, Honour, and Security of the Nation, in another Proportion than in any former Times it hath been obliged to: But I come to put you in Mind of the crying Debts which do every Day call upon Me; of some necessary Provisions

which are to be made without Delay for the very Safety of the Kingdom; of the great Sum of Money that should be ready to discharge the several Fleets when they come Home; and for the necessary Preparations that are to be made for the setting out new Fleets to Sea against the Spring. (1772, p. 42)

Thus by a clever *occupatio*—mentioning monetary needs he says he is not going to mention—immediate necessities are placed ahead of the long-term problem of how to raise the permanent revenue of the crown. National security, and of course those "crying Debts" that will be mentioned over and over again in subsequent speeches, trump a permanent solution. But then comes the admission of weakness:

I am very willing and desirous that you should thoroughly examine whether these Necessities be real or imaginary; or whether they are fallen upon us by My Fault, My own Ill-managery or Excesses, and provide for them accordingly. I am very willing that you make a full Inspection into my Revenue, as well the Disbursements as Receipts; and if you find it hath been ill-managed by any Corruption in the Officers I trust, or by My own Unthriftiness, I shall take the Information and Advice you shall give Me very kindly; I say, if you find it; for I would not have you believe any loose Discourses, how confidently soever urged, of giving away Fourscore Thousand Pounds in a Morning. (p. 42)

Thus the specter of accountability is raised almost from the start. And the infinitely more embarrassing specter of royal Unthriftiness, once summoned up from the dais in Westminster, would take more than better bookkeeping to banish it. At this stage, however, the Commons were not feeling particularly suspicious. On December 20, Turnor informed the king that "we have cheerfully and unanimously given Your Majesty Twelve Hundred and Threescore Thousand Pounds" (£1,260,000) (p. 44); and by the end of the session, on May 19, he added the disastrously unpopular hearth tax—"Two Shillings yearly for every Chimney-hearth in each House for ever." These bounties, which Clarendon would shortly call "two full Harvests in One Year" (p. 48), were to accompany, and be the king's consolation for, the first stage of the repressive religious settlement, the Act of Uniformity.

Between the second and third sessions (as would become typical) the king made a strong move without consulting parliament. He published his first Declaration of Indulgence on December 26, 1662. When parliament reconvened on February 18, 1663, he delivered a short speech solely dedicated to that Declaration, explaining the feelings behind it, and attempting to clarify what might be its impact. There was no accompanying speech by Clarendon, but again we can probably detect his style in what the king spoke. The opening sentence, however, smacks of the king's own brand of disingenuity:

> My Lords and Gentlemen:
> I am very glad to meet you here again, having thought the time long since We parted, and often wished you had been together to help me in some occasions which have fallen out; I need not repeat them unto you, you have all had the Noise of them in your several Countries, and (God be thanked) they were but Noise without any worse effects.

What Charles here referred to were the scattered protests at the ousting of the Presbyterian preachers from the pulpits at the end of August:[1]

> To cure the Distempers, and compose the differing minds that are yet among Us, I set forth my Declaration of the 26th of December, in which you may see I am willing to set bounds to the hope of some, and to the fears of others; of which, when you shall have examined well the Grounds, I doubt not but I shall have your Concurrence therein: The truth is, I am in my nature an Enemy to all severity for Religion and Conscience, when it extends to capital and Sanguinary Punishments, which I am told were begun in Popish times; therefore when I say this, I hope I shall not need to warn any here not to infer from thence that I mean to favour Popery.

Referring to the Catholics who had loyally served his father and himself, he admitted to hoping for some indulgence for them:

> But let me explain my self, lest some mistake me herein, as I hear, they did in my Declaration: I am far from meaning by this, a Toleration or qualifying them thereby to hold any Offices or Places of Trust in the Government; nay further, I desire some Laws may be made to hinder the growth and progress of their Doctrine.

As for the Protestant Dissenters: "if [they] will demean themselves peaceably and modestly under the Government, I could heartily wish I had such a Power of Indulgence, to use upon occasions, as might not needlessly force them out of the Kingdom, or staying here, give them cause to Conspire against the Peace of it."[2] Immediately published by Bill and Barker, this speech set the tone for the struggles over religion between king and Commons for the next decade. We can hear Charles (and probably Clarendon) cleverly balancing the claims of Catholics and Protestant Nonconformists to some degree of toleration in a way calculated to appease the representatives of each group.

The calculation failed. On February 19—a sign of the swiftness of dissemination—Samuel Pepys read this speech and gave his own skeptical account of it:

> Very short and not very obliging, but only telling them his desire to have a power of indulging tender consciences, not that he will yield to have any mixture in the uniformity of the Church discipline. And says the same for the papists, but declares against their ever being admitted to have any offices or places of trust in the kingdom—but God knows, too many have.

And on February 27 the Commons delivered to the king a well-thought-out (though to our ears displeasing) Address, rejecting the royal argument that indulgence would pacify the kingdom, telling him that there was no point in citing his Declaration from Breda, since those promises had subsequently been abrogated by a representatively elected parliament, and pointing out the contradictions in public policy: "It will no way become the Gravity or Wisdom of a Parliament, to pass a Law at one Session for Uniformity, and, at the next Session, (the reasons for Uniformity continuing still the same), to pass another Law, to frustrate or weaken the Execution of it" (1772, pp. 52–54). In a message delivered back to the Commons on March 16, the king declined to comment on the Address or its reasoning, except to say that "He finds what He had said much misunderstood" (p. 54). On April 1, having received a petition from both Houses that he act to control the spread of Catholicism, Charles sent a new (written) speech, read by the Speaker, Turnor, to both Houses, which ignored the contents of the petition, though it promised a speedy and satisfactory answer. Instead, it dealt with the rumor that the previous disagreement had led him to consider a dissolution. Three times Charles here used the term "jealousie" to refer to a hostile rumor, a term that would reappear again and again in subsequent speeches:[3]

> I have heard of one jealousie, which I will never forgive the authors of, that I was offended with Parliament to that degree, that I intended to Dissolve it. They say men are naturally most angry with those Reproaches which reflect upon their understanding, which makes them thought weak men: truly, I should appear a very weak man, if I should have any such passion, any such purpose: No my Lords and Gentlemen, I will not part with you upon those terms, never King was so much beholding to a Parliament, as I am to you.[4]

Whereupon he thanked them for proposing to begin a debate on his revenue. The next day, April 2, he sent a message to both Houses that, in effect, offered an apology for, if not a retraction of, his Declaration of Indulgence. He said he had "made some Reflections upon Himself, and His own Actions," and agreed to issue a proclamation to hinder the growth of popery, and to take care "that the same shall be effectual, at least to a greater Degree than any Proclamation of this Kind hath ever been"; an extremely clever and possibly ironic disclaimer.

There was still one more mid-term speech to come. On June 12, 1663, Charles sent for the Commons to attend him in the Banqueting Hall, and delivered quite a long speech almost entirely of reproach, though its opening words invoked an intimate friendship:

> I have sent for you this Day, to communicate with you, as good Friends ought to do, when they discover the least Jealousy growing, which may lessen their Confidence in each other: It is a Freedom very necessary to be used between Me and you; and you may all remember, that when there was lately a little Jealousy amongst you, upon somewhat I had said or done, I made all the Haste I could to give you Satisfaction.

"Jealousy" again, twice. The briefest of an allusion to the skirmish they had just concluded, in which the king had rather taken his time before capitulating; and then an extensive reflection on what had changed since 1661:

> You are the very same Men, who, at your first coming together, gave such signal Testimonies of your Affection and Friendship to my Person, of your Zeal for the Honour and Dignity of the Crown, . . . and of your Horror and Detestation of those Men whose Principles, you discerned, keeps them awake, to take all Occasions to disturb the Peace of the Kingdom. . . . And yet I must tell you, the Reputation, I had from your Concurrence and Tenderness towards Me, is not at all improved since the Beginning of this Session; indeed it is much lessened. . . . You cannot take it amiss (you shall use as much Freedom with Me, when you please) that I tell you there hath not appeared that Warmth in you of late, in the Consideration of My Revenue, as I expected.

From money to religion; from religion to money: so went the push and pull of the king's requirements, and too much time had already been spent on religion in this session. Delay had also been caused by the Commons taking up the invitation to inspect expenditures, during which it had been discovered how much less the hearth tax had brought in than was hoped. The king continued to stress his willingness to have his accounts inspected ("You will neither find My Receipts so great, nor My Expenses so exorbitant, as you imagine"). He raised a utopian thought: "God knows I do not long more for any Blessing in this World, than that I may like to call a Parliament, and not ask or receive any Money from them: I will do all I can to see that happy Day." He returned to the "man of sincerity" mode: "I must deal plainly with you; and I do but discharge my Conscience in that Plainness." And he concluded by explaining the unusual length and force of his speech—he wanted them to know what his *own* opinions were, as distinct from those of his ministers:

> I have enlarged much more to you upon this Occasion, then I have used to do; and you may perceive it hath not been very easy to Me: But I was willing you should understand, from Myself, what I desire and expect from you; and the rather, because I hear some Men have confidently undertaken to know My Mind, who have had no Authority from Me; and to drive on Designs very contrary to My Desires. (1772, pp. 56–58; misdated June 5)

In the Commons Journal, it is recorded that a copy of the king's speech, "all of his own Hand-writing" (possibly an indication that it was all of his own composition), was given to the Speaker to read to the House, which he did, twice.

Though it was ordered entered in the Journal, there does not appear to have been an official published version, which suggests that the king did not wish to tell the whole nation about his difficulties in obtaining money.[5] That same day the Commons voted generally to supply the king, but it was not until June 23 that they voted £120,000, or four subsidies, *nemine contradicente* (Marvell, *P&L*, 2:38).[6] On July 27, the king prorogued parliament, thanked it for the Supply, promised to be more careful in his expenditures, and said that he was surprised *not* to have been presented with bills against seditious conventicles and the growth of popery. He promised, in the next session, to "take Care to Present Two Bills to you to that End."

We happen to have an unusually alert witness to this prorogation. Samuel Pepys arrived at the House of Lords just as the Commons were entering, and so squeezed in "along with the Speaker—and got to stand close behind him" (4:249). The public were not admitted to this ceremony, but Pepys had a way with him, and we should be grateful for his impropriety. He proceeded to tell his *Diary* in detail what occurred, some of which was less than grandly ceremonial:

> The greatest matters were a Bill for the Lord's Day (which it seems the Lords have lost and so cannot be passed, at which the Commons are displeased)—the bills against Conventicles and papists (but it seems the Lords have not passed them); and giving his Majesty four entire Subsidys.

... After the bills passed, the King, sitting in his throne with his speech writ in a paper which he held in his lap and scarce looked off of it, I thought, all the time he made his speech to them.

Pepys reproduced the speech quite well—a tribute to his memory—and then gave his verdict on it:

His speech was very plain, nothing at all of spirit in it, nor spoke with any; but rather on the contrary, imperfectly, repeating many times his words, though he read all—which I was sorry to see, it having not been hard for him to have got all the speech without booke. (4:251)

It is on the basis of Pepys's testimony that the report has come down to us that Charles was a poor speaker. One must wonder whether, had Pepys been an auditor, he would have said the same about the intense and highly personal-ized speech of June 12. But it must be remembered that Pepys, who approached these performances as an addicted theater-goer, was essentially judging the king's elocution, not the speech's content.

In fact, when the fourth session opened on March 16, 1664, Charles said nothing about the two bills on religion he had promised to bring forward. His speech focused on a bold request for the repeal of the Triennial Act. This last had been delayed until March 21, "upon pretence," according to Pepys, "that many of the members were said to be upon the road," whereas in fact (according to Pepys) it was to prevent the beginning of parliamentary business until the earl of Bristol could be captured and prevented from attacking the chancellor. Once again, Charles began by inveighing against the rumors of a dissolution:

what good Meaning [could those] Men have, who, from the Time of the Prorogation to the Day of your Meeting, have continually whispered, and industriously infused into the Minds of the People, that the Parliament should meet no more; that it should be presently dissolved, or so continued by Prorogation, that they should be kept without a Parliament. (1772, p. 61)

This time Pepys, who had once again insinuated himself into the Lords, gave a much briefer account of the speech, with no derogatory comments. But on April 5, when the king spoke to mark the passing of the repeal bill (16 Car. II, c. I) and again Pepys "crowded in," he was disappointed: "he speaks the worst that ever I hear[d] man in my life—worse then if he read it all and he had it in writing in his hand" (5:112). I take this to mean that in this instance Charles was *not* reading from a text in his lap. The speech was so brief that he might have tried to memorize it; and because of its constitutional importance we should quote it. "You will easily believe," he began, "that I have come very willingly to give My Assent to this Bill." Indeed, since he had specifically asked for it!

> For the Act you have repealed could only serve to discredit Parliaments, to make the Crown jealous of Parliaments, and Parliaments of the Crown, and persuade Neighbour Princes that England was not governed under a Monarch: It could never have been the Occasion of frequent Parliaments. I do promise you, I will not be One Hour the less without a Parliament for this Act of Repeal. (*LJ*, 11:593)

Despite, or perhaps because of, its brevity, the speech was printed with an elaborate and explanatory title-page, as *His Majesties Gracious Speech to Both Houses of Parliament, on Tuesday April 5, 1664, at the Passing of Two Bills, The one Entituled An Act for the Assembling and Holding of Parliaments once in Three years, at the least; And for the Repeal of an Act Entituled, an Act for the preventing of inconveniences happening by the long Intermission of Parliaments.* The second act was an uncontentious legal reform, to prevent abatements of writs of error upon judgements in the Exchequer. Thus everyone in the country was alerted to the fact that the frequency with which parliaments were held was of constitutional significance. This may or may not have been good strategy.

At the end of this short two-month session, on May 17, Turnor, the Speaker, listed the achievements of the Commons, putting the repeal of the old Triennial Act first, followed by a review of the failure of the chimney-money tax to produce the expected revenue, followed by a fairly extensive rationale for bringing in a Conventicles Bill, precisely that which Charles had intimated would be welcome. The king's own speech was again extremely brief, and nothing but a celebration of the new harmony between himself and his Commons. Two days later he wrote to his sister:

> never any Parliament went away better pleased than this did. And I am sure that I have all the reason in the world to be well satisfied with them, and when they meet again, which will be in November, I make no doubt but that they will do all for me that I can wish.[7]

In the absence of counter-testimony (Marvell was out of the country, Grey had not yet started recording debates), it would seem that the king's reproachful speech of June 12 had been remarkably effective. Clarendon, however, has something to add about the strategy for this session:

It was very happy for his majesty, that he did cut out their work to their hand, and asked no money of them, and limited them a short time to continue together. It made their counsels very unanimous. . . . And as there was greater order and unanimity in their debates, so they dispatched more business of public importance and consequence, than any other parliament had done in twice the time. (*Life*, 2:46–47)

Thus Charles's utopian thought on June 12, that he might be able to call a parliament without demanding money, had been for strategic purposes instantiated.

What was to follow, however, reversed everything. This was the Second Dutch War. Responsibility for this unwise commitment on the part of England rests partly with the king, partly with some of his ministers, Bennet and Coventry in particular, and partly with the House of Commons, who got themselves in a warlike mood and promised to support the king "with their lives and fortunes" if he chose to confront England's greatest rival in trade and command of the seas. Before the previous session closed, in April 1664, as Seaward has shown, the government "obtained from a carefully directed committee of the Commons" a resolution condemning the Dutch, which both Houses approved (p. 120).[8] By the time the fifth session convened, on November 24, 1664, disagreements between the ministers had been ironed out, and even those who opposed an actual war, Clarendon and Southampton, saw the value of intimidating the Dutch in negotiations by obtaining a huge Supply. The figure of £2,500,000 to be requested had been decided in advance, and the devious strategy for obtaining it from the Commons had been settled, as described by Clarendon in his *Life*. In this context of well-planned deception, the king rose to speak in Westminster on November 24. Unsurprisingly, he began with the approach of war, the naval preparations for it, and the need for unqualified parliamentary support. There were two paragraphs, however, in which his distinctive voice emerged. In the first of these he asked for dispatch

lest that, by unnecessary Formalities, the World should think that I have not your full Concurrence in what is done, and that you are not forward enough in the Support of it; which I am sure you will be; and that, in raising the Supplies, you take such sure Order, that when the Expence is obvious and certain, the Supplies be as real and substantial, not imaginary as the last Subsidies were, which you all well enough understand. (p. 65)

Fair enough; except that he had just stated that the cost of the fleet would be £800,000, whereas the true figure was about £504,000, a discrepancy for which Pepys, along with Sir Philip Warwick and Sir George Carteret, was wittingly responsible.

The second and by now characteristic statement was defensive:

> I know not whether it be worth My Pains to endeavour to remove a vile Jealousy, which some ill Men scatter abroad . . . that when you have given Me a noble and proportionable Supply for the Support of a War, I may be induced by some evil Councellors (for they will be thought to think very respectfully of My own Person) to make a sudden Peace, and get all that Money for My own private Occasions. I am sure, you think it an unworthy Jealousy, and not to deserve an Answer. (p. 65)

"Jealousy" again, twice. A dark suspicion, now to be broadcast through the press. Those who had not imagined such a thought before must now confront it. The speech was promptly printed by Bill and Barker, though the accompanying narrative of worsening relations with the Dutch, almost certainly prepared by Clarendon and read by Charles from a written text (since the chancellor was ill), was not included in the pamphlet. Pepys, who was present to hear it, made no evaluative comment. The next day, outsmarted (or well managed) by Sir Robert Paston's surprise motion for £2,500,000, the Commons voted to raise that unprecedented sum, though the actual means of raising it was to occupy them for weeks.

Parliament would not meet again for nearly a year, and when it did, on October 10, it convened at Oxford on account of the plague. This sixth session was notable for its brevity (it lasted for only twenty days) and the length of the speeches with which it began. Charles himself, speaking on the 11th, was brief and to the point. He had entered the war on parliament's advice and encouragement, and "the great Supply" that it had given him for the purpose "is upon the Matter already spent" (p. 73). A sum that had been projected to suffice for two and half years of war had vanished. This startling information was followed by a speech by Clarendon of truly epic tone and proportions, chronicling what had led up to the war, the doubling of the size of the English fleet, the victory over the Dutch on June 3 of that year, and the preparations the Dutch were making for renewing the conflict in the spring. He quoted the king's words, "that the noble unparalleled Supply you have already given Him is upon the Matter spent," "upon the Matter" being a response to the "jealousy" Charles had mentioned in November of the previous year that money for one purpose would be diverted to another. He stressed the fact that some of the regicides were being harbored in Holland and had even fought on the enemy's side; and he reminded the parliament of continued seditious activity by republicans at home. Less than three weeks

later Turnor reported that the Commons had voted "for a present Supply" of
£1,250,000 to be levied over two years, along with the Five-Mile Act to
penalize the Nonconformist leaders. His Old Testament language is worth
noting:

> For the Prevention of this growing Mischief, we have prepared a
> Shibboleth, a Test to distinguish among them, who will be peaceable and
> give Hopes of future Conformity, and who of Malice and evil Disposition
> remain obdurate. The one we shall keep amongst us with all Love and
> Charity; the other we shall exclude from Cities and Corporate Towns, like
> those that have an infectious Disease upon them. (p. 81)

Poor attendance, jingoism, and another surprise motion (for that large figure)
by another innocuous country gentleman, repeating the Paston ploy, delivered
a court victory. Of course it helped enormously that at that point England
could be described as winning the war, even though the Battle of Lowestoft
had been far from decisive, because the duke of York, asleep on the job, had
failed to pursue the fleeing Dutch fleet.

When the seventh session convened on September 18, 1666, nobody was
talking victory. The country was staggering in the aftermath of the Great Fire
of London in the first week of September. In the Four Days' Battle of June
1–4, the infamous division of the fleet between two admirals, Monck (now
duke of Albemarle) and Prince Rupert, severely endangered Monck's fleet
and would lead to a parliamentary inquiry. Already in April the first of the
satirical "Advices to a Painter" was circulating, containing attacks on
Clarendon and on Paston, "whose belly bears more millions/ Then Indian
carracks," and complaining that there is nothing to show for all the money
raised—they are left with "four millions vainly giv'n as spent,/ And with five
millions more of detriment," and parliament's reputation in the country is
suffering. The king spoke alone on this occasion, two days after the session
opened, without the chancellor's backup, very briefly, but, of course, asked for
more money. By December 15, he had had no results, and sent a testy
message via Arlington that consequently there would be no Christmas recess
"except for the chief Festival Days." On January 18, 1667, accordingly,
Turnor informed the king that the Commons had voted £1,800,000, to be
raised by a poll tax, because land had been so heavily taxed hitherto. Turnor
was, however, far from exuberant, and far from his usual flattering self:

> Sir, looking narrowly into Things we found our Body Politic entering into
> a Consumption. Our Treasuries, that are the Sinews of War, and the Bond
> of Peace, as much exhausted; the great Aids which are given to Your

Majesty are but like the Blood in its Circulation, which will return again, and nourish all the Parts: But a great deal is yearly transported in Specie into France, to bring Home Apes and Peacocks; And the best Returns are but Superfluities and Vanities: We have therefore unanimously besought Your Majesty to stop this Issue of Blood. (1772, p. 84)

Apes and Peacocks! That sounds almost like satire. The king did not take this kindly. He replied to Turnor and both Houses as follows, and there is no mistaking his irritation:

I have now passed your Bills; and I was in good hope to have had other Bills ready to pass too. I cannot forget, that within few Days of your coming together in September, both Houses presented me with their Vote and Declaration, that they would give Me a Supply proportionable to My Occasions; and the Confidence of this made Me anticipate that small Part of My Revenue which was unanticipated for the Payment of the Seamen: And My Credit hath gone farther than I had reason to think it would; but 'tis now at an End.

This is the First Day I have heard of any Money towards a Supply, being the 18th of January; and what this will amount to, God knows; and what Time I have, you can well enough judge: And I must tell you, what Discourses soever are abroad, I am not in any Treaty. . . . 'Tis high time for you to make good your Promise; and 'tis high Time for you to be in the Country . . . and therefore I am resolved to put an End to this Session on Monday next come Sevennight, before which Time, I pray, let all Things be ready that I am to dispatch. I am not willing to complain you have dealt unkindly with Me in a Bill I have now passed, in which you have manifested a greater Distrust of Me than I have deserved. I do not pretend to be without Infirmities: But I have never broken My Word with you, and, if I do not flatter Myself, the Nation never had less Cause to complain of Grievances, or the least Injustice of Oppression, than it hath had in these Seven Years it hath pleased God to restore Me to you. I would be used accordingly.

Probably unwisely, this speech was promptly printed as *His Majesties Most Gracious Speech to both Houses of Parliament, The Eighteenth Day of January 1666*, with a rather splendid royal coat of arms on its title-page.

If the speech was meant to be intimidating, it was also, like several that had preceded it, defensive. Charles does not pretend to be "without Infirmities." "What Discourses soever are abroad" that he intends to make peace with the Dutch are to be ignored. And with another nice *occupatio*, "I am not willing to

complain you have dealt unkindly with me," he does indeed complain about
the proviso introduced by William Garroway to the Poll Bill which brought
accountability to the forefront. As Marvell, back in his seat and a member of
the committee for drafting the Poll Bill, had reported to Hull on December 3:

> It was yesterday perfected, ready for ingrossing but that in the conclusion
> there was offerd an inacting Provisoe that for the better satisfaction of the
> people, &c: great sums of mony having been already granted there should
> by this Act be constituted so many Commissioners of Lords and Commons
> to inspect and examine thorowly the former expense of the 2500000 l^i, of
> the 1250000 l^i, of the Militia money, of the Prize goods. The debate here-
> upon was very long, and at last upon division of the House those that were
> against it being but 83, those for it 119, 'twas carried for the Provisos being
> committed . . . which I hope will be of very good service to the publick.
> (*P&L*, 2:47)

Samuel Pepys seems by this time to have lost his intense interest in hearing
the king's speeches delivered, but he still learned about them at second hand,
and was interested in their interpretation and reception. On the evening of
the 18th, he recorded:

> Sir W. Pen told me this night how the King did make them *a very sharp speech*
> in the House of Lords today, saying that he did expect to have more Bills;
> that he purposes to prorogue them on Monday come se'nnight; that wheras
> they have unjustly conceived some jealousys of his making a peace, he
> declares he knows of no such thing or treaty; and so left them. (Italics
> added)

According to Pepys (or his source, Penn), the royal demand for dispatch had so
little effect that the Commons wasted time by debating whether to put aside
the debate on Supply! "[T]his shews," Pepys added, "that they are not pleased,
or that they have not any awe over them from the King's displeasure." Earlier,
on the 7th, he reported that the duke of York himself had told him

> how the Parliament is grown so jealous of the King's being unfayre to them
> in the business of the Bill for examining Accounts, Irish Bill, and the busi-
> ness of the Papists, that they will not pass the business for money till they
> see themselves secure that those Bills will pass.

This explains the scenario whereby the king passed the Poll Bill, complain-
ingly, *in order* to get the Commons to move on to the money bill. And at the

end of January Pepys reported that the parliament was prorogued, "having given the King money with much ado, and great heats, and neither side pleased."[9] This was the first serious breakdown in relations between Charles and his great council.

Having now reached the watershed year of 1667, it would be tedious to pursue this pattern of close-reading for every speech that followed. We must, however, take note of some of the more important ones, if my claim that the royal speeches constitute a form of parliamentary history is to be properly tested. Certainly one of the most revealing, in short compass, was the speech Charles gave on July 29, 1667, at his prorogation of the shortest of all the sessions, the intermediate session he had called, against Clarendon's advice, after the disastrous attack by the Dutch on the English fleet at Chatham. When the Commons convened on July 25, the king unwisely deferred meeting them until the following Monday, and the Speaker proposed an immediate adjournment till then. But rumors that peace was imminent led Thomas Tomkyns to outsmart the Speaker, and he quickly moved that the troops be disbanded. The motion passed *nemine contradicente*. On Monday the king came to the House and prorogued it, saying he no longer needed its advice, since peace was concluded, and members could go home—but not before hearing one of his by now characteristic complaints: "He wondered what One Thing He had done since his coming into England, to persuade any sober Person that He did intend to govern by a Standing Army: He said he was more an Englishman than so" (1772, p. 88).

Once more, we owe to Pepys our understanding of what caused this rather petulant complaint. Again, he had a verbal report, more detailed than the last, from Sir William Penn of what had happened on the 25th:

> [He] told me that, contrary to all expectation by the King that there would be but a thin meeting, there met above 300 this first day, and all the discontented party; and indeed, the whole House seems to be no other almost. . . . [And] before they would come to the question whether they would adjourn, Sir Thomas Tomkins steps up and tells them, that all the country is grieved at this new raised standing army; and that they thought themselves safe enough in their trayn-bands. Then rises Garraway and seconds him, only with this explanation, which he said he believed the other meant; that, as soon as peace should be concluded, they might be disbanded. Then rose Sir W. Coventry, and told them that he did approve of what the last gentleman said; but also . . . he durst be bold to say, he knew . . . the king's Mind, that as soon as peace was concluded he would do it of himself. Then rose Sir Thomas Littleton, and did give several reasons for the uncertainty

of their meeting again but to adjourn . . . and the possibility of the King's having some about him that may endeavour to alter his own, and the good part of his Council's advice, for the keeping up of the land army.

Hence the vote *nemine contradicente* that the king should be informed of the House's opposition to any such policy. Pepys, who had approved of the recalling of parliament, now discerned what it might produce if it was allowed to sit: "They will fall foul upon the faults of the Government; and I pray God they may be permitted to do it, for nothing else, I fear, will save the King and Kingdom than the doing it betimes."

On the 29th Pepys went to the Painted Chamber, "thinking to have got in to have heard the King's speech," but decided it would not be worth risking the crowd! At second hand he heard a poor report of it, which he passed on:

> The King having made then a very short and no pleasing speech to them at all, not at all giving them thanks for their readiness to come up to town at this busy time; but told them that he did think he should have had occasion for them, but had none, and therefore did dismiss them to look after their own occasion till October; and that he did wonder any should offer to bring in a suspicion that he intended to rule by an army, or otherwise than by the laws of the land. . . . Thus they are dismissed again to their general great distaste, I believe the greatest that ever Parliament was, to see themselves so fooled, and the nation in certain condition of ruin, while the King, they see, is only governed by his lust, and women, and rogues about him. The Speaker, they found, was kept from coming in the morning to the House on purpose, till after the King was come to the House of Lords, for fear they should be doing anything in the House of Commons to the further dissatisfaction of the King and his courtiers. . . . Here I saw old good Mr. Vaughan, and several of the great men of the Commons, and some of them old men, that are come 200 miles, and more, to attend this session of Parliament; and have been at great charge and disappointments in their other private business; and now all to no purpose, neither to serve their country, content themselves, nor receive any thanks from the King.

Pepys then proceeded to retail precisely the rumor that Charles had dismissed as implausible, stating that the duke of York, Lady Castlemaine the king's reigning mistress, and Baptist May, a courtier close to the king, now all advised Charles to "rule by an army." As for the speech, our knowledge of its wording derives from the "Effect of His Majesty's Speech" recorded in the Lords Journal and transferred to the 1772 collection. Thus Marvell's expectation that it would be made public was mistaken. In this case, at least the king decided not to broadcast an entirely misjudged piece of parliamentary management.

For the opening of the eighth session, Charles evidently decided to avoid making a similar mistake. His speech consisted of two neutral sentences, mentioning some "Things" he had done since the last prorogation that might "not be unwelcome" to them. These included, of course, the dismissal of Clarendon; and he then referred all details to Lord Keeper Bridgeman, whose speech would be published alongside the king's elliptical one as, in effect, its real substance. Bridgeman attempted to explain not only the unfortunate July prorogation, but to proffer now the compliments and thanks to parliament that had been so curtly omitted at that time. Needless to say, he asked for money, even though the war was over, but promised that the Commons should be able to do a full accounting for themselves, since previous commissions to that end had been ineffectual. "[The king] is willing you should follow your own Method, examining them in what Way and as strictly as you please. He doth assure you, He will leave everyone concerned to stand or fall, according to his own Innocence or Guilt." It must have been this speech of the lord keeper to which Pepys referred on October 12, when he reported that "the King did make them a very kind speech, promising to leave all to them to do, and to call to account what and whom they pleased . . . the Parliament is mightily pleased with the King's speech, and voted giving him thanks for what he said and hath done," especially with respect to Clarendon. To complicate matters, however, Pepys also tells us on the 14th that Charles himself *insisted* that the Commons should formally thank him for putting away the chancellor (thereby laying the ground for his impeachment); and that he "commends my Lord Keeper's speech for all but what he was forced to say, about the reason of the King's sending away the House so soon the last time, when they were met, but this he was forced to do." Pepys's informant here was Lord Crew; and the entire episode gives us a sharp view of what was at stake, phrase by phrase, in these speeches.

At this point we lose Pepys's *Diary* as a key to how the royal speeches were *heard* at the time; but his glosses, as a loyal servant of the administration, validate the interpretive protocols to be used hereafter. We need only mention in passing the misstep of October 24, 1670, when all the king did was introduce Bridgeman to do the work. It was this presentation, thanks to Bridgeman's tactless dwelling on the Triple League and other alliances, that was ordered by Arlington *not* to be printed, but that was so carefully recuperated by Marvell for his *Account of the Growth of Popery*. On October 25, 1670, John Starkey also took the trouble to send the "substance" of Bridgeman's speech to Sir Willoughby Aston on the grounds that it was forbidden!

But we should certainly dwell on the statements that accompanied the opening of the eleventh session, after a very long recess. To be precise, parliament had been prorogued on April 22, 1671, and reprorogued several times, having assembled only to hear that news. In the interim, there had occurred several royal coups: the Stop of the Exchequer, on January 1, 1672; the king's second Declaration of Indulgence, on March 15, 1672; a declaration of a third war against the Dutch, two days later; and the replacement of Bridgeman by Shaftesbury as the king's chief minister. *Another* war with the Dutch, after the last had proved so financially disastrous? *Another* Declaration of Indulgence, after the first had had to be nullified in response to protests from the Commons? One has to ask, what was the king thinking? The speech tells us nothing about his motives, but a good deal about his state of mind, which was truculent:

> I am glad to see you here this Day [an echo of May 1661]. I would have called you sooner together, but that I was willing to ease you and the Country till there were an absolute Necessity.
>
> Since you were here last, I have been forced to a most important, necessary, and expensive War; and I make no doubt but you will give Me suitable and effectual Assistance to go through with it. . . .
>
> You will find, that the last Supply you gave me did not answer Expectation for the Ends you gave it, the Payment of My Debts: therefore I must, in the next Place, recommend them again to your especial Care.
>
> Some few Days before I declared the War, I put forth my Declaration for Indulgence to Dissenters, and have hitherto found a good Effect of it, by securing Peace at Home when I had War Abroad. There is One Part in it that hath been subject to Misconstructions, which is that concerning the Papists; as if more Liberty were granted to them than to the other Recusants, when it is plain there is less; for the others have public Places allowed them, and I never intended that they [the Catholics] should have any, but only have the Freedom of Religion in their own Houses, without any Concours of others.

Charles then repeated the rationale of 1663, that this was the least he could do for those Catholics who had loyally served himself and his father. But having admitted the possibility of "misconstruction," a by now typical move, he added: "Having said this, I shall take it very ill to receive Contradiction in what I have done. And, I will deal plainly with you [another echo of 1663], I am resolved to stick to my Declaration" (1772, pp. 106–07).

He then adverted to "One Jealousy more, that is maliciously spread abroad, and yet so weak and frivolous, that I once thought it not of Moment enough to mention." But mention it he does, and it is a recurrence of the standing army rumor. Finally, he promised to "preserve the true Reformed Protestant Religion, and the Church as it is now established in this Kingdom, and that no Man's Property or Liberty shall ever be invaded." So familiar had these rhetorical moves become that it is amusing, as well as informative, to hear Shaftesbury begin his speech by saying: "The King hath spoken so fully, so excellently well, *and so like Himself,* that you are not to expect much from me" (italics added). If this is not in fact a statement to the effect that Charles had written his own speech, then it is a peculiarly barefaced lie. It is doubly amusing to read the king's speech of March 8, when, after having done everything he could to avoid retracting his Declaration of Indulgence, including appealing to the Lords, he offered the evasive assurance that nothing that had occurred as a result of it should "for the future be drawn either into Consequence or Example" (1772, p. 114). Like a naughty boy with his eye on Saturday's pocket money, the king wriggled out of a candid retraction. It was left to Shaftesbury to admit that the original Declaration had been canceled in the king's presence and the Great Seal removed from it.

Charles was not only disingenuous in his speeches. He was capable of telling outright lies. On January 7, 1674, when rumors of the secret Treaty of Dover had already leaked, and were known to Shaftesbury, who had changed sides accordingly, Charles astonishingly said:

> I know you have heard much of My Alliance with France; and, I believe, it hath been very strangely misrepresented to you, as if there were certain secret Articles of dangerous Consequence; but I will make no Difficulty in letting the Treaties, and all the Articles of them . . . to be seen by a small Committee of both Houses, who may report to you the true Scope of them: And I assure you, there is no other Treaty with France, either before or since, not already printed, which shall not be made known. (p. 120)

About this paragraph Lord Conway wrote to the earl of Essex in Ireland as follows (but originally in cipher):

> I beseech Your Excellency to consider the last part of King speech [sic]. It was the consultation of many days and nights that produced it. He fumbled in delivering it, and made it worse then in the print; yet there you may observe 'tis incoherent, and all this is for fear of D. of Yorke.[10]

On January 27, Conway wrote again: "the King's last speech hath been the subject both of the privat cabals and the Publick debates these two last dayes." He concluded that the effect of the speech on the Commons had been largely negative, and that parliament would "sit a great while, and give money, but with great opposition. They know their own strengths so well that Mr. Sacheverell told me he was confident they [the Court] would carry the point of money only by five votes."[11] In fact, no money was granted.

On April 13, 1675, the session in which Danby planned to bring in his Non-Resisting Bill, the king delivered a short and empty speech. The plan was, as Burnet reported (2:63), to ask no money now, but only to build good-will for an autumn session. Marvell too had learned of this plan, and saw it as part of Danby's strategy, writing to William Popple that

> the King should ask, forsooth, no Money, but only mention the building and refitting of Ships. And thus the Parliament meets, and the King tells them 'tis only to see what farther is wanted for Religion and Property. The Commons were very difficultly brought to give him Thanks for his gracious Expressions. (*P&L*, 2:342)

"Forsooth" in the circumstances is a wonderfully ironic locution. In the Lords, also, suspicions arose that something was afoot. Two questions were put: the first, "Whether the humble Thanks of this House shall now be presented to His Majesty, for His Gracious Speech"; and the second, "Whether the humble Thanks of this House shall be presented to His Majesty, for His Gracious Expressions in his Speech." One has to look closely to see the difference, but it is significant. The second motion implicitly distinguishes between gracious intentions and merely gracious expressions which may conceal darker intentions. And when the first motion passed, ten lords dissented, "because of the ill Consequence we apprehend may be from it," and their names were listed in protest: "Winchester, Stamford, Salisbury, Clarendon (jr), Shaftesbury, Will. Pagett, Mohun, Halifax, P. Wharton, Delamer." All of these would subsequently appear in the recorded protests against Danby's Test.[12]

In the Commons, however, a reluctance to give thanks was followed by more effective forms of protest, according to Marvell:

> Straight they poured in Bills for Habeas Corpus against Imprisonment beyond Sea; Treason to levy Money without, or longer than Consent of Parliament; and that it should be lawful to resist [;] New Test, and Way of Proceeding, for speedyer Conviction of Papists; and, which is worse, for appropriating the King's Customs to the use of the Navy; and worse of all, voted one Morning to proceed on no more Bills before the Recess ... Address upon Address against Lauderdale. Articles of Impeachment against the Treasurer [Danby], but which were blown off at last by great bribing. (*P&L*, 2:342)

Thus an innocuous-seeming speech, but one that was known to be part of a devious plan, produced exactly the opposite of what Charles and Danby hoped for.

On October 13 that same year, the request for money came pat as planned. Echoing his promises of budgetary reform of May 19, 1662, the king replayed his two great themes, money and religion, in a lighter and more genial tone. On his budget, he acknowledged that "I have not been altogether so good an Husband as I might have been" (1772, p. 134) and resolved once more to do better. The Commons, however, voted 172 to 165 *not* to supply the king on the grounds of anticipations of his revenue. And some of them must have been thinking with amusement of the Mock-King's speech which had been circulating in manuscript since early March of that same year, in which the habits of speech and strategy that we have been following were gloriously and persuasively parodied.[13] I cite here only some of the most salient moments:

> But some of you may perhaps thinke it dangerous, to make mee too rich, but doe not feare it, I promise you faithfully, whatever you give mee, I will always want & although in other things my word may be thought but slender Security, yet in that you may rely on me that I will not breake it.
>
> . . . I have a pretty good Estate, I confesse; but Gods-Fish I have a great charge upon itt, here is my Lord Treasurer [Danby] can tell you, that all ye Money designed for ye next Summers Guard must of necessity be applied to ye next yeares Cradles, & Swadling Clothes; what shall wee doe for Ships then? I onely hint it to you, for that is your businesse, & not mine: I know by experience, I can live without them.
>
> . . . Therefore looke to it, & take notice, that if you do not make me rich enough to undoe you, it shall lye att your doores.
>
> . . . I desire you, to beleave of mee, as you have found mee, & I doe solemnly promise, that whatever you give mee, shall be especially managed with the same Conduct, Thrift, Sincerity, & Prudence, that I have ever practiced, since my happy Restauration.[14]

"I tell you plainly"; "You know, I never broke my word with you": the pose of the man of sincerity who is doing his best for the country in the face of a recalcitrant parliament. On February 15, after the Long Prorogation, he said: "I am now resolved to let the World see, that it shall not be My Fault, if they be not made happy by your Consultations." Three times he mentioned his determination to speak "plainly," and concluded by saying: "if any of these good Ends should happen to be disappointed, I call God and Men to witness this Day, that the Misfortune of that Disappointment shall not lie at My Door" (1772, pp. 135–36). On May 23, 1677, he would say: "I tell you plainly, it shall be your Fault, and not Mine, if our Securities are not provided for" (p. 129). On January 28, 1678, he said, twice mentioning "jealousies": "It shall not be My Fault, if That be not obtained by Force, which cannot be had otherwise" (p. 142).

If Charles had seen a copy of the Mock-King's speech in 1675, he had not learned anything from it. Andrew Marvell had been listening to the king's speeches for over a decade, and he got the tone exactly right.[15] In fact, on May 24, 1677, he wrote to his Hull constituents a letter containing the full text of the king's speech of the previous day (rather than waiting for a printed copy, which in fact never emerged). This was an extra speech, expressing impatience at the combination of deferred Supply and Addresses demanding a change in foreign policy. On the 23rd, Charles had summoned the Commons to the Banqueting Hall, and there delivered the speech, which he read, "to prevent mistakes," delivering a copy to the Speaker (now Sir Edward Seymour). Marvell's version varies slightly from the version printed in the Commons Journal:

> Gentlemen, I sent for you hither to prevent mistakes and mistrusts, which I find some so ready to make, as [if] I had calld you together onely to get mony from you for other uses then you would have it imployed. I do assure you in the word of a King that you shall not repent any trust you repose in me for the safety of my Kingdomes and I desire you to believe I would not breake my Credit with you. But as I have already told you that it would be impossible for me to speake or act those things which should answer the ends of your several Addresses without exposing my Kingdomes to much greater dangers, so I declare to you againe that I will neither hazard mine own safety nor yours until I be in a better condition then I am able to put my selfe, both to defend my subjects & offend my enemyes. I do further assure you that I have not lost one day since your last meeting in doing all I can for our Defense. And I tell you plainly it shall be your fault and not mine if our Security be not Sufficiently provided for. (*P&L*, 2:201–02)

Marvell thought this speech important enough to be cited in full in his *Account* (p. 347). The Commons thought it irritating enough to be defied. In a new Address of May 25, they found themselves "obliged (at present) to decline the granting your Majesty the supply your Majesty is pleased to demand, conceiving it is not agreeable to the usage of Parliament, to grant Supplyes for maintenance of Wars, and Alliances, before they are signified in Parliament." It was this last Address that provoked the furious, indeed absolutist, speech that Charles delivered to the Commons on May 28, 1677, which Marvell also inserted in full into the *Account*, making the point that "this Severe Speech" was published in the next day's *Gazette*, thereby completing the process by which Charles had increasingly humiliated and hamstrung his House of Commons. Meanwhile "none of their own transactions or addresses for the Publick Good are suffered to be Printed" (p. 369).

What Marvell did not point out, though he was certainly smart enough to have done so, was that the royal monopoly over print in the case of parliamentary proceedings was rebarbative. Too many people saw what the king had said, and too often he had drawn attention to, and fixed in print, rumors or criticisms of his government that might otherwise have vanished into thin air. *Litera scripta manet.* But the publication of what came to be known in Chandler as "the king's resenting speech" was a better-calculated risk than some of its predecessors. That speech was brilliantly written. It abandoned the *mea culpa maybe* mode, and the defensive harping on negative rumors and mistrusts, replacing both with an all-out statement of royal prerogative and barely concealed threat. The only reason it was followed by a notice of adjournment, rather than prorogation or dissolution, is that the king and Danby needed to prevent the release of Shaftesbury from the Tower, which these stronger moves would have triggered.

Who Wrote the King's Speeches?

Did Charles II write his own speeches? This question itself became an issue in later sessions of the Long Parliament. The foregoing analysis is designed to suggest that indeed he did, at least in part, and especially the shorter ones. He undoubtedly consulted his ministers as to what he should ask for, and got his figures from them. But his ministers changed, and his locutions remained the same. There were some speeches, however, that we know to have been ghostwritten. Those at the very beginning of the reign, when Charles was uncertain of himself, were surely written by Clarendon. For the meeting of April 29, 1678, Danby approached Sir William Temple and asked him to write a speech for the king, presumably because it had at last to reveal details about the international situation, of which Temple was the master. In the event, this speech was delivered not by Charles, but by Heneage Finch. For the meeting of June 18 of that same year, we have more detailed information from Charles Hatton, writing to his brother Sir Christopher. He reported Sir William Scroggs had been sent for

> to confer with His Majesty and the Lord Treasurer and to receive instructions for making a speech for the King to the Parliament, who wase to meet the Thursday following and had, a little before, for their peevishnesse, been

prorogu'd by his Majesty. Sir William made a speech, but there were in it some expressions against popery, which were by one person disliked and therefore the whole speech rejected. Ther were 3 speeches made for His Majesty, one by the Lord Treasurer, one by the present Chief Justice, and one by Sir William Temple, which last wase approved of at ye cabinet and wase the speech the King spoke, which I sent you in print.[16]

Both these utterances of 1678 are remarkably different in tone and vocabulary from the short speeches analyzed above, both deal with the details of negotiations in Europe, and both share a conciliatory rhetoric most likely attributable to Temple, though that of June 18 concludes with the astonishing demand for a permanent revenue of £3,000,000 per annum.

If we know that some of the foreign policy speeches were ghostwritten, we need not assume that Charles was always just reading what he had been handed by a minister. There are manuscript copies in the king's own hand of several speeches. That of November 20, 1661 (HLRO Main Papers), although based on a draft in Clarendon's hand (Clarendon MS. 75, f. 308), contains at least one correction made by Charles himself to the wording, as distinct from correcting a copying error: from *vigour* to *judgement.* The speech on October 11, 1665, delivered at the Oxford parliament and also in the royal hand (SP 29/134/71), has some very interesting corrections, at least one of which is an important second thought. Instead of telling the parliament that he had assisted the bishop of Munster with "one hundred thousand pounds," the figure cited by Clarendon as the initial agreement (*Life*, 2:75), Charles crossed that out and replaced it with "a very great summe of ready mony," the phrase that Clarendon later used in his paraphrase of the speech (2:164). By the time the Oxford parliament heard of it, the English were already experiencing difficulties in coming up with the third, or August, installment, and would eventually fail to deliver it in full.[17] Another long clause in the part of the speech that deals with the tricky matter of the royal husbandry of the great sum originally voted for the war, a clause that began "and you will" but that is too efficiently scribbled over to be legible, also suggests caution.[18] It seems that autograph versions of the royal speeches were more the norm than the exception. The printed speech at the prorogation on November 4, 1673 was sent by Bridgeman to Essex, to correct a version he had received from Arlington. Bridgeman reported that the printed speech "I am sure is verbatim the same with the originall written in the king's owne hand" (Stowe MS. 203, f. 167).

There is a manuscript copy of the crucial speech of February 15, 1677 in Finch's hand, but that may mean no more than that the king checked his oratorical and strategic intentions with his new chancellor before a session for which everybody had come particularly well prepared. Charles's speech on this occasion sounds entirely like himself. Three times he declared himself come to speak "plainly" to them, and twice he said that if matters did not improve it would not be *his* fault.

There were several moments when the question of who wrote the royal speeches was raised in the Commons. One was on the occasion of the speech delivered by Finch on April 29, 1678, which was roundly attacked in the Commons. But Sir William Coventry had first to develop the premise that the king was not in any sense responsible for it:

> Pardon me, if I say, when the King speaks to us, or sends us a Message, I look upon it as the advice of others written for him by an inferior penman. What the King says, or signs, is the work of other men. No man can imagine any things so low, as that the king is the penman of other men's Speeches. That part of the King's Messages, or Speeches, in which are gracious expressions of the King . . . of his people, is the King's own. . . . The gracious part is the King's only. The glosses, and varnish upon it, are of his penman's doing. (Grey)

This was evidently absurd, and also back to front, but it allowed Coventry to deconstruct the arguments, the chronology, and indeed the veracity of the explanations proffered.

On May 4, Colonel Birch delivered a (for him) long speech, preparatory to moving to reject the league with Holland. He reminded his audience of their debates of the previous May, and their frustration at the recall of the English troops from French service. "When we did speak home, there was never such a thing said to the Commons of England, and we were sent away with the Speech, you remember, pinned to our backs." On May 7, Birch reverted to that notorious speech, and blasted those who advised it. To which Sir Edward Dering replied, inadvertently adding fuel to the fire: "As to that spoken of the King's Speech, I cannot distinctly remember the points of it, but possibly some of his Council advised one part of it, and some another, and what part of it would you advise against?" Williamson made things worse by apologizing: "I am sorry that any point in the King's Speech should be sharp, but beyond that one expression mentioned, there is not any thing to give offence to the House; and there being but one sharp point, methinks it should not be so fastened upon." Whereupon Cavendish rightly observed that Williamson had laid the responsibility back with the king. Finally, to make sure that nobody failed to remember "distinctly the points of it," Sir Thomas Meres quoted the "resenting speech" and reminded his audience of what had happened to it:

The words in the King's speech were, "I am confident it will appear in no age (when the Sword was not drawn) that the Prerogative of making Peace and War hath been so dangerously invaded." . . . And this Speech of the King's was put into the *Gazette*, [placing the Commons] amongst run-away servants, and a lost shock-dog

—a quotation from Marvell's recently published *Account* (p. 369). Meres also pointed out that two of the king's answers (those of February 4 and May 6) had used the same word, "surprised." "The penman that drew the one did the other," he believed. Perhaps he also believed, though chose not to risk suggesting, that Charles was the penman in both cases.

I conclude, then, that the king was indeed the author of most of his speeches and answers, and certainly in control of their tone. We can, as Marvell did, learn to recognize his particular locutions and attitudes, and particularly to distinguish those delivered *"stylo minaci & imperatorio"* from more genial attempts at persuasion. But the story that the royal speeches in sequence and in context tell is entirely consonant with the larger account of the Long Parliament with which we began: that initial goodwill on the parts of both king and parliament was soon squandered by the Second Dutch War, then briefly rebuilt in 1670 (at least in terms of Supplies granted), then dissipated again with the deeper distrust engendered by the Third Dutch War and fear of the king's engagements with France. The peculiar way the speeches tell that story seems to have been invisible to parliamentary historians hitherto, perhaps because it requires a different style of reading—a style that considers style, tone, tics, and the possibility of slips, if not Freudian ones. Looking back, it is surprising how little efficacy the speeches after 1665–66 had in getting the king what he wanted, and how many of them were actually counterproductive. The persona Charles developed for himself as an orator was so patently in dishar-mony with events that mistrust grew even as it was urged against.

In a manuscript collection of satires owned by Sir Samuel Danvers (d. 1683) there are two items that belong in this chapter. The first is dated 1678, "A Dialogue between the King and the Duke," in which James's role is to urge his brother to go to war and not to worry about his parliament so long as he keeps his army:

> But if Rabbles Command
> Shall make you disband
> You may bid absolute Power goodnight
> Great Grandfather's huff
> And your Boyes in the buff
> Will make [the] Clownes alter their Votes.

And the king replies:

> Well to please those brave Men
> *I'le speech them againe*
> And huffe them much more then before
> But if that will not doe
> Let the Ministers goe
> For by Christ I'le travel no more. (Italics added)[19]

Later in the same manuscript appears another mock-speech, dated March 21, 1680; that is, the opening day of the Oxford parliament. Marvell was dead; but whoever wrote this speech to herald the parliament had paid careful attention to that circulated in 1675, a copy of which in fact precedes it in the manuscript.[20] The parody is clever enough to deserve extensive quotation:

> My Lords and Gentlemen:
>
>   . . . .
> In the first place I must tell you that the last Parliament were very unkind to me and my Brother, & you know there is but us two in the World, besides my Lord Anglesey tells me they were a Pack of very saucy fellows that meddled with what they had nothing to doe in. Now I would have you avoid all those things, that we unite & be happy, for my Lord Hallifax Vows, that unless we doe soe, neither you nor I can stand long in the Government & you may be sure I will take care to secure my selfe. My Lord Clarendon saith, If Popery must come in, We had as good have the Credit of it. . . . Nay some of my Subjects have given me good Encouragement to set up a standing Armye to inslave you all. But I was resolv'd not to doe it till I had advise'd with you soe to doe. . . .
> . . . As to those who were accus'd of the Plot formerly, I sufferd them to be Executed, tho I must needs say in my Conscience they knew no more of the Plott then I doe. . . .
> There is another thing I must begg of you again, not to trouble your selves about my Brother, for I can assure you he hath had such hard usage the last two Parliaments that he is almost distracted. . . . 'Tis in Vain to perswade him, He's resolved not to part with his Title, & I have sworn to him not to alter the Succession, & you know I always love to keep my Oath. . . .
> . . . I doe therefore assure you, upon the Word of a King, for I intend to inslave you, that your welfare & happiness shall no longer lye att my dore and therefore you must looke to it, and be quick in dispatching the supplyes.

No doubt more than a few members had already read this, thanks to the strategy of scribal publication, when they met to hear the king deliver the real speech inaugurating the Oxford parliament. They would not have been disappointed by it, either, for this was both anticipatory parody of what they knew would be the royal position on the exclusion, and a reprise of two decades of being "speeched." To the Opposition, it must have been a constitutional breath of fresh air: Stuart concepts of monarchy could evidently be, if not yet outflanked or outmoded, at least for a moment outsmarted.

CHAPTER 4

❖

Up Close and Personal
The Memoirists

"At doomsday we shall see whose a—is blackest"—Charles II,
citing a Scotch proverb.

The problem with memoirs as a source of parliamentary history is the veil of ego. This is the mirror image of their strength. A man who writes a memoir about his role in public events does so because he believes he has been, if not always at their center, then at least watching from a privileged vantage point. The first person singular therefore is almost omnipresent—because, in a sense, the author was. Bias is therefore easier to discern than it is in a diary or journal. But the memoirist of the later seventeenth century is also aware of providing insider information, giving his work an aspect of secret history, which by its nature is not subject to verification. This gives his testimony a frisson—a bait for the reader, and you know what happens when you swallow a bait: you get hooked.

There were two great memoirists of the Restoration era whose recollections happened to include substantial accounts of parliamentary history, Edward Hyde, earl of Clarendon, and Gilbert Burnet, later bishop of Salisbury. They were widely opposed in character and political ideology, but not entirely dissimilar in the way they handled their material. Martin Greig, author of the article on Burnet in the *Dictionary of National Biography*, suggests that Burnet's recasting of his *History of His own Time* was influenced by the publication in 1702 of the first volume of Clarendon's *History of the Rebellion*; but in fact the analogy is rather with Clarendon's *Life*, first published in 1727, well after Burnet's death. Burnet got the inspiration for writing his own Life in 1710, as he tells us in its opening pages, not from Clarendon, but from Jacques de Thou;[1] and for parliamentary history, it is Burnet's *History of His own Time* that we need. What really connects the two memoirists is the pleasure each derives from being inside not just the corridors of power (if that is how one regards parliament) but even the king's cabinet; though Burnet's access to the cabinet was only sporadic, and less important to him than his access to Westminster. A third memoirist who enjoyed some of the same privileges of access but put them to less interesting use was Sir John Reresby, a country gentleman who soon became a reliable Court party supporter. And a fourth, Sir William Temple, dropped remarks about Charles's relations with parliament in the course of laying out the byzantine story of the king's foreign policy during the late 1670s. Between them, Clarendon, Burnet, Reresby, and Temple will carry us from the opening of the Long Parliament to its dissolution, in each case providing an intriguing personal perspective along with a review of those eighteen years.

And precisely because it is the personal perspective we are after, the memoirists require unusually generous quotation. We should think of them as raconteurs, whose every word is meant to intrigue us, and whose narrative skills are at least as important as the "facts" they relate.

Clarendon's *Life:* All about Me

Edward Hyde, eventually earl of Clarendon, was undoubtedly the most famous politician in the service of Charles I and Charles II, although the amount of information he left us about himself has, of course, helped to aggrandize him. Ironically, it was his periods of exile from the center that allowed him to write the legend of his own importance. As Charles I's primary advisor and de facto protector of the heir to the throne he was sent first to Jersey, when the royalist forces in the west of England were routed, and then in 1648 to Paris. During his two years in Jersey, he began his *History of the Rebellion*, starting way back with the king's accession, and nearly brought it up to what was then the present situation; but when he moved to France the *History* had to be put on hold. At the Restoration the reward for that first exile was to become lord chancellor, increasingly the hottest of all hot seats to be in as the euphoria of the Restoration dissipated, financial conditions worsened as an unwise war against the Dutch created endless conflicts with parliament, and the moral tone of the court grew visibly atrocious. By late 1667, Clarendon's exposed position, still more exposed by the shotgun marriage of his daughter to the duke of York, led to a campaign in parliament to impeach him, and he was finally persuaded, by messages from Charles II, not to risk standing trial, but instead to flee to France. In 1669, after being rudely shunted from place to place by the no longer welcoming French, he settled in Montpellier. By now he was sixty years old. In the next five years he would do more significant writing than most of us achieve in a lifetime.

As soon as he settled in Montpellier, Clarendon began the work of self-justification that we now know as his *Life*. This was completed up to the

Restoration by 1670. In 1671, his son, Laurence, brought him his papers, which probably included the *History of the Rebellion* as so far constructed, and Clarendon proceeded to complete it, too, up to the Restoration. He then returned to the *Life,* and continued it through his Restoration triumphs to his ultimate disgrace.[2]

The *Life* is one of our finest sources for the Second Dutch War and the impeachment of Clarendon that followed, but there are other important witnesses (Pepys, Marvell, the letters of John Nicholas to his father, and *The Proceedings in the House of Commons touching the Impeachment of Clarendon,* a pamphlet written at the time but not published until 1700). These events are also fully covered by Seaward and Witcombe. But here we see, in slow motion, parts of the story of parliament that only Clarendon recorded for us in the process of his self-vindication. The first part, however, which deals with the funding for the Second Dutch War, serves rather to indict him.

After the Commons had obliged the king during the fourth session by revoking the Triennial Act and giving him the chimney-money tax, they were prorogued on May 17, 1664, initially until August. During that short fourth session, Clarendon remarked:

> they, who were very solicitous to promote a war with Holland, forgat not what they had to do; but they quickly discerned that it was not a good season to mention the giving of money, (which the king himself had forborne to mention, that the people might see one session of parliament pass without granting new impositions . . .) [.] And therefore it would be as unseasonable to speak of a war.

Meanwhile conflict with the Dutch had increased (and was exaggerated by the reports of Sir George Downing). In January 1664 (Clarendon's date seems too early), "the king commanded the chancellor and the treasurer to meet with those members of the house of commons, with whom they had used to consult, . . . and to adjust together what sum should be proposed." Clarendon states that "the chancellor and treasurer (who were known to be averse from the war)" warned that if war was inevitable the only way to handle it was "by raising a great present sum of money, that the enemy might see that we were prepared to continue it as well as to begin" (*Life,* 2:61). But this advice was challenged:

> They who were most desirous of the war, as sir Harry Bennet and Mr. Coventry, (who were in truth the men who brought it upon the nation,) with their friends, were of the opinion "that there should not be a great sum demanded at present, but only so much as might carry out the fleet in

the spring, and [that] sufficient provisions might be made for the summer service: and then, when the war was once thoroughly entered into, another and a better supply might be gotten about Michaelmas, when there was reason to hope, that some good success would dispose all men to a frank prosecution of the war."

But Clarendon and Southampton carried the argument.
They concluded

that a less sum than two millions and a half ought not to be proposed, and being once proposed ought to be insisted on and pursued without consenting to any diminution; for nobody could conceive that it would do more than maintain the war one year, which the parliament could not refuse to provide for in the beginning. (2:63)

The rest of the group agreed on the figure, but protested

that they could not advise that so prodigious a sum should be as much as named; and that they did not know any one man, since it could not be thought fit that any man who had relation to the king's service should move it, who had the courage to attempt it, or would be persuaded to it.

They decided therefore to name "some of those members, who were honest worthy men, and looked upon as lovers of their country, and of great fortunes, unsuspected to have any designs at court," and Clarendon and Southampton engaged to find and persuade them. From the list they chose "three Norfolk gentlemen" who were already friends. One was Sir Robert Paston; the other two, since neither Grey nor Marvell was reporting at this time, must remain unidentified by us. *House of Commons* states that Paston looked for a peerage for himself, or at least "some financial reward to offset his increasing pecuniary embarassment." The fifth session of parliament was postponed to November 24.

On November 25 (*House of Commons* says the 24th), Paston made his move. This is Clarendon's own description:

When the house was in a deep silence expecting that motion, sir Robert Paston, who was no frequent speaker, but delivered what he had a mind to say very clearly, stood up, mentioned shortly the obligation, the charge of the war, and "that the present supply ought to be such as might as well terrify the enemy as assist the king; and therefore he proposed that they might give his majesty two millions and a half, which would amount to five and twenty hundred thousand pounds." The silence of the house was not broken; they sat as in amazement, until a gentleman, who was believed to wish well to the king, . . . stood up, and moved that they might give the king a much less proportion. But then the two others, who had promised to second, renewed the motion one after the other; *which seemed to be entertained with a consent of many, and was contradicted by none.*[3] (italics added)

So the Speaker put the question, and the "affirmative made a good sound, and very few gave their negative aloud, and it was notorious very many sat silent" (2:66).

Now, if Clarendon were the only witness to this debate (Marvell was with the earl of Carlisle on his embassy abroad, and Grey had not yet entered the Commons), we would be left with a brilliant but hardly self-exculpatory account of Clarendon's chief responsibility for the Second Dutch War, to be balanced against his statement that he and Southampton were opposed to it. We have no reason to doubt his account of how the figure was arrived at and Paston recruited. Witcombe, however, observes that the Commons Journal recorded a division, 172 to 102, "not indeed on the motion for supply, but on the no less important motion, that 'the question be now put.' " The discrepancy between Clarendon's account of a great silent victory and this evidence of dispute can be resolved by a letter written by Thomas Clifford, a supporter of the war, to Secretary Coventry on the evening of November 25.[4] Clifford had obviously been asked by Coventry to report to him on how things went in the Supply debate, and it is equally obvious that Clifford was not in on the secret maneuvers by which Paston was selected to do the court's work.

Holland first began of the necessity of a supply but mentioned nothing of the summe. Sir Robert Pastern [sic] spoake next and after a great speech against the Duch which was in sence and expression beyond expectation he very handsomely, and as he said like a country gentleman insinuated the summe of two millions and a halfe as necessary for the carrying on of the war in behalfe of the country whose interest it was—and not as a supply to the Kinge. The summe gave at first a great consternation and silence in the house till the house by the Debate were netled into so great an animosity against the Duch (for there was not one person but freely declard for the war whatever his motion else tended unto) that it seemd a cleare case that that great summe was fit to be raisd.

"Men of that interest," however, i.e. the Country party, attempted to insist that the amount of the subsidy not be decided before they had worked out, in committee of the whole House, how to raise it. Clifford mentions Sir Edward

Walpole and Sir John Goodricke as making this reasonable proposal, "so that it was a difficult matter to turne the streame." But turned it was:

> And the house seemd so much inclined to give the first great summe nam'd that Mr. Vaughan spoake in the presence of god he was so much convinced of the necessity of the war that during the continuance of it he would be content to be reducd to bread and water rather then the reputation and honour of the Kinge or the interest of the nation [should suffer] and to this tune Sir Richard Temple and Mr. Garroway also chanted and therefore they desired only a previous Vote that the naming the summe should not be a restriction at the committee as to the manner of raising it which being easily yielded unto Mr. Vaughan himself even contrary to his own professions takes the boldness to enveigh against the war and in fine concludes that the summe certain should be but five hundred thousand pounds which was in it selfe so ridiculous and in relation to his particular avowments so contrary to honour or honesty and is so apparent to all that I believe his worke is done for one while.

In the interest of objectivity, we need this discrediting portrait of John Vaughan, one of the greatest speakers in the Opposition, who had spoken for an hour and a half against repealing the Triennial Act, but who here seems to have lost his way. Then others, including Sir Henry North, Sir John Holland, and Sir Edward Walpole, argued for a lesser sum at this stage. "So that," Clifford continued, "with great difficulty we came to this question whether the question for the great summe should be now put or noe and we carried it in the affirmative by 70 voyces more than the negative and when the main question was put there were not above five or six noes to it." "Sir Thomas Littleton spoake the shrewdest of the other side and Mr. Trevor has the day upon ours. I hope you will let me know who does great daring things when you have a sea fight. I wish it as successful as we have bin." For both Clifford and Clarendon, though the processes they describe are quite different, the vote on Paston's motion (though the division only occurred on the procedural issue) was a triumph of parliamentary management. Clifford's account is most useful for identifying the speakers pro and con, and for giving a sketch of John Vaughan's[5] rhetorical flourishes and subsequent proposal of a Supply one-fifth the size, though Clifford cannot explain what caused Vaughan's turnabout. That Temple and Garroway "chanted" reminds us of how irritating political debates can sound—to the other side. But beyond the bare facts, his analysis of the House's psyche, and how the war fervor overcame the fiscal caution, is worth close-reading. The House was "netled" into animosity against the Dutch. The "great summe" is repeated fourteen times,

telling a modern reader just how alarming a figure it seemed. But Clifford's
hopeful assumption that inconsistency had discredited Vaughan is contradicted by the fact that Vaughan was named chair of the committee to put the
Supply into practice. Yet we forgive him because of his self-effacement (he
does not describe himself as a speaker, though surely he must have been)
and for the analogy he draws between the sea fights that are about to begin
in earnest and the "great daring things" performed within the walls of
Westminster: a brief parliamentary epic!

Great daring things or devious manipulation? There is one more witness
to call in evaluating this question. On November 25, Samuel Pepys recorded
in his *Diary* that he was all morning at his office "to prepare an account of
the charge we have been put to extraordinary by the Dutch already; and I
have brought it to appear 852700 l; but God knows, this is only a scare to the
Parliament, to make them give the more money" (5:330). He then took his
figures to Westminster and handed them to Sir Philip Warwick. The king's
speech of the preceding day had mentioned £800,000, and Pepys had evidently
been asked, most likely by Coventry, to provide backup documentation.

This "brave vote," in Clarendon's words, was the high point of his influence in both court and parliament, but the *Life* makes it sound braver than it
was. Between this moment and his painfully full account of his loss of favor
with Charles and vulnerability to the growing intrigues against him come a
series of melancholy reflections on how the initial goodwill of the Restoration
had been squandered. But to round off our own account of Clarendon as
historian of parliament, we now turn to the final disaster of the Second Dutch
War, the midsummer assault by the Dutch on the English fleet at Chatham,
and the national panic that followed. Nobody knew whether the Dutch would
return for another attack. Parliament had been prorogued on February 8 to
meet again on October 10. At court, Clarendon reported,

> they who had most advanced the war, and reproached all them who had
> been or were thought to be against it, "as men who had no public spirits,
> and were not solicitous for the honour and glory of the nation," . . . were
> now the most dejected men that can be imagined . . . and wished "that a
> peace, as the only hope, were made upon any terms."

These views, in quotation marks, probably reflect what Clarendon actually
heard in the Privy Council in June 1667.

> In this perplexity the king was not at ease, and the less that every man took
> upon him to discourse to him of the distemper of people generally over
> the kingdom, and to give him counsel what was to be done: and some men

had advised him to call the parliament, which at the last session had been prorogued to the 20th of October [Clarendon misremembered the date]; and it was now the middle of June. And surely most discerning men thought such a conjuncture so unseasonable for the council of a parliament, and that the crisis should be let pass and be dealt with in "a more contracted council."

There was also a legal difficulty. After a prorogation a session could not be called before the day appointed (though William Prynne had declared to the king that this might be gotten around). The king decided to stage a Privy Council debate on the question of whether to recall parliament by proclamation, although Clarendon soon grasped that he had already made up his mind to do so.

At the council, he told them

"that they all saw the straits he was in, the insolence of the enemy, and the general distemper of the nation. . . . That he had no money, nor knew where to get any; nor could imagine any other way to provide against the mischiefs which were in view, than by calling the parliament to come together." Three or four of those who sat at the lower end of the board, and who were well enough known to have given the counsel [to recall the parliament], . . . enlarged themselves in the debate, "that the soldiers could not be kept together without money; and they could not advise any other way to get money but by the convening the parliament, which they were confident might justly and regularly be done." (2:421)

This, remember, is a meeting of the *Privy* Council, whose debates were strictly confidential. And yet here is Clarendon quoting the words of his colleagues.

The chancellor pointed out that the "temper" of the Commons was well known, and unlikely to be improved by an irregular midsummer session, and that they might take the opportunity to raise other concerns which would only confuse matters more. He cited the legal problem. And he concluded by proposing that, if it were absolutely necessary to hold a parliament, the current one should be dissolved by proclamation and writs issued for a new one, which could well be elected before October. We know now, and Clarendon must have known at the time, that neither the king nor his then closest councilors were willing to risk new elections; but his advice for a dissolution would soon be imparted to parliament, and became the first article in his impeachment.

Clarendon is surprisingly vague as to what happened next. When parliament convened on July 25, the king unwisely deferred meeting it until the following Monday, and the Speaker asked that it adjourn. But, quick as a flash, Thomas Tomkyns, who had begun as a loyal Country party cavalier, reacted to the rumors that a peace with the Dutch had already been negotiated by moving to disband the troops, lest suspicion arise in the nation that the king intended to govern by a standing army. The result was a motion *nemine contradicente* that the Privy Councilors in the Commons carry this request to the king. On Monday 29, Charles came to the House and curtly prorogued it to the original date of October 10. Andrew Marvell wrote to his Hull constituents with some of these details, though without mentioning Tomkyns and his seconders (*P&L*, 2:56). Clarendon, who might very well have said, "I told you so," merely reports, inaccurately, that "they separated without any debate" (*Life*, 2:430). And, on August 30, Clarendon was asked to surrender the seals, the symbol of his position as chancellor.

The saddest part of Clarendon's story, however, is not the impeachment itself, but the secret of which he was either ignorant or that he chose not to understand: that the king had not only decided to abandon his old chancellor to his enemies, but actively pursued his impeachment by his own influence. John Nicholas's letters to his father begin now, and on November 13 he wrote: "My Lord Clarendon hath one unhappines beyond my late Lord Strafford my Lord of Canterbury or my late Lord. of Bucks. If it be true what common report sayes, that the King interesses himself very much in the busines & encourages the prosecution. Beatus ille qui procul negotiis &c."[6] Citing Horace's second Epode, so important to the morale of cavalier poets during the Civil War, provides some emotional distance. On November 14, Nicholas wrote: " 'Tis strange to see with what passion and malice that poore Lord is pursued, the King hath a Liste given him of all those who voted against this violent course and hath severely checkt severall of them" (f. 139v).

Gilbert Burnet's *History of His own Time*

"Damn him, he has told a great deal of truth, but where the devil did he learn it?"—Francis Atterbury

Gilbert Burnet, who became bishop of Salisbury under William III, was in almost every way a contrast to Clarendon. Raised by a strict Presbyterian father, he was a wily Scottish upstart who decided to enter the church instead of the law, and thereafter expressed himself forcibly in print on all affairs of church and state that interested him. At the age of twenty-three he drafted a *Memorial of Divers Grievances and Abuses* in the Scottish church, and sent copies to the highest-ranking bishops. This earned him the attention and special favor of John Maitland, earl of Lauderdale, a member of Charles II's five-person Cabal, who at this stage had a policy of moderate indulgence for Dissenters.

In the summer of 1673 Burnet was in London, where Lauderdale presented him to the king, who was so impressed by his conversation that he made him one of his chaplains. Burnet also made friends with the duke of York. In June 1674, he returned to discover that he had badly alienated Lauderdale, lost his royal chaplaincy, and was in serious danger of imprisonment if he returned to Scotland. From this point on until 1683, when Burnet again got himself into serious trouble by supporting Lord Russell and Essex during their trials for the Rye House Plot, he lived in London supporting himself as a preacher at the Rolls Chapel, with time to write as he pleased.

Burnet states in his autobiography that in London he lived next door to Sir Thomas Littleton, a far from insignificant coincidence. This may have been the most important fact about his London period:

> I soon found that he was one of the considerablest men in the Nation. He was at the head of the opposition that was made to the Court and living constantly in Town he was exactly informed of every thing that past. He came to have an entire confidence in me so that for six year together we were seldom two daies without spending some hours together. I was by his means *let in to all their secrets.* . . . We argued all the matters that he perceived were to be moved in the House of Commons till he thought he was a master of all that could be said on the subject, and it was observed of him that in all debates in the House of Commons he reserved himselfe to the conclusion and what he spoke commonly determined the matter (p. 485; italics added)

Thus from 1674 to 1681–82 Littleton practiced his parliamentary arguments on Burnet. Allowing for Burnet's characteristic stress on his own appeal as a confidant, this has a certain plausibility; though in fact, so far as we can tell from Grey's *Debates*, Littleton was sometimes the *first* to speak in the most important debates.

Burnet decided to write what he himself called his "secret history" in 1683 at the time of the Rye House Plot, and worked on it for two years until he prudently left for Europe in May 1685. He continued it at The Hague, and had brought it up to date in October 1688, before returning with William III to England. At that point he left directions in his will for it to be published no sooner than six years after his death. But after the Glorious Revolution he continued it from 1691 to 1703, at which point he decided to recast the whole work so as to make it less of a personal memoir and more of an objective history, and to distinguish it more clearly from his autobiography. Eventually it ended at 1713 with the Treaty of Utrecht. It was first published in several small volumes from 1724 to 1734, with no publisher's name and a false London imprint (it was actually printed at The Hague).

The parts of the *History of His own Time*, then, that concern us were all written long after the event. And Burnet's sources were, almost invariably, word-of-mouth ones: personal conversations with others in the know. X told me that Y told him. . . . About his first visit to England he wrote: "I was in the court a great part of the years 1662, 1663, and 1664; and was as inquisitive as I could possibly be, and had more than ordinary occasions to hear and see a great deal" (1:345). This attitude, and these opportunities, continued all his life, and made his *History* the remarkable document it is.

But not having been on the spot does not deter him either. For the Dutch War period, he admits he "must write more defectively, being then so far from the scene" (1:375), and it is obvious he had none of the insider information about its funding that obsesses other writers. In 1664, he writes: "The house of commons was so far from examining nicely into the grounds of the war, that without any difficulty they gave the king two millions and a half for carrying it on" (p. 375), thereby obscuring the maneuvers described by Clarendon and Clifford and enacted by Sir John Paston to get that vast sum through the Commons. On the other hand, Burnet supplies a detailed account of the Five-Mile Act, in regard to which he seems to have had access to debates both in the Commons and the Lords (1:390–92). During Clarendon's impeachment, Burnet talked to some of the chancellor's friends. "The lord Burlington and bishop [George] Morley both told me" that they had asked Clarendon to warn them of any dark secrets in his administration so that they might best know how to defend him (1:441). In discussing the Stop of the Exchequer in 1672, he remarks:

> the earl of Shaftesbury was the chief man in this advice. *He excused it to me, telling me what advantage the bankers had made . . . and added, that he never meant the stop should run beyond the year.* He certainly knew of it beforehand; and took all his own money out of the bankers' hands, and warned some of his friends to do the like. (1:532–33, italics added)

Just when this conversation took place is never explained. Burnet was in Scotland at the time.

Nor was he in London in February 1673 when parliament reassembled in the wake of the Stop of the Exchequer, the declaration of war against the Dutch, and the king's Declaration of Indulgence. But he still gave a rather large account of the doings of that parliament, including several statements that were later inserted into the footnotes to Grey's *Debates*. This gives Burnet's *History* double status, as it were, since his presence as a commentator on Grey requires us to compare what might at first seem irreconcilable versions. Describing the king's speech at the opening sessions, and Shaftesbury's expansion of it,

Burnet wrote: "But no part of his speech was more amazing than that, speaking of the war with the Dutch; he said, *Delenda est Carthago*. Yet, while he made a base complying speech in favour of the court and of the war, he was in a secret management with another party" (2:4). Everybody knew about *Delenda est Carthago*; but who except Burnet knew at the time it was made in bad faith?[7] One could of course say that this knowledge was merely hindsight. But the *History* will shortly show him to have been, at least to some extent, in Shaftesbury's confidence.

Burnet was also informed of behind-the-scenes negotiations as to how the court managed to get another huge supply of about £1,250,000 through the Commons in 1673:

> Garroway and Lee had led the opposition to the court all this session . . . so they were thought the properest to name the sum. About eighty of the chief of the party had met over night, and had agreed to name 600,000l. But Garroway named 1,200,000l. And was seconded in it by Lee. So this surprise gained that great sum, which enabled the court to carry on the war. When their party reproached these persons for it, they said, they had tried some of the court as to the sum intended to be named, who had assured them, the whole agreement would be broke, if they offered so small a sum. . . . They had good rewards from the court: and yet they continued still voting on the other side. They said, they had got good pennyworths for their money. (2:13)

The pennyworths included the Test Act (25 Car. II, c. II), described at the time as the "bill against popery," which eventually passed the Lords on March 29, 1673. As soon as the "money bill" was finally passed, also on March 29, Charles adjourned the parliament until October 27.

The next session of parliament to which Burnet's attention was drawn was one that involved him personally:

> In April 1675 a session of parliament was held, as preparatory to one that was designed next winter, in which money was to be asked: but none was now asked; it being only called to heal all breaches, and beget a good understanding between the king and his people. (2:63)

This was the fourteenth session, which followed a fourteen-month prorogation, and lasted only until June 9, when it was prorogued till October. This lack of immediate fiscal business gave the Commons an opportunity to attack Lauderdale, and Burnet was summoned before them to reveal conversations he had had with Lauderdale in the past, which he had unwisely talked about, and which could be used to incriminate the minister. With that major breach of confidence Burnet again lost the favor of the court, and the several Addresses by the Commons against Lauderdale went nowhere.

But Burnet was more interested in what was going on in the Lords, where, on the third day of the session, Danby, in collaboration with the bishops, had introduced a new oath or loyalty test, to be taken by all members of parliament. In fact, as observed in the scofflaw pamphlet *A Letter from a Person of Quality*, it was moved by the earl of Lindsey, lord high chamberlain, who was in this respect "imposed upon" by the real instigators. The central issues of the Test were reported to Hull on April 22 by Marvell, who was appalled by it: "I AB do declare that it is not lawfull upon any pretense whatsoever to take Arms against the King and . . . I do sweare that I will not at any time endevour the alteration of Government either in Church or State" (*P&L*, 2:148–49). Burnet too saw this as an important moment in the history of parliament, and spent some time summarizing the debate:

> To all this great opposition was made. It was plain, the duke did not like it: but the king was so set on it, that he [the duke] did not declare himself against it. . . . The lords Shaftsbury, Buckingham, Hollis, Hallifax, and all those who were thought the country party, opposed this mightily. They thought there ought to be no tests, beyond the oath of allegiance, upon the elections to Parliament: that it being the great privilege of Englishmen, that they were not to be taxed but by their representatives; it was therefore thought a disinheriting men of the main part of their birthright, to do any thing that should shut them out from their votes in electing; all tests in public assemblies were thought dangerous, and contrary to public liberty . . .

At this point, Burnet both partly reveals his source, and makes a considerable contribution to our knowledge of the debate:

> Lord Shaftesbury distinguished himself more in this session than ever he had done before. He spoke once a whole hour, to shew the inconvenience of condemning all resistance upon any pretence whatsoever. . . . since there might be cases, though so far out of view that it was hard to suppose them, in which he believed no man would say, it was not lawful to resist. If a king would make us a province, and tributary to France, and subdue the nation by a French army, or to the papal authority, must we be bound in that case tamely to submit. Upon which he said many things that did cut to the quick. And yet, though his words were watched, so that it was resolved to have sent him to the Tower if any one word had fallen from him that had made him liable to such a censure, he spoke both with so much boldness

and so much caution, that, though he provoked the court extremely, no advantage could be taken against him. (2:72–74).

This summary of Shaftesbury's speech, which must have been related to Burnet, or shown to him, possibly by Shaftesbury himself,[8] is perhaps most important for its clue as to Shaftesbury's most provocative remark, his instance of what might constitute a legitimate reason for resistance, "If a king would make us a province, and tributary to France," a claim that *England's Appeale* had come very close to making. Where Burnet got the information as to how closely Shaftesbury's words were listened to by the court, and how carefully he controlled them, we can only guess, but again, Shaftesbury himself seems the most likely source. The other sources for this debate are the Journal of the House of Lords, which printed those protestations and the names of those who made them, and the famous *Letter from a Person of Quality, to His Friend in the Country*, which will be discussed in Chapter 5; but Burnet's report adds another perspective.

Burnet knew, as the author of the *Letter* did not,[9] that the Test would be defeated not by a vote but by the disruption caused by the Shirley/Fagg case, which led to such a dispute between the two Houses over their prerogatives that the king prorogued them on June 13. "I am not sure," wrote Burnet,

> if this was laid, or if it happened by accident. Lord Shaftesbury said, it was laid by himself. But others assured me, it happened in course, though it produced great effects: for there never was a strength in the court to raise this debate of the test in any subsequent session. (2:75)

Indeed, "it dyed the Second Death," wrote Marvell, "which in the Language of the Divines, is as much as to say, it was Damned" (*Account*, p. 286).

On October 13, parliament reconvened for its fifteenth session. And here again Burnet has an interesting tale to tell:

> the king laid before the commons the great difficulties he was in by the anticipations of his revenues. It was then generally thought, that the king was in such straits, that, if money could not be obtained, he must turn to other counsels and to other ministers. The debate went high in the committee of the whole house . . . the previous question being then put, whether the main question should be then put or not, the votes were equal. So sir Charles Harbord, who was in the chair, gave it for putting the main question. But, some of the country side coming in between the two questions, the main question was lost by two or three. So near was the court to the carrying so great a point. (2:76–77).

A tied procedural vote; late arrivals; a big defeat for the king. Though Grey has a very full account of this debate, which took place on Tuesday, October 19, and reported the main question as moved by Cavendish, he left no record of the tied procedural vote. Marvell, however, reported it to Hull that evening (*P&L*, 2:165). The procedural tie had been 166 to 166. The final vote on the main question was 172–165 against the taking off the "anticipations" on the king's revenue, a word that had led to some ironical reflections. So if we follow this carefully, one of the Court party changed sides after the six latecomers showed up, and the defeat of the motion could be anticipated.

And Burnet has more insider information:

> Harbord was much blamed for this. . . . A lively repartee was made by his own son to him in the debate. He had said, the right way of dealing with the king, and of gaining him to them, was, to lay their hands on their purses, and to deal roundly with him. So his son [William] said, he seconded the motion: but he meant, that they should lay their hands on their purses, as he himself did, and hold them well shut, that no money should go out of them. (2:77)

Thanks to Burnet, this Oedipal drama entered the archives, and was passed on in *House of Commons*; at this point, William Harbord, it seems, became a staunch supporter of the Opposition.

And at this point, it also seems, Burnet himself, though without a seat in parliament, joined that group. First, he related the failed attempt in the Lords, headed by Shaftesbury, to vote an Address to the king to dissolve parliament, citing in the process many of Shaftesbury's own arguments (2:78). Then, he used the long gap between sessions—the fifteenth session was prorogued on November 22, 1675 until February 1676—to tell us how that opposition in the Commons was formed and stabilized.

According to Burnet, it was the corruption of those members of the House who did *not* wish for a dissolution, since they would lose their jobs and their income, that produced a reorganization or consolidation: "In opposition to these a great party was formed, who declared more heartily for the protestant religion, and for the interest of England. The duke of Buckingham and the earl of Shaftesbury opened many of their eyes, and let them know the designs of the court" (2:79). As well they might, having recently changed sides, and hence tactics, themselves. In their "great party," according to Burnet, were Sir William Coventry, Colonel Birch, Edmund Waller, Lord William Russell, William, Lord Cavendish, Sir Thomas Littleton, Henry Powle, Sir Thomas Lee, and Edward Vaughan. (In the notes he wrote in his copy of Burnet's *History*, Arthur Onslow remarked that Burnet ought also to have included in his list of Opposition spokesmen William Sacheverell.) Character sketches of these men were supplied by Burnet, and were followed by a telling rationale: "All this I thought to lay together, and to fill as it were an empty place in my history: for, as our main business lay in preparing for, or managing a session of parliament, so we had now a long interval, of above a year" (2:84). *Our main business? We* had now a long interval? Burnet's view of the Long Prorogation is that of someone who feels himself to have joined the fray, wishing it would begin again.

One would expect, therefore, that Burnet would be closely concerned with the session that eventually began on February 15, 1677. But on this occasion he tells us nothing that is not available from other reporters, especially Marvell's *Account*, and, from a very different perspective, from Daniel Finch's long letter to his uncle. Where Burnet does become again a spectacular and unique witness is during the eighteenth session, the last gasp of the Long Parliament, where he is rather more than a witness: in fact, more like a go-between.

The sixteenth session of the Long Parliament had consisted, in the Commons, of a struggle between the Opposition members and the king as to what kind of relations, whether of friend or foe, the country should have with France. Despite, or because of, its intransigence, parliament was prorogued on May 13 until May 23, 1678. The seventeenth session was then prorogued on July 15, till August 12, and thereafter by several prorogations to October 21. By the Peace of Nijmegen the efforts the Commons had made to force the king to declare war on France were nullified, and so, wrote Burnet, "all people looked on the next session as very critical":

> The party against the court gave all for lost. . . . And many did so despair of being able to balance [Danby's] numbers, that they resolved to come up no more, and reckoned that all opposition would be fruitless, and serve only to expose themselves to the fury of the court. But of a sudden an unlooked for accident changed all their measures. (2:144)

This was the astonishing (and fraudulent) testimony of Titus Oates. It all began, according to Burnet, when "three days before Michaelmas Dr. Tonge came to *me*," with talk of "strange designs against the king's person" (2:144). Burnet, suspecting a trap, informed the secretary, probably Sir Joseph Williamson, "Since I would not be guilty of misprision of treason," and then discovered that Tonge had already carried his tales to that higher authority.

> I told this next morning to Littleton and Powel. And they looked on it as a design of lord Danby's, to be laid before the next session, thereby to dispose

them to keep up a greater [military] force, since the papists were plotting against the king's life. . . . But lord Hallifax, when I told him of it, had another apprehension of it. He said, considering the suspicions all people had of the duke's religion, he believed every discovery of that sort would raise a flame, which the court would not be able to manage. (2:145)

Later, Tonge arranged for Burnet to meet with Titus Oates, who had already delivered his incredible testimony before the Privy Council. A fortnight later Sir Edmund Berry Godfrey disappeared, and was then found murdered. "The session of parliament was to be opened within three days: and it may be easily imagined in what a temper they met. The court party were out of countenance. So the country party were masters this session" (2:154). Burnet then intervened in the trial of "the popish banker Staley" (2:160), who he knew was being shafted by a Scot named Carstairs, and for his pains earned the ill-will of Jones, the attorney general. He also talked to Holles, Halifax, and Shaftesbury about how incredible the evidence was, and "wished they would not run too hastily to the taking men's lives upon such testimonies" (2:161). He did not save Staley, who was executed, but the king sent for him secretly. Throughout December Burnet met with Charles alone. "We agreed in one thing, that the greatest part of the evidence was a contrivance" (2:168). This is a very different *we* from the one that praised the heroes of the Opposition during the Long Prorogation.

Meanwhile, parliament was preparing its own response. A bill was brought into the Commons requiring all members of both Houses, and anyone with access to the king, to take a test against popery. It passed easily. When it came back from the Lords, however, it contained a proviso exempting the duke of York. Burnet somehow had access to that part of the debate in the Lords, and put his own inimitable gloss upon it:

The duke got a proviso to be put in it for excepting himself. He spoke upon that occasion with great earnestness, and with tears in his eyes. He said, he was now to cast himself upon their favour in the greatest concern he could have in this world. He spoke much of his duty to the king, and of his zeal for the nation: and solemnly protested that, whatever his religion might be, it should only be a private thing between God and his own soul, and that no effect of it should ever appear in the government. The proviso was carried for him by a few voices. And, contrary to all men's expectation, it passed in the house of commons. (2:165)

Grey briefly reported this debate on November 21. It was dominated by a long speech in support of James by Secretary Coventry. Despite brief objections from Sir Thomas Meres and William Cavendish, the proviso passed by 158 votes to 156. The bill itself got bogged down in other amendments from the Lords respecting the queen's servants. But Burnet's account of what happened in the Lords, with the duke's dramatics, with hindsight so hypocritical, was appended as a footnote to this section of the *Debates*, and thereby delivered, as it were, a double whammy.

For the later parliaments of Charles II Burnet remained marginally involved, behind the scenes. Before the Oxford parliament, he had secret conversations with Littleton about expedients to avoid the absolute exclusion of James from the succession. After the parliament's sudden dissolution, Burnet realized that it was time for his own retreat. "I had been much trusted by both sides: and that is a very dangerous state; for a man may come upon that to be hated and suspected by both" (2:275). There was one more interview with the king arranged by Halifax from which Burnet, who was disgusted with Shaftesbury for his role in bringing about the executions of the supposed Popish Plot conspirators, might have profited. But when he refused to stop consorting with Essex, Russell, and Jones he was out in the cold again. Finally, after the executions of Essex and Russell for the Rye House Plot, Burnet was summoned before the Privy Council to explain his role in attending them, and his complicity in the writing and dissemination of Russell's last speech. James never forgave him for reading aloud to the council the journal he had compiled of Russell's last days. And it was in that year, 1683, that Burnet began to write the *History of His own Time*, the journal of an era.

Sir John Reresby: or, "How I Kept my Seat"

When, in 1936, Andrew Browning edited the *Memoirs* of Sir John Reresby, who entered the House of Commons in 1675, he suggested that they were first published in 1734 by Tories hoping to counter the continued impact on politics of Burnet's *History*:

> With a general election imminent, and the long-anticipated second volume of Burnet's *History* . . . holding out an immediate promise of ammunition for the Whigs, it was presumably felt that the moment had come for the Tories to furbish up any historical weapons they might possess. What was wanted was not a violent Tory pamphlet . . . but a moderate account of the part played by the Tories in previous reigns, which should commend their attitude to as large a circle as possible.[10]

To see Burnet and Reresby as rival interpreters of their era makes a certain amount of sense. Reresby was a country gentleman of mildly royalist persuasion.

But it might be more accurate to say he was of no persuasion at all. Beginning as a young supporter of Buckingham, though his election was not promoted by Buckingham but by a rival faction, he rapidly became a friend and confidant of Danby, who had in 1674 become lieutenant of the West Riding of Yorkshire and "immediately sent me a commission for deputy lieutenant" (p. 94). His *Memoirs* are, however, in no sense a secret history, but the candid comments of a mild observer of the parliamentary scene. Thus at the time he stood for election in 1673, he recognized it as a turning-point in the history of the parliament:

> The state of that Parlament was this at that time, that all things had been carryed on from the time of its being called . . . with great calm and success for the advantage of the Crown. They had given the King a very great revenue . . . ariseing to above three times more per annum then any other king of England had before. This began to weigh heavy upon the country, and to make them repine, which stirred up some gentlemen in both Houses to oppose this currant (which was called the Country party, in opposition to thos others whom they called the Court party). The first of thes pretended to protect the country from being overburdened in their estates, in their privileges and libertys as Englishmen, and to stand by the religion and government as established by law. The other declared for that too, but at the same time for the King to have a sufficient revenue and power for the exercize of his regall authority. (p. 90)

This difference in perspective now led, Reresby saw, to a new interest in by-elections, which were becoming hotly contested—he himself had five competitors. (His election remained contested until 1678.) He added that there were other reasons than principle that made men eager to become members of parliament: "Such as were in debt found protection by it (this Parlament haveing sitt soe long, and meeting soe ofton), and others had gotten great places and presents from Court to stand by that interest" (p. 90).

We know now that Reresby oversimplified matters, by exaggerating the level of the king's actual revenue; but his perception of the resurgence of party politics at this point seems correct. It is worth noting that, though not a member of parliament himself at the time, Reresby gave an account of the slitting of Sir John Coventry's nose (though he has the timing slightly awry) and its result in "that Act against malicious maimeing and wounding" (p. 81). When he actually takes his seat in April 1675, he notes that "the two factions [are] extream warm one against the other," but that "most part of the time being spent in debates *pro* and *con.*, little was effected, for the two partys were soe near equall that neither of them durst put it to a question" (pp. 96–97). After the session was prorogued (Reresby says "adjourned"), he makes a telling admission: "During this short time of sitting in the Hous I confess I thought the country party had great reason in their debates; but I was care-full how I voted, the merit of my cause being yet behind" (p. 97): that is to say, the committee of elections had still to decide finally on his right to his seat. Reresby is a perfect candidate for a revisionist interpretation of early modern politics, with its focus on self-interest.

At any rate, his position was soon to change. When Reresby returned to London after the Long Prorogation, just before parliament met on February 15, 1677, Danby sent for him. Here is Reresby's account of the interview:

> [I] found him lamenting that his countrymen would not give him opportu-nity to serve them near the King; made several protestations that all the jealousies of such as called themselves of the country party were ground-less; that the King to his knowlege had no design but to preserve the religion and government established by lawe; ... that if ther was any danger to the goverment [sic], it was more from thos that pretended to be zealous for it, who, under that colour, were straining matters to soe high a pitch on that side (by pinching the Crown in supplys and in the prerogative) as to create discontents betwixt the King and his people, that confusion might be the issue; and therfore desired [me] to be carefull not to imbarke with that sort of people. (p. 110)

Reresby responded by asserting his intention to be "moderate and healing between the two extreams, and to have a due regard to the King's prerogative as well as the liberty of the subject," and he added that, until Danby's analysis of the motives of the Country party, "I had much more beliefe of their thruth and sincerity." Accordingly, when the debates on Supply resumed, and the Country party proposed only £400,000, while the Court party suggested a million, the "moderate men were for six hundred thousand." "For which sum I gave my voat," wrote Reresby. In response, Danby carried him to kiss the king's hand. Charles, meanwhile, gave Reresby in person his own version of Danby's analysis, which was still more cynical:

> Thos members of Parliament, said the King, that pretend this great zeale for the publique good, are of two kindes, either such as would subvert the government themselves and bring it to a commonwealth again, or such as seem to joine with that party and talke loud against the Court, hopeing to have their mouths stopped by places or preferments. (p. 112)

For the rest of his parliamentary career under Charles II, Reresby enjoyed the same degree of intimacy with Danby, with the king, and also with the duke of

York, all of whom intervened from time to time to protect his claim to his parliamentary seat. In the autunm of 1678, when the Popish Plot broke, and the Commons sent up a bill to the Lords to prevent Catholic lords from sitting if they refused the oath of allegiance, the Lords, as Burnet recorded in quite a different tone of voice, sent down as an amendment a proviso exempting the duke. As Reresby tells us, the proviso was accepted in the Commons on November 21 by only two votes. The vote was 158 to 156. "If this had been carryed against him," Reresby wrote, "he would also have been voated from the King's presence. I spoake for the Duke in this debate, and had his Highness his thankes when I waited upon him" (p. 160). If Reresby had voted in the other direction, it would have been a tie. Although Grey reported this day's debate with considerable fullness, Reresby's intervention goes unmentioned.

It is a mystery to me how Browning, having edited these *Memoirs*, could so confidently defend Reresby against the charge of trimming. His friendship with Danby, Browning asserts, "is not in the least to his discredit," and "in spite of the very troublous times which followed 1677 nothing in Reresby's conduct after that date provides any foundation for a charge of real lack of principle" (p. xxvii). One might agree with this defense, provided that the idea of principle can be reduced to an ideal of moderation for its own sake, as well as for one's own sake. When Danby fell in 1679, Reresby's conclusions were as follows—not very different from John Nicholas's Horatian reflection on the fall of Clarendon:

> This confirmed me in the opinion that a middle state was ever the best, not soe low as to be trodden upon nor soe high as to be in danger to be shaken with the blast of envie, not so lazie as not to endeavour to be distinguished in some measure from men of the same ranke by ones own industry nor soe ambitious as to sacrafice the ease of this life, and the hopes of happiness in the next, to clime over the heads of others to a greatness of uncertain continuance. And I take this to be the fitt and just care of a father of children. (p. 174)

Using these principles, Reresby easily survived the reign of James, in whose parliaments he was very active and with whom he was moderately intimate. He dreaded the arrival of William, whom he regarded with deep suspicion as an unsettler. He declined to seek election in the Convention Parliament, and died in May 1689, at the age of fifty-five. At almost the same time Gilbert Burnet was appointed by William to the see of Salisbury, and became one of the most active members of the episcopal bench in the Lords.

The value of Reresby's *Memoirs* consists in large part of what they do *not* provide. Despite his intimacy with Danby, the king, and the duke of York,

Reresby does not supply us with insider information unavailable from other sources. Nor, given his decision, quoted above, to summarize rather than report debates, does he give us the *texture* of the business of the Commons. The "I" in these memoirs is not insidious, but it is omnipresent; the work could have been retitled *My Parliamentary Career*. But as an example of an ordinary country member whose votes were appropriated, if not actually dictated, by the crown, if not by the Court party, Reresby confirms what the critics of the pensioners in the Long Parliament had been saying; or rather, he explains how one might come to be a pensioner oneself.

Sir William Temple: Diplomat "Behind the Curtain"

Sir William Temple, as J.J. Davies tells us in *House of Commons*, attended Cambridge in the 1640s and used his time at the university "to become a moderately accomplished tennis-player." This skill would serve him perfectly in his career as Charles II's chief ambassador to the Netherlands, a role he first undertook in 1667, towards the end of the Second Dutch War, when the French invaded the Spanish Netherlands, and the English king had to rethink his allegiances. Temple's great achievement was to broker the famous Triple Alliance between England, Holland, and Spain for the defense of the Spanish Netherlands against France, which was achieved with remarkable speed in the early spring of 1668. No sooner was this shift in English foreign policy in place, however, than Charles secretly reverted to his friendship, cemented by familial ties, with Louis XIV. A glutton for punishment, Temple nevertheless accepted the role of ambassador to the Netherlands at the end of the Third Dutch War. He helped to broker the marriage of William of Orange, with whom he had become good friends, to Mary, daughter of the duke of York, and so had a much greater influence on future English history than he could ever have dreamed.

This chapter is concerned, however, only with Temple's activities between 1675 and 1678, when relations between the European powers were again under stress as Louis XIV embarked on a rapid and brilliant course of territorial expansion, creating the specter of a French "universal monarchy." Temple's *Memoirs of what passed in Christendom from 1672 to 1679*, published in 1691, became one of the founding texts of Whig secret history, since it laid out with devastating frankness both the deceits that Louis had practiced on other heads of state, and those that Charles II had cultivated with respect to his parliament, especially in the long sixteenth session when the Commons engaged more directly than ever before with English foreign policy.

The value of Temple's testimony is that his personal conversations with Charles II, Danby, and others help us to ascertain what these men were actually thinking, as distinct from what they were saying to parliament. This period begins with Temple's very general summary of the fourteenth session, in which Shaftesbury, having lost his position on the Privy Council, "had run desperately into the popular humour," and Arlington was so jealous of Danby's rise "that he fell in with the common humour of the Parliament, in fomenting those jealousies and practices in the House of Commons, which centered in a measure agreed among the most considerable of them, not to consent to give the King any money" whilst Danby was in power.[11] Attacks on Lauderdale and the quarrel between the two Houses led the king to prorogue them "about the end of June," actually June 9, 1675. Then Temple heard the king's reasons from his own mouth:

> Upon my arrival soon after, his Majesty, telling me the several reasons that had moved him to it, said, That he doubted much, while the war lasted abroad, it would give occasion or pretence for these heats that had of late appeared in the Parliament, and make him very uneasy in his revenue, . . . that some of the warm leaders in both Houses had a mind to engage him in a war against France, which they should not do for many reasons; and, among the rest, because he was sure, if they did, they would leave him in it, and make use of it to ruin his Ministers, and make him depend upon them more than he intended, or any King would desire. (p. 317)

Shades of Clarendon. Charles asked Temple to attempt a reconciliation between Danby and Arlington, which failed lamentably, especially on Arlington's side: "Thus the seeds of discontents, that had been sown in Parliament under the counsels of the Cabal, began to spring fast and root deep." The result, Temple averred, was that England's allies abroad believed the war fervor in parliament and the nation "would at last engage the King in their quarrel, which they knew would force France to such a peace as they desired" (p. 318). This belief was further fostered by the next session of parliament,

> which grew so high against the French, or at least, upon that pretence, against the present conduct of his Majesty or his Ministers, that the King prorogued them about Christmas [actually November 22, 1675], before any of the matters projected by the warm men amongst the House of Commons were brought into form. (p. 339)

In July 1676, there opened the international congress at Nijmegen, an attempt by the European powers with a stake in the current situation to decide whether the response to the French advances should be a confederacy for war against Louis or a new general peace treaty that included him. The negotiations at Nijmegen were endless and intricate, much time being spent upon the formalities of precedence, etc. The Dutch were exhausted and wanted peace. The French, wrote Temple, were "willing, like gamesters that have won much, to give over, unless obliged to play on by those that had lost" (p. 371).

Temple is rather short on, or imprecise about, dates, but we can tell that he is still speaking of the sixteenth session of the English parliament when he explains that Spain was interfering in it by way of its minister Don Bernard de Salinas, "who did indeed very industriously foment the heats that began about this time to appear in the Parliament . . . which moved them, about the end of March [actually March 10, 1677], to make an address to the King" against the French advances (pp. 411–12). Salinas "told some of the Commons, that the King was very angry at this address, and had said upon it, that the authors of it were a company of rogues." Charles ordered Salinas to leave the country, but "about a month after [actually May 25], the Parliament made another address, upon the same occasion; desiring his Majesty to make a league offensive and defensive" with Holland. This was the Address that occasioned the most extraordinary royal speech of the reign, which Temple describes as "an angry answer" (p. 412). Importantly, he misdescribes what followed. Charles, he reported, "prorogued the Parliament until the winter following" (p. 412), whereas in fact he adjourned it, three times. It finally reconvened on January 28, 1678.

In the interim, the prince of Orange was in England to celebrate his marriage and negotiate, as he thought, support from Charles against Louis. William was particularly concerned lest a peace with the French leave Flanders without a frontier, open to another encroachment when Louis felt ready. But between them William, Charles, and the duke of York worked out the terms of a peace that might satisfy all. "However, [the prince] went not away without a great mortification, to see the Parliament prorogued to next spring; which the French Ambassador had gained of the King, to make up some good mien with France after the Prince's marriage" (p. 437). Naturally, there were objections to the marriage from Louis, but also in Holland, where it was feared that the prince had been drawn over entirely to England's interests.

When parliament reconvened after the series of adjournments on January 28, Temple felt that it "seemed to import something of great consequence," and inserted an overview of the Long Parliament's shape at this stage:

> The King acquaints them with the league he had made in Holland, and asks them money upon it for putting himself in a posture to carry on the war if the peace failed; which the Parliament gave him, upon the hopes of the war, and not of the peace [£1,000,000 voted on February 21]. The Constitution of this

Parliament, that had sat seventeen years, was grown into two known factions, which were called, that of Court and Country: the Court-party were grown numerous, by a practice introduced by my Lord Clifford, of downright buying off one man after another, as they could make the bargain. The Country party was something greater yet in number, and kept more in credit upon the corruption of others, and their own pretence of steadiness to the true interest of the nation, especially in the points of France and popery. When these came in question, many of the Court-party voted with those of the Country, who then carried all before them; but whenever the Court seemed to fall in with the true interests of the nation, especially in those two points, then many of the Country-party, meaning fairly, fell in with the Court, and carried the votes, as they now did, *upon the King's pretence to grow bold with France,* and to resolve upon the war if the peace were refused. (p. 441; italics added)

Temple then reports on his personal knowledge of the huge bribe offered to Charles by Louis. "About this time I happened to be with my Lord Treasurer one evening in his closet when a packet came to him from Mr. Montague ambassador at Paris," informing him that France and Holland had agreed on a separate peace and Louis had made "his Majesty the offer of a great sum of money for consent," i.e. for non-interference. According to Temple, Danby was also offered "a very considerable sum for himself" in exchange for keeping the deal secret. Danby rejected it for himself and appeared to reject it for his master too, saying to Temple "that he thought it was the same thing, as if it should be made to the King, to have Windsor put into the French hands . . . and that we had nothing to do but to go on with our treaty with the confederates" (p. 443). Meanwhile, parliament had been adjourned and readjourned since March 27, and would not meet again until April 29, 1678.

For the meeting on the 29th, special provisions were made. Danby, Temple tells us, came to him on the 20th "and desired me to prepare what the King was to say to the Parliament upon this occasion; which I did" (p. 445).[12] This is a remarkable piece of information. In fact, Charles made no speech on this occasion, but a very long speech was delivered by Chancellor Finch, which brought the two Houses up to date on what had been happening in Europe, and announced the grave fact that "at this very Time" the Dutch were about to sign a separate peace with France. A very conciliatory tone is exhibited throughout, utterly different from the angry speech of May 28 of the previous year. Finch (as the mouthpiece of the diplomatic Temple) offered to show the Commons the terms of the "League offensive and defensive" made with Holland, which previously the court had adamantly refused to reveal.

In fact, an envoy from the prince of Orange had just arrived in England with very different news, that Holland would still be willing to go to war if they could be convinced that England was in any way sincere. Temple reported this to the king, "who seemed positive to declare the war, in case the Parliament advised him, and promised to support it."

> When an unlucky peevish vote, moved by Sir T[homas] C[larges] in spite to my Lord Treasurer, passed the House of Commons, that no money should be given, till satisfaction was received in matters of religion. This left all so loose and lame, that the King was in a rage, reproached me with my popular notions, as he termed them; and asked me when, or how, I thought he could trust the House of Commons to carry him through the war, if he should engage in it? And indeed I had not much to say. (p. 446)

Temple attributes this move, which occurred in the debate on the Finch/Temple speech on April 29, not only to Clarges (where Grey does not name the mover) but also to personal spite at the loss of Clarges' court offices, which are unspecified in *House of Commons*, and in any case occurred much earlier, after the affair of Sir John Coventry's nose, in which Clarges had been instrumental in bringing charges against the guardsmen. Clarges had been an active and consistent opponent of the court's policies from the start of the Long Parliament. But to claim that one "peevish vote" (which was carried 129 to 89, a large margin) irrevocably altered the course of history is patently absurd. In Chapter 8 we will follow step by step the stages by which the Commons became increasingly suspicious of the king's intentions, leading to the prorogations of both the sixteenth and seventeenth sessions, and ultimately to the dissolution of January 1679. It is easier to believe that Charles was just seeking excuses for avoiding a war that he had originally told Temple he had no intention of waging.

> The turn that the King gave all this was, that, since the Dutch would have peace upon the French terms, and France offered money for his consent to what he could not help, he did not know why he should not get the money; and thereupon ordered me to treat upon it with the French Ambassador. (p. 447)[13]

Enough has been cited from Temple's *Memoirs* to establish their tone and (with the obvious caveats) their value as testimony. This chapter has necessarily oversimplified the intricacies of international diplomacy, and indeed there were still more twists and turns to come, to which Temple, though a little hard to follow, is not a bad guide. We leave him, and he us, with one of his several summaries:

Thus was the peace gained with Holland. His Majesty was excluded from any fair pretence of entering into the war, after the vast expence of raising a great army, and transporting them into Flanders. . . . Spain was necessitated to accept the terms that the Dutch had negotiated for them; and this left the peace of the empire wholly at the mercy and discretion of France, and the restitution of Lorrain (which all had consented in) wholly abandoned and unprovided. . . . The King's disposition inclined him to preserve his measures with France, and consequently to promote a peace which might break the present confederacy: the humour of his people and Parliament was violent towards engaging him in a war. . . . From these humours arose those uncertainties in our counsels, that no man, *who was not behind the curtain*, could tell what to make of, and which appeared to others still more mysterious than indeed they were. (p. 468; italics added)

"Behind the curtain"; a fine metaphor for the stance of the relator of secret history. The question is: how can you ever be sure, when you believe yourself to be behind the curtain, that there is not another curtain behind that.

CHAPTER 5

❖

Under Cover
Scofflaw Pamphlets

Whenever there was a crisis in the Long Parliament, and members of the Opposition in either House believed that disseminating what had occurred in one session might improve their chances in the next, scofflaw pamphlets published the proceedings of parliament. There were five such moments. The first was during the eighth session of 1667–68, when the debacle of the Second Dutch War was being discussed in the Commons. The second was during the second part of the eleventh session, when in October 1673 the Commons reconvened to learn that during their adjournment the duke of York had contracted to marry the Catholic duchess of Modena. The third, which was fought out instead in the Lords, was created by Danby's notorious Test Bill in April 1675, brought in as a surprise at the opening of the fourteenth session, and only killed by the procedural struggle between the Houses over the Shirley/Fagg case, which led to their prorogation. The fourth, hardly a moment, was the product of the extremely long and contentious sixteenth session of 1677, which began with the doomed protest by the four Whig lords as to the legality of the Long Prorogation and ended with a mighty challenge in the Commons—a challenge directed to the king himself—over foreign policy. Finally, the fifth crisis was, of course, the furor over the supposed Popish Plot in 1678, which completely changed the temper of the eighteenth session and ended in parliament's dissolution.

Each of these moments spawned illegal pamphlets; but, as mentioned earlier, it is important to distinguish between printed protests and pamphlets that actually recorded, instrumentally, in the interests of protest and future strategy, chunks of the recent history of parliament. The former often *became* themselves part of the history of parliament, as when Dr. Nicholas Cary was summoned in 1677 to the Lords to explain his responsibility for *The Grand Question Stated & discussed concerning the Prorogation*. But the *Grand Question* itself tells us nothing about the debates in either House on this issue.

In the latter category, for the 1667 war crisis, we should count as a legitimate form of parliamentary history Andrew Marvell's *Last Instructions to a Painter*, which might have been planned as a pamphlet. An unusually long verse satire, this poem devoted nearly a quarter of its almost one thousand lines to the debates in the Commons on October 12, 1666 over a new general excise tax, introduced by the court as a surprise on a foggy morning before most members were seated. Presented as a mock-epic battle, the poem names the then heroes of the emergent Country party and their opponents (though for what they actually said we would need an equivalent of Grey's *Debates*, which does not start till the following year). The poem also glances at other events that happened later, such as Edward Seymour's attack on the Canary patent on October 29, or Sir Richard Temple's dubious victory in banning Irish cattle in January 1667. In the battle of the Excise, Colonel Giles Strangeways is particularly praised for having been in his seat first thing in the morning "when the house was thin," and delivering a filibuster, "fighting it single till the rest might arm" (l. 262). We have, however, no evidence of a published version of the poem prior to 1689. A manuscript at the University of Nottingham (Portland MS. Pw V 299), which contains only this poem, appears to be a copy text,[1] but it might have been meant for a later attempt at publication. If there had been a printing early in 1668, it could easily have disappeared altogether. On the other hand, when Clarendon fled the country on November 29, 1667, the poem's chief rationale, which was to paint him as the principal villain of the war's funding, if not of its mismanagement, expired.

This may also explain the existence, as a 1700 imprint only,[2] of *The Proceedings in the House of Commons, touching the impeachment of Edward, late earl of Clarendon, lord High-chancellour of England, anno 1667. With the many debates and speeches in the House.* Once Clarendon's enemies had achieved their ends, the publication of such a pamphlet in late 1667 might have seemed gratuitous; but, independent of its motives, it makes an invaluable contribution to our knowledge of who said what during the impeachment. *Proceedings* is vastly more detailed than Grey's *Debates*, which was perhaps originally generated by the Clarendon affair, and is at this stage sketchy and curt by comparison. It is not impossible that Grey got the idea of taking shorthand notes of debates from whoever was responsible for *Proceedings*. This might have been John Vaughan, whose long and legalistic speeches are reported therein at disproportionate length.

A much bigger provocation for scofflaw publication, however, was presented in 1673. In that year it was the Modena marriage that generated the most anxiety. The incentive and the model for scofflaw publishing then may have been created by Peter du Moulin's *England's Appeale from the Private Cabal at White-hall to the Great Council of the Nation, The Lords and Commons in Parliament*

Assembled, which was known to be on its way to England from Amsterdam in January. Though it surely contributed to the Commons' unwillingness to finish up the Supply debates in the eleventh session, *England's Appeale* was focused on England's double-dealing with respect to Holland, and gives information only en passant about how the English parliament was misled about the king's foreign policy. Not long afterwards, however, somebody published, from Middleburg, *My Lord Lucas his Speech in the House of Peers, Feb. The 22. 1671, upon The Reading of the Subsidy Bill the second Time, in the presence of his Majesty*. It takes a little patience to realize that the title-page's assertion, "London, Printed in the Year 1670," is a barefaced lie, since the pamphlet concludes with a list of all the bad things that have happened subsequently, including the "Strict Alliance with France," "Shutting up the Exchequer," and "His Highness ... marrying a Papist (Niece to a Cardinal)." "Making French Carwell an English Dutchess" is the penultimate item, dating the pamphlet after July 15, 1673. But as a contribution to parliamentary history in itself, *My Lord Lucas his Speech* is quite brilliant, recording for posterity a protest about over-supplying the king that the House of Lords had determined should be blotted from the record. The publication was ordered burned by the public hangman. The speech would subsequently appear in full in Archdeacon Echard's *History of England*, published in 1718,[3] thereby being authorized and absorbed into the general history of parliament for the eighteenth century and thereafter.

But Lord Lucas's speech was not the only scofflaw pamphlet hoarded and preserved by Archdeacon Echard. On November 24, 1673, Robert Yard, an under-secretary of state, informed Sir Joseph Williamson at Cologne of the appearance, "some days since," of another scofflaw pamphlet: *Votes and Addresses of the Honourable House of Commons assembled in Parliament, made this present year 1673, concerning Popery and other Grievances*.[4] This is a small eight-page tract which deals with two brief pieces of business in the Commons during the eleventh session: an Address to the king, of March 29, 1673, about grievances connected with the billeting of soldiers and problems in Ireland; and a second Address, of October 20, protesting against the Modena marriage, after which parliament had been immediately prorogued to October 27. The pamphlet concludes with the disturbances that took place on November 4, which the publisher thought needed to be set out in all their embarrassing detail, when parliament was once more prorogued. It was this part of the tract that Yard quoted to Williamson—an unusual sign of how important he imagined it would be to his correspondent:

The House of Commons having ordered an Address to be made to his Majesty, shewing that the standing Army was a Grievance, ... did intend that day to wait on his Majesty to present it; But his Majesty was in his Robes in the House of Peers, and Lords hastening to him, the Black-Rod being sent to the Commons House to command the Speaker and the Commons to come to his Majesty to the House of Peers; but it so hapned that the Speaker and the Black-Rod met both at the Commons-House door; the Speaker being within the House, the door was commanded to be shut, and they cryed to the Chair, others said the Black-Rod was at the door . . . but the Speaker was hurried to the Chair. Then was moved.

1. That our Alliance with France was a Grievance.
2. That the evil Counsel about the King was a Grievance to this Nation.
3. That the Lord Lauderdale was a person that was a grievance to this Nation, and not fit to be intrusted or imployed in any Office of Place of Trust, but to be removed. Whereupon they cryed, *To the Question*. But the Black-Rod knocking very earnestly at the Door, the Speaker rose out of the Chair and went away in confusion. (p. 7)

The last word of the pamphlet, then, before "FINIS", was "confusion."

The purpose of this publication was evidently to show that the relationship between king and parliament had broken down to the point where even the most ritualistic of actions had become symbolic of anarchy. So effective was it that Echard copied it more or less word for word into his *History*, the only changes being in the direction of still greater drama. Thus in Echard we find additionally: "the King unexpectedly and of a sudden appeared at the House of Peers with his Robes and Crown"; "Some of the Members suddenly shut the Door, and cryed out *To the Chair, to the Chair!*" There was "a General Cry, *to the Question, to the Question*"; and the Speaker "leapt out of the Chair, and the House rose in great Confusion"(p. 337).

Grey's *Debates* gives a very truncated version of this scene. So it is all the more entertaining, in following the story forward, that when the *Debates* was published in 1763 its editor thought fit to insert Echard's dramatic account into the footnotes. He then added an evaluative comment taken from James Ralph's *History of England*, published in 1745:

What a dreadful picture have we here of the disorders of these times! Though there was sufficient cause for a close enquiry into the state of the nation, and a firm opposition to the favourite view of the Court; and though the alliance with France, and the ruin of Holland, were equally inconsistent with the interest and safety of England; yet surely such violence and fury, without any previous remonstrances or endeavours to bring the Court to reason, more resembled the turbulence of a faction, than the regularity and decorum of a Senate.

Thus from 1673, when the pamphlet appeared, through 1718, when Echard raised its temperature, through 1745, when Ralph expressed a somewhat prissy dismay, to 1763, when the editor of Grey's *Debates* believed we should revisit it once again, the events in question came to stand for much about the Long Parliament that the authorities would have preferred to forget.

The third scofflaw pamphlet of 1673 was far more ambitious. Entitled *A Relation of the most material matters handled in Parliament: relating to Religion, Property, and the Liberty of the Subject. With the Answers unto such Addresses as were made unto his MAJESTY, in Order to the Redressing the several GRIEVANCES complained of, and the Behaviour and Carriage of the Popish and French Court Party*, it left no potential purchaser in any doubt that it contained forbidden information, which it would deliver with an Oppositional gloss. "Printed in the Year, 1673," it carried no obvious sign by which printer or publisher might be detected. A larger publication than *Votes and Addresses*, forty pages long, it also focused on the failure of the eleventh and twelfth sessions, but began the story earlier, when the Commons reconvened in February 1673 and tackled the king on the subject of his Declaration of Indulgence, which he was forced to withdraw in early March. The Commons' Address on this issue, the king's first unsatisfactory answer, their second Address on it, and the king's final speech of defeat are published in full (pp. 4–13). But these are folded around interpretive passages that speak to the growing fear of France abroad and of popery at home, as well as containing information about what happened in the Lords. At this point the *Relation* printed the Address about Ireland which had opened *Votes and Addresses*, followed by a narrative of the Modena marriage and the Commons' attempt to prevent it, which led to their prorogation. But instead of reporting that scene of chaos, the *Relation*, whose theme was that "the Court . . . only stands in need of Parliaments to raise money" (p. 24), cited in full the king's disingenuous speech at the prorogation, with its conclusion: "I will not be idle either in some things which may aid to your Satisfaction, and then I shall expect a suitable Return from you" (p. 26).

"You see here," wrote the anonymous author, saucily, "his Majesties unwillingness to part without Money, and also to leave the French, his trusty Friends":

> Therefore Recollect yourselves, that it is resolved, that *Delendo est Carthago*,[5] and to Advance the French Interest, that there be no need of Parliaments; Religion is concerned it seems (but which we know not) and Reformation promised, such as will make us all his Debtors. Let's therefore state the Accounts, that you may pay what is owing (pp. 26–27).

And the last five pages of the pamphlet were devoted to listing, as a parodic accounting of what the Commons might owe the king or had already paid: such as £500,000 "For Marrying his Highness (the undoubted Successor to the Crown) to an Adopted Daughter of the Pope and the French King" (p. 28). Readers were invited to amuse themselves by comparing the pension paid to the Lord O'Brian (one of Sir John Coventry's assailants) of £700 with the one pound and eightpence set aside "For Redressing Grievances in Ireland according to the late Address" (p. 31).

This is about as scofflaw as one can get. The Relator impugns the king directly: "The King's Answer pleased too the Major part, though the most intelligent questioned the performance thereof, knowing there was very little Security in his Majesties Promises and Engagements" (p. 11). It must have been from the *Relation* that Archdeacon Echard had access to the text of the second Address against the Modena marriage (Friday, October 31, 1673), which appears verbatim in his *History*. There is no record of the text in Grey, though it must have been read aloud in the House.

The eleventh session of the Long Parliament also spawned a scofflaw pamphlet, rather elegantly printed under the following provocative title: *A Journal of the Proceedings of the House of Commons the last Session of Parliament, Beginning Jan. 7 Anno Domini 1673 [i.e. 1674] and ending Feb. 24, 1673. Containing all the publick Transactions Of the House of Commons. To which are added four of the Grand Bills Prepared to be enacted that Session. Printed at Rome By the Especial Command of his Holiness, at the request of his Highnesse the Duke of York* (1674). This short session was prorogued on February 24, to be followed by a recess of fourteen months, and the pamphlet uses its ire against the prorogation to record, on a day-by-day basis, what the Commons had been trying to achieve in those few weeks, only to have their efforts rendered nugatory. Impeachment proceedings against Lauderdale, Arlington, and Buckingham are detailed. The four "Grand Bills" are printed in full: Habeas Corpus, "An Act for a Test to distinguish between Protestants and Papists," "An Act for the better prevention of illegall exaction of money from the Subject," and (shades of the twenty-first century) "An Act to prevent Imprisonment of the Subject in illegal & Secret Prisons, or places beyond the Seas." The *Journal* concludes with an address to the "Courteous Reader," which is lively enough to deserve ample quotation, not least since, despite its presence among the Thomason Tracts, it seems to be virtually unknown:

> it will not be improper to enquire into the Causes of the Prorogation, which has made abortive all those wise and healing Councels which this languishing Nation has so long groaned for, Let us therefore in the first place consider his gracious Majesties Speech, and try what reasons may be extracted from it to satisfy the People, that this Prorogation was more reasonable, just and necessary than the former Prorogations. ... he tells the Parliament *that*

the Peace was ratified &c. I wonder by what illumination his sacred Majesty knew this; certainly it must be by some Correspondent of another world that revealed this secret of State to him whilst he was speaking to the Parliament: for the same day (& almost the same minute) . . . the States of the United Netherlands were ratifying the Peace: In the next Place his Majesty is pleased to tell the Parliament *That the Spring was coming on so fast, &.* . . . This, I must confesse, was neither Reason nor Inspiration: But they must be Prorogued and whosoever is not satisfyed with his sacred Majesties Reasons and Revelations, let him read on.

I presume all sober men of unbyassed judgements look upon the Kings speech but as a flourish of Wit and Eloquence, which some of the Cabal had put into his mouth, hoping thereby to veyl their designs.

The *Journal* then proceeds to give its own reasons for the prorogation: to prevent the passing of the bill against popish recusants; to prevent parliament from inspecting the condition of Ireland; "to prevent the Parliament taking any further notice of the Duke of Yorks obstinate temerity in marrying a Papist"; to prevent an Address for the immediate removal of the English forces in the French service; because the Houses were (for once) in good agreement; because Arlington was in danger; because the Commons were slow in giving money, "which the Court thinks their Duty and the onely thing they are fit soe to meet and consult about."

The agents of the prorogation were then listed: the duke of York, Lord Arundel of Wardour, "the Pope's Nuncio"; Arlington; Lord Treasurer [i.e. Danby]; Anglesey; the duchess of Portsmouth; and the lord keeper, Heneage Finch. Then the *Journal* returns to the timing of the prorogation, and its relation to the treaty with Holland:

What if the States had happened to deferre the ratification, and in the interim heard the King had prorogued his Parliament? I fear our case had been litle better than that of the Sheep, who were perswaded to send home their faithfull friends, the Doggs, because they were in Treaty with the Wolves; you know what followed. (p. 43)

And having floated his Aesopian fable of European politics at the time, the author returned scathingly to the king's reference to the speedy approach of spring. In fact, as he pointed out, "the very extremity of the weather, & the badnesse of the ways detained them a month in London after the Prorogation."[6] Thus the *Journal* engaged simultaneously with the king's manipulation of the length of sessions, clearly by this time a grievance, and the deceptive function (which a published critique could reveal) of the royal speeches.

A Letter from a Person of Quality, to His Friend in the Country

The sixteenth session ended in frustration, as Archdeacon Echard put it, "without having granted or voted any Money, or having one single Act passed" (3:354). When parliament reconvened on April 13, 1675, after a recess of almost fourteen months, the hounds of indignation were straining at the leash. This despite the fact, as Gilbert Burnet informed his eighteenth-century readers, no money was to be requested in the king's speech this session, "it being only called to heal all breaches, and beget a good understanding between the king and his people" (2:63). There was skepticism about this. In March, a parody of the king's expected speech, now usually attributed to Andrew Marvell, was circulating in manuscript, and in a letter to his nephew dated July 24, 1675, Marvell reported on the opening days of the session, and the (to him) sinister plans that had led up to it: the creation, by negotiation behind the scenes, of an "Episcopal Cavalier Party," the reinvigoration of the laws against Dissenters, and the agreement "that the King should ask, forsooth, no Mony, but only mention the building and refitting of Ships":

> And thus the Parliament meets, and the King tells them 'tis only to see what farther is wanted for Religion and Property. The Commons were very difficultly brought to give him Thanks for his gracious Expressions. Strait they poured in Bills for Habeas Corpus . . . Treason to levy Mony without, or longer than, Consent of Parliament; and that it should be lawful to resist. (*P&L*, 2:342)

The scene now shifts to the House of Lords. Danby, who had, according to the *Relation*, given a violent speech there against the Commons' Test Act against Catholics (p. 13), decided to counter it with his own Test Act, to be directed against almost anybody who might disagree with the will of the king or his ministers. This Test Act, invidiously introduced under the title of "An Act to prevent the Dangers which may arise from Persons disaffected to the Government," but more commonly referred to as the "Non-Resisting Bill," was introduced into the Lords on April 15 by Lord Lindsey, Danby's brother-in-law. It eventually produced one of the two most famous scofflaw pamphlets of the reign, the *Letter from a Person of Quality, to His Friend in the Country*, which appeared in print in mid-October 1675, in time for the opening of the fifteenth session on October 13, providing the public with a close view of what had happened in the fourteenth. During this last session the proposal for a new Test Act was strenuously debated in the Lords, and those who opposed it, primarily Shaftesbury, Buckingham, Halifax, Holles, and Wharton, kept the resistance (against an anti-resistance bill) going until the end of May. Danby's party, however, had the majority, in large part constituted by the bishops whom he had lined up before the session began. They were no doubt influenced by the king's presence among them, especially during the long debate on May 31. The bill was only prevented from being sent down to the Commons for final approval by the dispute between the two Houses over the Shirley/Fagg case, which so interrupted business that the king prorogued the parliament on June 9. During the recess, the *Letter* was compiled, printed, and distributed through the complex machinery of clandestine publication, which involved many small agents, including women. The more people involved the better, spreading responsibility. On Monday, November 8, the Lords' Journal reported that a complaint was made in the House about the *Letter*, which was ordered to be burned by the hangman in two separate public locations. One of the first people called in to be questioned by the Lords themselves was John Starkey the bookseller (*LJ*, 13:17). The wardens of the Stationers' Company began a major search, but none of the people in whose houses copies were found could or would provide any clues as to their origin or originators.

We are fortunate now to have a complete account of the planning for Danby's Test Act and of the *Letter from a Person of Quality* from J.R. Milton and Philip Milton, who included the *Letter* as a possible work by John Locke in collaboration with Shaftesbury in a volume of the new Clarendon edition of Locke's works.[7] They dispose effectively of the suggestion that when, on November 12, Locke left London for France, where he would remain for the next three and a half years, he left in haste, to avoid being questioned about the *Letter*, and they emphasize not only his preparations for the journey before the *Letter* was condemned, but also aspects of Shaftesbury's role in its compilation. They point out the similarities between parts of the *Letter* and the long speech delivered by Shaftesbury against the Test. They do not, however, speak about the reportorial quality of the *Letter* as a contribution to parliamentary history, and its efforts to make that history a continuous narrative of conspiracy, of which the Test was "this STATE MASTER-PIECE."

The idea of placing a current event in a longer narrative that suggests a sinister design had already been broached in the *Relation* of 1673. The author (or authors) of the *Letter* take this explanatory mechanism further. It begins with the passing of the legislation we refer to as the Clarendon Code: the Corporation Act, the Act of the Militia, the Act of Uniformity, and finally the Five-Mile Act passed at Oxford in 1665. What linked all of these, according to the *Letter*, was their hostility to Dissenters and their dependence on oaths; and it was pertinent to the author's case that the Oxford session had also very nearly passed an earlier version of the Non-Resisting Bill, which only failed to pass by three votes, two of them being cast by Danby himself and Lord Lindsey. That there was something wildly ironic about all this was grist to the

Letter: "they have since made ample Satisfaction for whatever offence they gave the Church or Court in that Vote" (p. 340).

The *Letter* then turns to discussing Charles II's ill-fated second Declaration of Indulgence, which it attributes to the influence of Clifford and the support of Shaftesbury. Dramatically, the writer now presents himself as on confidential terms with both Clifford and Shaftesbury, each of whom imparts to him in conversation his theory of why the king chose this route. In the case of Shaftesbury, we are given a long explanation, in reported speech, of why the Declaration was not illegal or dangerous, but good for Protestantism and good for the Anglican church, "for the narrow bottom they [the Anglican bishops] had placed themselves upon, and the Measures they had proceeded by, [were] so contrary to the Properties, and Liberties of the Nation [as] must needs in short time, prove fatal to them" (p. 342). A rigid conformity is itself the danger. The "Shaftesbury" of the conversation manages to imagine a time when "that power of our Church should come into the hands of a Popish Prince" (p. 343) and the doctrine of coercive uniformity be turned upside down.

The *Letter* next turns to the outcry against the Declaration, which it attributes to lobbying by the bishops and their fear of popery, which so influenced the Commons that in the 1673 session they had produced both their own Test Act against Catholics (the one against which Danby railed in the Lords) and "an act in favor of the dissenting Protestants," which lapsed "for want of time," a somewhat inaccurate account of what actually happened. "In this posture, the Session of Parliament that began Oct. 27. 1673 found Matters, which being suddenly broken up, did nothing" (p. 345). This mild reference to the indecent prorogation of November 4 connects the *Letter* quietly to *Votes and Addresses*. The difference between them is that for the *Letter* religion is the only issue, and the shifts in public policy are dictated by the bishops, who keep changing their strategy. The session that began in January 1674 likewise ended "without doing any thing," because of the behind-the-scene negotiations. Whereupon the *Letter* proceeds to describe the deal that was struck at Lambeth Palace on January 26, 1675, between Danby, Finch, Lauderdale, and "six or seven of the Bishops," to create a new alliance between Old Cavaliers and conservative bishops, an alliance that could control both Catholics and Protestant Dissenters, and take over "all the places of Profit, Command, and Trust" (p. 347). There is a close correlation between the *Letter* at this point and Marvell's letter to William Popple of July 24, 1675: "In order to make their Episcopal Cavalier Party, they contrived beforehand a politic Test to be inacted . . . they discoursed of none having any beneficial Offices but Cavaliers, or Sons of Cavaliers" (*P&L*, 2:341). Since the *Letter* was not published until October at the earliest, the talks at Lambeth Palace must have been leaked.

The rest of the *Letter* is devoted to detailing the resistance to Danby's bill waged by individual members of the Lords, both at its first introduction, and then clause by clause. "The debate lasted Five several days before it was committed to a Committee of the whole House, which hardly ever happened to any Bill before" (p. 349). Perhaps the most important service that the authors of the *Letter* provided for their readers was in printing the full texts of the protestations made and signed by the dissenting lords at various stages—a record of great names conjoined in protest, names made greater by the way the *Letter* honors them. The second protestation, signed by Buckingham, Bristol, Shaftesbury, Winchester, Howard of Berks, Wharton, Salisbury, Clarendon's son, Mohun, Denbigh, Stamford, and Delamer, itself caused a violent debate:

> the great Officers and Bishops raised a *storm* against the Lords that had Subscrib'd it; endeavouring not only some severe proceedings against their persons, if they had found the House would have born it, but also to have taken away *the very liberty of Entring Protestations with Reasons* . . . the Debate ran for some hours either wholly to raze the Protestation out of the Books, or at least some part of, the Expression of *Christian compassion to Protestant Dissenters* being that, which gave them most offence. (p. 351)

The *Letter* especially commends Denzil Holles, not only for his able defense of the protestation, but also for insisting that his name be added to it, "because his sickness had forced him out of the House the day before." A third protestation, defending the "absolute freedom of Protesting," was signed by twenty-one lords; and a fourth protestation was necessary because, though the Opposition lords had managed to get two votes passed that seemed to protect the rights of peers to sit and speak in parliament, whatever should come of Danby's bill, the committee of the whole House overrode this proviso, and further cut off protestations by refusing to report its own votes at the time they were taken. By this time the bill was a mess, so that Lord Keeper Bridgeman asked permission to reorganize it; whereupon the *Letter* suddenly placed the whole affair in the perspective of biblical history—the attempts by the Egyptian pharaoh to keep the fleeing Israelites in slavery: "But it was observable the Hand of God was upon them in this whole Affair; their Chariot-wheels were taken off, they drew heavily: A Bill so long design'd, prepared, and of that Moment to all their Affairs, had hardly a sensible Composure." The reference is to Exodus 14:23–26: "And the Egyptians pursued, and went in after them to the midst of the sea. . . . And . . . the Lord looked unto the host of the Egyptians through the pillar of fire and of the cloud. . . . And took off their chariot wheels, that they drave them heavily." What followed in the biblical story, but not in the parliamentary one, was that the pursuers were trapped in the middle of the Red Sea when the temporarily parted waters returned and overwhelmed them.

Clause by clause the bill was then dissected, and its premises rejected by the Opposition lords, so that various amendments were made, none of which addressed the central issue. It proved impossible to define satisfactorily in the words of the bill which religious tenets or practices were being protected thereby: what exactly one meant by "Protestantism," for example! And then the *Letter* set aside for special consideration the fact that, even if the freedom of speaking and voting in parliament were preserved by a proviso, the oath remained as a prohibition "either by Speech, or Writing, or Address" outside the walls of parliament, and "takes away all *private Converse* upon any such affairs" (p. 369). This point was made by Oliver St. John, earl of Bolingbroke, and seconded by Delamer. "Upon this all the great Officers showd themselves [and] told the Committee in plain terms, that they intended, and designed to prevent Caballing, and conspiracies against the Government," even to the point that members of parliament were to be "deprived of discoursing one with another, upon the matters that were before them" (pp. 369–70).

"Three years ago," someone observed, "it was *All Liberty and Indulgence*, and now it is *Strict and Rigid Conformity*, and what it may be, in some short time hereafter, without the Spirit of Prophesying might be shrewdly guest by a considering Man" (p. 372). When none of the Court party responded to this summation, Buckingham brought the defense to a close with a speech that, though we have no other record of it, has become immortal—thanks to the clever style of the author(s) of the *Letter*:

> This being answered with silence, the Duke of Buckingham, whose Quality, admirable Wit, and unusual pains, that he took all along in the debate against this Bill, makes me mention Him in this last place, as General of the partie, and coming last out of the Field, made a Speech late at night of Eloquent, and well placed Non-sense, showing how excellently well he could do both ways, and hoping that might do, when Sense . . . would not. (p. 372)

Thus the metaphor of parliamentary debate as epic battle, first broached in Marvell's *Last Instructions*, reappears; though the *Letter* quickly changes the literary genre, stating "This was the *last Act* of this *Tragi-Comedy*, which had taken up sixteen or seventeen whole days debate" (p. 372). Archdeacon Echard obviously had a copy of the *Letter* in front of him when he wrote his *History of England*, for he also mentions that the debate lasted "sixteen or seventeen days": "In the Conclusion of which, the duke of Buckingham, as General of the Party and last in the Field, made a famous Speech consisting of eloquent, regular, and well-plac'd Non-Sense, hoping that it might prevail when Nothing else wou'd" (3:383).

Suddenly remembering that its framing genre is that of an epistle "to a friend in the country," a phrase loaded with party meaning, the *Letter* explained its own status and place in the chronology of the Long Parliament. "Thus Sir, You see the Standard of the *new Partie* is not yet set up, but must be the work of another Session" (p. 374). From this we can infer several things; first, that Shaftesbury (as a likely author of the *Letter*) *expected* another session, during which the published *Letter* would serve as the standard of his own party; second, that it was completed after the prorogation on June 9; third, that it was in print before October 13, when the new session convened (although the uproar it caused did not begin until early November). Fortunately, Shaftesbury was wrong about the danger that Danby's bill would be reintroduced. It died a quiet and shameful death between sessions. And Shaftesbury and Buckingham would very soon be engaged in a campaign for the dissolution of the parliament, a campaign no more successful than Danby's. On October 20, when the Shirley/Fagg dispute revived, perhaps at his instigation, Shaftesbury spoke in the Lords to the effect that the Long Parliament had become useless because of the intransigence of the Commons. This speech was promptly printed as a scofflaw pamphlet, entitled *Two Speeches*, with a false Amsterdam imprint, the second speech being a very brief one made by Buckingham on November 16, asking for leave to bring in a bill of indulgence for Protestant Dissenters. The pamphlet filled itself out with "A List of the Lords who were present at the Vote for an Address to the King for Dissolving the Parliament, November the 20th, 1675," another roll-call of honorable names. It thereby fulfilled the criteria of recording for posterity a speech of Shaftesbury's that would otherwise have disappeared, and of showing the public how severely divided was that House, since the proposed Address failed by only two votes, sixteen of which were cast by episcopal proxies.[8] Finally, *Two Speeches* printed "The Protestation, with Reasons of several Lords for Dissolution of this Parliament, entred in the Lords Journal, November 22, 1675, the day the Parliament was prorogued."

The Long Prorogation Tracts

Between the prorogation of November 20, 1675 and the next calling of parliament in the spring of 1677, fifteen months elapsed. Very close to the time when the new session was expected, there was a spate of tracts arguing that the Long Prorogation was illegal, and that parliament was, or should be, dissolved: *The Long Parliament Dissolved* (1676), attributed to Denzil Holles;[9] *Some Considerations upon the Question, whether the Parliament is dissolved* (1676);[10] *A*

Seasonable Question, and an Usefull Answer (1676); and *The Grand Question concerning the prorogation of this Parliament for a year and three months stated and discussed* (dated 1676, but actually published on or about February 9, 1677), for which Dr. Nicholas Cary was questioned before the Lords and, for refusing to divulge the identity of the author, imprisoned in the Tower.[11] This last prorogation tract caused the most uproar, in part because of Cary's imperviousness to threats and his mention of "great head-pieces" being involved. He was even questioned in private by the king himself, but to no avail.[12] Bringing up the rear was a high-spirited tract sometimes attributed to Andrew Marvell: *A Seasonable Argument to perswade all the Grand Juries in England, to Petition for a New Parliament. Or, A List of the Principal Labourers in the Great Design of Popery and Arbitrary Power* (Amsterdam, 1677). This was just what it claimed to be: a long list of members of parliament and courtiers who had received gifts, pensions, positions, or other favors from the government, and what they had done to deserve them. Its tone reflected the satirical piece of bookkeeping that closed the *Relation.* Thus Sir Robert Sawyer is described as "a Lawyer, of as ill reputation as his Father,[13] [who] has had for his attendance this Session 1000l. and is promised (as he insinuates) to be Attorney-General, and Speaker of the House of Commons" (p. 4). And Sir Robert Howard, who had defected from the Country party, is now skewered as "Auditor of the Receipts of the Exchequer, worth 3000l. per annum, many great Places and Boons he has had, but his W[hore] Uphill spends all, and now refuses to Marry him" (p. 9). Amusing, perhaps, though not for Sawyer and Howard; true, it seems; and, if a form of parliamentary history, a very eccentric one.

None of these pamphlets contributed to the historiography of previous sessions. With the exception of the last, they were abstruse legal and constitutional arguments to the effect that the king had broken the rules maintained even in the amended Triennial Act, not to mention the medieval statutes enacting annual parliaments. This strategy of informing the parliamentarians of their precarious situation before they reconvened may have backfired, because Danby and his supporters were thereby informed of the arguments that would be used. The result was that when Buckingham and Shaftesbury challenged the legality of the session on February 15, the Court party lords and bishops were prearmed. We know a great deal about what happened next thanks to the scofflaw pamphlet *A Narrative of the Cause and Manner of the Imprisonment of the Lords: Now close Prisoners in the Tower of London,* which appeared with a false Amsterdam imprint, dated 1677, and the initials J.E. by way of an authorial identification. It was probably printed by John Darby. It too gestures at the device of being a letter to a distant friend. It must have appeared shortly after the arraignment of Nicholas Cary in the Lords on March 1, for that episode, and Cary's imprisonment in the Tower, appear as the pamphlet's logical, if depressing, conclusion. The *Narrative* also placed on its title-page a quotation from Psalm 37: "Fret not thy self because of him who prospereth in his ways, because of the man who bringeth wicked devices to pass. For yet a little while and the wicked shall not be: Yea, thou shalt diligently consider his place, and it shall not be."

Wishful thinking, however venerable. But the rest of the *Narrative* is actually very down-to-earth. It effectively and extensively quotes Buckingham's speech, and the startling and immediate response:

No sooner had the Duke ended his Speech, but the Lord Freschvil mov'd to have him call'd to the Bar, and then proceeded against as should be thought fit. The Lord Salisbury said, *That was to take away the Freedom of Parliament.* And maintain'd the Duke in his assertion with great Reason. . . . The Lord Arundel of Trerise seconded the Lord Freschvil's motion. The Lord Halifax said, The Parliament was not in his Opinion Dissolved, but that it was so far from a Crime in the Duke to move it, that it deserved Commendation, because this was a proper place for the motion, and the Determination of it would be of advantage, which way soever the House should determine of it. The Lord Berkshire spoke against calling to the Barr, and made a jest of it. The Lord Shaftsbury said, The calling the Duke to the Barr were to take away all liberty of speech in Parliament; he very judiciously opened the state of the case with relation to the *Dissolution*: He shewed, That by the common law there ought to be *Annual Parliaments*; That divers Statutes had provided for *Annual Parliaments*; That we have right to our laws, and these are the laws that preserve our Rights. . . . That tis dangerous to remove *Old Landmarks.*[14] That many Inconveniences have ever been the consequences of *long Parliaments*; And after many Arguments and answering all Objections to the contrary, he concluded the *Prorogation* was *illegal.* The Marquess of Winchester said, The Parliament was not *Dissolved*, but thought the Duke, who moved the business, desired thanks. The Marquess of Dorchester carried on the debate of the *Dissolution*, and argued against it. After this (which was about an hour) the debate of the Dissolution was continued about four hours, the Lord Chancellor [Finch] undertaking to answer the Arguments which were or should be urged for it. (pp. 7–8)

Thus the *Narrative* gives us an insider's view of a crucial debate in the Lords about which we would otherwise have no information, not least since the version published in the Lords Journal erased all trace of what would follow: the condemnation and imprisonment of the four lords for raising the question. This is, in effect, a version of Grey for the Upper House, however brief;

and it is promptly followed by an equally brief account of the parallel
debate in the Lower House, where we have Grey for comparison. For—and
this is a piece of secret history—the five hours of debate in the Lords seem to
have been prolonged in order to allow Danby's party to determine what the
Commons were going to do:

> But as soon as they had notice that the Commons were up, and had not
> suffered any Question to be put upon it, but had run the Debate upon a
> Question that had no ground either in law or Reason, which they had not
> determined neither, but had adjorned to the next day; They from this took
> right measures to conclude, that the major part of the Commons were
> unwilling to part with their Seats, and thereupon took confidence to shew
> them, that they had the major part of the Lords too: and having so in both
> Houses, they need not fear to do whatever they had a mind to. (p. 8)

So the duke of Ormond moved that Buckingham should be "questioned," that
is, condemned for his motion, and Danby moved that this proposal should be
extended to include Salisbury, Shaftesbury, and Wharton too. "This motion of
these Lords (as I thinke I have been told)," writes J.E., "was seconded
by the Duke of York" (p. 8). "As I thinke I have been told" is an interesting locution, matching in its evasiveness the strategies of Dr. Cary and the printers and
booksellers who were currently being interrogated.

The *Narrative* is also valuable in providing a fairly long account of the speech
by Anglesey, the lord privy seal, in defense of parliamentary freedom of
debate, arguing pragmatically that if the majority had gone the other way, he
did not believe that those who argued the parliament was *not* dissolved would
have agreed to be called to the Bar for maintaining *that* opinion. Besides, why
were only four of the speakers in favor of dissolution to be punished? But
nothing could now stop the proceedings. The four lords were sentenced to the
Tower, to be kept in close imprisonment, denied communication with each
other, and allowed no visitors except their personal servants. In defiance, all but
Wharton asked (and gained) permission to have their own cook, a request that
reportedly infuriated the king because it implied they feared being poisoned!
J.E. rounds off his letter with heroic language in praise of the four lords, satiric
disdain for the "*New Tripple-League*, (Viz.) *Bishops, Court and Popish Lords*," and a
rather shrewd observation that if the majority can imprison the minority, "only
for proposing and debating," "Twenty-six may Imprison Twenty five by the
same reason," and so on, till they come to two, when the stronger will imprison
the weaker, and we are back in a state of anarchy (p. 19).

There is more to the story of the *Narrative*, however. I suggested above that
it was a one-off version of Grey's style of reporting for the Upper House. In

fact, we know who did the reporting. Among the manuscripts owned by Lord Wharton is a large collection of materials relating to this moment in the history of the Lords, containing arguments for the dissolution, complaints about the illegality of the way the four lords were treated, and, unusually, several versions of the proceedings of February 15–17. Wharton himself took brief notes on Buckingham's speech and those that followed, then wrote them up in two longer and more legible drafts, one with and one originally without the names of speakers (but later added in the margin). These are followed by a copy in another hand (which omits Wharton's own speeches) and was probably the copy submitted to the author of the *Narrative*, which plays down Wharton's role.[15] Another Wharton manuscript contains the full text of the speech delivered by Buckingham, from which, no doubt, the *Narrative* drew its extensive quotations.[16] All manuscript versions share the important quotation from Halifax, and Shaftesbury's caution against removing the "old Landmarks." All versions except the *Narrative* quote Lord Berkshire's short speech against calling Buckingham to the Bar, "that it was little way thither but a Lord ought to be a good while a going to it." The *Narrative* says, more effectively, since the joke was so poor, "The Lord Berkshire spoke against calling to the Barr, and made a jest of it" (p. 7).[17]

An Account of the Growth of Popery and Arbitrary Government

This famous tract by Andrew Marvell was, as it were, an *omnium gatherum* of most of the scofflaw pamphlets that had preceded it. We can now read it as brilliantly edited by Nicholas von Maltzahn, who discovered that it was constructed as a collage of disparate materials, the most important of which were manuscript journals recording what happened in the parliament of 1677 in relation to foreign policy, careful accounts of the debates that might themselves have been intended for scofflaw publication.[18] The *Account*, however, becomes even more interesting if we note that its strategy—of placing the 1677 session in a longer, explanatory narrative suggesting a long-term design by the Court party—was anticipated (slightly) by the *Relation* of 1673 and (considerably) by the *Letter from a Person of Quality* in 1675. It seems clear that Marvell at first intended to write only a report of the 1677 session, but gradually realized that its impact would be more powerful if he started, as it were, from the beginning—that is, the "vast supplies" granted for the Second Dutch War . . . "and yet after all, no Fleet set out" (*Account*, p. 241), resulting in the Chatham disaster. Marvell obviously consulted Du Moulin's *Appeale* for England's disingenuous dealings with the Dutch leading up to the Third Dutch War, including his description of how the pretenses for that war were set up, and the timing of its declaration. And he was certainly indebted to the printed *Narrative of the* . . .

imprisonment of the Lords, of which he gives a heightened, if shortened, redaction. Sir Roger L'Estrange assumed that the *Account* was connected in origin to the "libels" from the previous March now locked away in the Lords' records, and hoped, by getting access to those, to trace similarities, whether of text, paper, or font.[19]

The title of the *Account* also echoes the second half of the title of *A Seasonable Argument . . . or, a List of the Principal Labourers in the Great Design of Popery and Arbitrary Power*, which, according to Sir Robert Southwell, writing to the duke of Ormond, came out at the same time. The two tracts were, together, twice advertised in the *Gazette* as treasonable, on March 25 and 28 (Nos. 1288 and 1289), and a reward of £50 offered for the discovery of the printer, £100 for the discovery of "the hander to the press," that is, hopefully, the author. Southwell was writing towards the end of February 1678,[20] but the first copies of the *Account* were seized on February 21. Marvell's printer was John Darby, who had been involved in his earlier tracts on toleration, *Rehearsal Transpros'd* and *Mr. Smirke*.

The *Account* actually appeared in two quarto editions, both (like *Two Speeches* and *A Narrative*) with a false Amsterdam imprint, and both dated 1677. In 1679 after the Licensing Act had expired, and after Marvell's death, his party brought out a folio edition as a further statement of defiance. The *Account* produced an enormous reaction, more even than the *Letter from a Person of Quality*, no doubt in part because of the inflammatory nature of its title, and in part because the story it told of the connections between domestic and foreign policy was so compelling. Marvell was not the first of the scofflaw writers to propose a conspiracy theory, nor the best-informed; but he was for the most part a better writer, with a vein of irony that gave the *Account* staying power in the later history of parliament, as we shall see.

Marvell's *Account* will reappear in Chapter 8, when we can compare his report on the long sixteenth session with that of Daniel Finch, who wrote from the opposing political perspective. Here I want to deal only with three components of what von Maltzahn has rightly called its "assembled text" (*Account*, p. 207). One of these seems anomalous and disproportionate, so it is worth looking more closely to see what the motive was for its inclusion. This is the full text of *An Act for further securing the Protestant Religion, by Educating the Children of the Royal Family therein; and for the continuance of a Protestant Clergy*. This was sent down from the Lords on March 15, 1677, along with another bill about religion which was promptly quashed in the Commons "because the Body of the Bill was Contrary to the Title" (p. 312). This one, however, received a first and second reading in the Commons and was sent to committee for further discussion. Marvell was named to the committee, no doubt because he had spoken at unusual length against it on the second reading (Grey, Tuesday, March 27). He therefore had access to its full text, which takes up twelve pages in the modern edition. It helps to understand this stumbling block of legalese if you have read Marvell's succinct account of the bill to his Hull constituents; it contained, he wrote, "certaine provisions in case of a Popish King, for the Education of the Royal Children and for the Election of Bishops" (*P&L*, 2:188–89): that is, it assumed that there *would* be a Catholic successor, and wrote an insurance policy for the survival and dominance of the Protestant bishops in that event. In his speech in the Commons on March 27 (Grey), Marvell made the point clear: the bill "supposes 'that possibly the Crown may devolve on a Popish Government,' which ought not to be supposed easily and readily." In the *Account* Marvell summed up its fate: "it dyed away, the Committee disdaining, or not daring publickly to enter upon it, some indeed having, as is said, once attempted it in private, and provided R[obert] S[awyer] for the chairman, but were discovered" (*Account*, p. 323). Thus Robert Sawyer, of *Seasonable Argument* infamy, who had spoken in favor of the bill on the first reading, was caught behaving the way that other pamphlet suggested he was likely to do. And Marvell ensured that the proposed text of the bill would not disappear from the public record, but survive in perpetual ignominy.

Preceding this odd piece of documentary storage was another example of the same: the entire text of the speech of Lord Keeper Orlando Bridgeman at the opening of the tenth session, on October 24, 1670. Marvell alerts the reader to the historiographical service he is performing in bringing it to public view:

> It is not without much labor that I have been able to recover a written Copy of the Lord Bridgemans speech, none being printed, but forbidden, doubtless lest so notorious a Practice as certainly was never before, tho there have indeed been many put upon the Nation, might remain publick. (p. 244)

On November 28, Marvell had written to Popple that both the king's and the lord keeper's speeches were "forbid to be printed, for the King said very little, and the Keeper, it was thought, too much in his politic simple Discourse of foreign Affairs" (*P&L*, 2:318). The point was that Bridgeman had enlarged at length upon the success of the king, or rather of his ambassador Sir William Temple, in establishing the Triple League of friendship between England, the Dutch, and Sweden, along with other recently agreed leagues with Spain and Denmark, at the very moment that Charles was secretly abandoning the Triple League and embarking instead on a clandestine relationship with France. Why was it forbidden? In part because it was causing talk in Europe. The Venetian ambassador reported that Spain and Holland liked what they heard, or read in scribal copy, but the French ambassador, Colbert, requested its suppression.[21] Why did Marvell resurrect it (probably by accessing the papers of friends, whether John Rushworth, who had been Bridgeman's secretary at the time, or Lord Wharton, whose papers in the Bodleian include a complete text)?[22] Because it showed how even the lord keeper had been kept in the dark about what the king really intended. And Archdeacon Echard got the point. He transferred the speech more or less verbatim to his *History*, remarking: "This Speech was thought fit, to be suppressed, and not suffered to be printed, nor is it in the Journals of the House of Commons; *therefore it is the more necessary to have it in full length here, without any Abridgement*" (p. 256; italics added). A pun on Bridgeman and Abridgement is not out of the question.

Previous scofflaw pamphlets had preserved for the record speeches by Opposition members, or members temporarily in an Oppositional mode, such as Lord Lucas. Here, Marvell preserved for the record what the administration itself said—and then attempted to suppress. However, he included only two of the king's speeches. One of these was in no danger of disappearing, and indeed appears in the Commons Journal. On May 28, 1677, the king replied to the most recent Address from the Commons requesting him to engage in a "league defensive and offensive" with the Dutch, the offensive, of course, to be now directed at France. This is what he memorably said—and the opening phrase is brilliant in the way it raises and then dismisses the notion of restraint:

> Could I have been silent, I would rather have chosen to be so, then to call to mind things so unfit for you to meddle with, as are contained in some parts of your last Addresses, wherein you have intrenched upon so undoubted a right of the Crown, that I am confident it will appear in no Age (when the Sword was not drawn) that the Prerogative of making Peace and War hath been so dangerously invaded. . . .
>
> Should I suffer this fundamental Power of making Peace and War to be so far invaded (though but once) as to have the manner and circumstances of Leagues prescribed to Me by Parliament, its plain that no Prince or State would any longer believe that the Soveraigntie of England rests in the Crown. (*Account*, pp. 367–68)

The rhetoric is perfect. Not a word is wasted. There is a clever allusion to the failures of his father in maintaining the prerogative in an age when the sword *was* drawn. The big words—"undoubted," "right," "prerogative," "fundamental," and especially "Power"—are balanced by the nursery tone of "meddle with." And the repetition of "invaded," a military word if ever there was one, now used to describe an accepted parliamentary process, when "encroached on" would have served, is particularly threatening. One can still hear, after all these years, in what tone of voice Charles spoke.

Marvell included this speech not only for its humiliating tone, however. He wanted to make permanent the point about why scofflaw histories of parliament were necessary. For "that which more amazed" the Commons than the unceremonious and improper manner in which the Speaker adjourned them was that

> while none of their own transactions or addresses for the Publick Good are suffered to be Printed, but even all Written Copies of them with the same care as Libels suppressed: Yet they found this severe Speech published in the next days News Book. . . . Thus were they well rewarded for their *Itch of perpetual Sitting*, and of *Acting*, the Parliament being grown to that height of contempt, as to be *Gazetted* among Run-away Servants, Lost Doggs, Strayed Horses, and High-way Robbers. (p. 369)

This explains why the *Account* carefully includes the text of all the critical Addresses, so that the balance of power in terms of publication might be slightly redressed. But Marvell's sardonic language took on a life of its own, being echoed in contemporary correspondence and later debates, and, more importantly for the long term, imported into James Ralph's *History of England*. From there it was transported into the footnotes of Grey's *Debates*, though the most important point—the unequal access to publication—was lost in translation.

Because Echard's *History* has been for so long invisible, it is important to note that, for the fifteenth and sixteenth sessions of parliament, Echard becomes dependent on Marvell's *Account* to an astonishing degree, often copying it verbatim for long passages. He fairly indicates his debt in the margin; and, more to the point, he virtually insists that by including it he places himself on the scofflaw side. Here is what he reports about Charles's preparation for the continuation of the sixteenth session:

> His Majesty thought fit to do some Things Terrifying as well as Popular, to shew his Authority as well as his Clemency, in suppressing Libels and seditious Discourses, which very much encreas'd about this Time. Particularly the Dangers of Popery, and the Advances of the Popish Interest at Court, were so boldly and reflectingly represented by Mr. Andrew Marvel in his *Account of the Growth of Popery*, that his Majesty caused an Order to be publish'd in these Words . . . "£50 reward to Discoverer of Printer or Publisher, £100 to Discoverer of the Hander of it to the Press." (3:439)

What the king attempted to suppress, Echard, collector of scofflaw pamphlets, saved for posterity.

Finally, it was not only Echard who collected the scofflaw pamphlets of the reign. In 1689, there appeared a collection of such items under the title *State Tracts: Being a Collection of several Treatises Relating to the Government. Privately Printed in the Reign of K. Charles II.* The printer, or compiler, who remained discreetly anonymous, but was very probably Richard Baldwin, offered the public a gloss, both disingenuous and self-contradictory, on what was meant by "Privately Printed":

> If these Collections shall chance to fall into the hands of some Persons for whom they were not design'd, it will be requisite to inform them, That they were not intended to be made Publick, but were Printed at the request, and for the sole use of some particular Gentlemen, who set an extraordinary value and estimate upon them; and that not undeserv'dly: For they contain, 1st. The most material Passages of State, which hapned in the Reign of King Charles II . . . with the secret Springs that set them in motion. 2ly. In them is the Constitution of the English Government truly Stated and Asserted: and a clear demonstration, how much it is the Interest of England to preserve the Balance of Europe, by opposing the growing greatness of the French king . . . etc, etc.

Included in this collection were: *England's Appeale; A Relation; A Letter from a Person of Quality; Two Speeches; Two Seasonable Discourses; An Account of the Growth of Popery*; and *Lord Lucas's Speech*. Also included were tracts we have not yet encountered: *Coleman's Letters; The Character of a Popish Successor*; and *A Letter from a Person of Quality, in answer to King Charles II's Declaration, for dissolving his last two Parliaments*. Thus the story of the Opposition was continued, by a post-Revolution publisher. And thus those who were active in working out the new constitution, as well as eighteenth-century historians, could access most, but not quite all, of the scofflaw pamphlets of the Restoration in one convenient package.

The collection of scofflaw pamphlets in one volume suggests that they were soon perceived as a new kind of publication, supposed to be read seriatim. Crucial to the genre was a subversive form of parliamentary reporting; authorial anonymity; and, increasingly, a sense that the pamphlets formed a chronological series, which both indicated the root causes of current problems and gave encouragement to others to continue the story. The scofflaw pamphlets (never called such at the time) rub shoulders with other recognized "literary" genres, especially the epic (*Lord Lucas, A Narrative*), drama (*Votes and Addresses*), and of course the device of "A Letter to a Friend" much in use at the Restoration. Several of them feature a salient biblical quotation, suggesting that God is on their side. Though most have a strong satirical component, nobody could doubt their seriousness. Though Marvell's *Last Instructions* is the exception as being poetry (and part of another series, the satirical *Advices to a Painter*) its inclusion here, as the chapter's opening frame, alerts us to how "literary" some of the scofflaw pamphlets are. The closing frame is the *Account of the Growth of Popery and Arbitrary Government*, which though it sets out as merely "a naked Narrative" (p. 241) of the 1677 session, by its end is revealed as a "Tragedy" waiting for its fifth act (p. 375).

PART THREE

SESSIONS

❖

CHAPTER 6

Parliament and the Control of Religion

1661–1674

Now that we have distinguished and partly evaluated the different kinds of sources available for writing the history of Charles II's Long Parliament, we can begin to marshall them as witnesses to the conflicts that characterized this parliament, between different interest groups or parties, between its two Houses, and between parliament and the king. Wherever there are conflicts there will be rival accounts, and this is, not surprisingly, clear from the beginning of the reign, since what was first at stake was the nature of the new religious settlement, after the defeat of Presbyterianism. That proportion of the population which was unwilling to accept the hegemony of high Anglicanism, bishops and all, was referred to as Dissenters. In theory, both low-church Protestants and Roman Catholics were Dissenters. In practice, the term came increasingly to apply to Presbyterians, Quakers, and others in between, while Roman Catholics were referred to by the still more derogatory term, papists.

The king's relationship with his new parliament was quickly snagged on the issue of how much toleration of divergent religious beliefs and practices— for practices were what really made people stubborn—could be allowed. By passing the Act of Uniformity in May 1662 the Anglican majority in the House of Commons determined that toleration should be rigorously discouraged. The king countered with not one but two Declarations of Indulgence (for tender consciences, as the phrase went), both of which were challenged and effectively cancelled by the Commons. This struggle, with various compromises proposed and resisted, lasted until 1674. By that time, the religious issue had shifted, to focus on the king's over-intimate relationship with Catholic France, his lack of a legitimate heir, and the avowed Catholicism of the heir therefore presumptive, James, duke of York. Religious concerns thus dovetailed with foreign policy, the focus of later chapters.

We must begin, however, with what might seem like a narrow and obsessive focus on the religious question, because that was what the battles were fought over, narrowly and obsessively. This chapter will set beside each other, as competing voices, the Anglican John Milward, the enigmatic tolerationist Andrew Marvell, the nascent Whig Anchitell Grey, and, for balance, the skeptical newsmonger and gossip, John Starkey, who seems to favor the Dissenters. The first three were all members of the Commons, Starkey an outsider with, however, excellent connections, including Grey the diarist. In the case of Grey, we hear not his own voice but those of the debaters he chose to quote, as close to verbatim as possible.

There is a consensus among historians that the parliament that convened on May 8, 1661 was very different in its religious affiliations from the Convention Parliament that preceded it. The strength of the Presbyterian group in the Commons was dramatically reduced by the new elections, and the impetus of those Presbyterian members who remained had been weakened by the failure of the Presbyterian Bill brought in on November 6, 1660. But the convenience of referring to the repressive legislation that followed the Act of Uniformity (May 19, 1662) as the Clarendon Code, whereas in fact Clarendon himself was variably inclined to some degree of toleration, tends to submerge the particular in the general;[1] and there has been a corresponding tendency to assume that the Lower House, with its majority of royalists who had suffered during the Interregnum, was holistically of a "persecuting temper." A closer look—or a more careful listening—also throws light on what Charles II himself wanted, a matter still debated among historians. Was he genuinely in favor of what he called "indulgence" for all "tender consciences," for leaving the laws elastic and subject to exception? Or was he rather seeking primarily to improve the lot of his Roman Catholic subjects? The former, more generous interpretation is the one I favor for this earlier period. But the rigorous persecution of Protestant Dissenters after Charles had dispensed with parliament will ultimately need to be faced.

The king's general dislike of religious persecution was expressed not only in his Declaration at Breda in 1660, which might be considered a tactical statement to allay fears but also, and more decisively, in his two Declarations of Indulgence, both of which were published *between* sessions of parliament. The first, which tends to get overlooked in comparison to the flurry created by the second, was announced in print on December 26, 1662, and was clearly intended to modify the effects of the Act of Uniformity. This Declaration quotes "the very words . . . from Breda," with respect to the incoming king's desire for "A Liberty to Tender Consciences, and that no man shall be disquieted or called in question for differences of Opinion in matters of Religion, which do not disturb the Peace of the Kingdom" (p. 8). This was unacceptable to the newly powerful heads of the Anglican church, especially Archbishop Sheldon. Walter Simon states that "the conflict between Charles and his bishops on this point raged through the first fifteen years of the reign."[2] But it was the cavalier majority in the Commons who, in their Address of February 27, forced him to retract it indirectly, and only after considerable delay.[3]

But even to use the phrase "the cavalier majority" is to oversimplify, as this chapter will show. It implies that the battle was lost at the general election, when the votes against toleration were permanently secured. A complicating figure was Philip, Lord Wharton, a staunch Presbyterian, who made no secret of his now unpopular allegiance, and actually had conventicles meeting at his residence at St. Giles-in-the-Fields. Wharton, though seemingly isolated in the House of Lords, was in fact from 1661 organizing support for toleration (for Protestants) in the Commons, and created for the Convention Parliament lists of possible supporters or "moderates" whom he divided into regional groups to be canvassed by men he could count on. This discovery was made by G.F. Trevallyn Jones, using the Wharton Papers in the Carte Collection in the Bodleian Library, a vein of gold still incompletely prospected,[4] and reinforced by Douglas Lacey's work on the same papers and Andrew Swatland's account of Wharton in *The House of Lords.* According to Swatland, Wharton may even have played the role of the king's manager for the debates on the Uniformity Bill, and "most of the nine amendments surviving among his papers accorded closely with the king's preferred settlement of the church."[5] For the Lords debate on the first Conventicles Bill of 1664, according to Jones, he "drew up a detailed plan including every conceivable argument, delaying tactic or possible source of jealousies concerning privileges,"[6] efforts that were then nullified in the Commons. Lacey notes similar activity by Wharton in respect of the second Conventicles Act of 1670.[7] Eventually he would be joined as a tolerationist leader (for Protestants) in the Lords by Buckingham and Shaftesbury.[8]

If Wharton was the leading figure in organizing, however unsuccessfully, a stand against too harsh a religious settlement, it was primarily to Gilbert Sheldon, working behind the scenes, rather than Clarendon, that the Restoration church owed its punitive legislation and attempts at enforcement. In 1663, just after his elevation, Sheldon wrote to Ormond: "'Tis only a resolute execution of the law that might cure this disease—all other remedies have and will increase it—and 'tis necessary that they who will not be governed as men by reason and persuasion, should be governed as beasts by power of force."[9] The central role of Sheldon in keeping up the defenses against, or attacks on, Nonconformity was fully outlined by Simon in his study of the Restoration episcopate. Most of the bishops in the Lords were with him, he had several close friends in the Commons, and various tools among his chaplains, deacons, and prebendaries.

Though attempts were made to silence Lord Wharton by implicating him in the Derwentdale Plot, he still fervently attacked the Five-Mile Bill in October 1665, and made the longest speech of any of the peers who opposed it.[10] But by that time the nation was embroiled in the Second Dutch War, and parliamentary attention shifted to what seemed more urgent questions. The war ended unsatisfactorily (for England) on July 29, 1667. From that point forward, all consideration of the religious issue would have to be intertwined with, or alternate with, recriminations against those who had mismanaged the war, with Clarendon the primary scapegoat.

Nevertheless, plans were being laid for revisiting the religious settlement. Was the latter fair, and could it conceivably hold? In October 1667, Sir Robert Atkyns was approached by two moderate bishops about the possibility of a degree of comprehension, that is, mitigating the Act of Uniformity to allow moderate Presbyterians to be brought within its gates. Atkyns was an outspoken defender of Clarendon, and appears three times in Wharton's list of "friends." Herbert Croft, dean of Hereford, himself a convert from Roman Catholicism, joined the project, and Bishop Thomas Barlow, another moderate, was instrumental in both working out the necessary compromises and recording them for posterity.[11] The plan was directed at Nonconformist ministers already ordained who might be willing to subscribe to the Thirty-six Articles dealing with matters of faith, not discipline, and would thereby be permitted to preach. Colonel John Birch agreed to move the bill in the Commons; though eventually a staunch Oppositionist in the 1670s, he was at this time seen, despite his Presbyterian upbringing, as a Court party supporter, and therefore a plausible sponsor. But the bill never reached the floor of the Commons, because, according to Simon, Birch lost his nerve and delayed introducing it until the December adjournment arrived.[12]

"Behind the Curtaine": Strategy and Counter-Strategy

Since mid-December, however, there had been rumors of another attempt to bring in a Comprehension Bill. This time the group of moderates was much larger, and had the direct support of the king. Its primary mover was John Wilkins, recently appointed one of the king's chaplains, and shortly to become bishop of Chester. It was he who had drafted the bill, with the support of Buckingham, Sir Orlando Bridgeman, the new lord keeper, Matthew Hale, the lord chief baron, and Robert Montagu, earl of Manchester.[13] Wilkins met with the king on January 10 for a private conference, and shortly afterwards with some leading Nonconformists, including Richard Baxter and Thomas Manton, the leader of one of London's most important conventicles, to see what compromises might be possible. The plan was then discussed with a group of moderate bishops, including Herbert Croft. Unfortunately, according to Simon, Wilkins shared its contents with his Oxford friend Seth Ward, who informed Archbishop Sheldon, who was thus in a position to lead a fightback.

At this point we can call on an outside but well-informed source for important information, and what we might well call "attitude." On December 31, John Starkey reported to Sir Willoughby Aston that "The Arch Bishop of Canterbury is in so much disfavour with the King, that he forbad him to preach on Christmas day and appoynted the Bishop of Hereford in his roome" (f. 56). The bishop of Hereford was by now Herbert Croft, already identified as a spokesman for comprehension. Thus the king's ostentatious display of favoritism towards Croft (he was made dean of the chapels royal on February 8) carries much wider significance than the fact that Charles liked his preaching.

By January 23, 1668, Starkey's newsletters have begun to take note of the rumors about the new move for comprehension, making it clear that this had support in the very highest circles. "The Comprehensive bill about religion is a fresh discurst on, and hath beene so much debated by the king and Counsell, that it will be offered to the parliament" (f. 59). On January 28, Starkey added: "the comprehension bill is agreed on at court, and assented to by some Bishops and many presbyterians, to whom it only extends and will be offered to the parliament" (f. 60). But on January 29, Herbert Thorndike published a pamphlet that showed that he had had access to the proposed bill and that refuted all of its propositions. Two days before the meeting of parliament, however, on February 4, Starkey was still optimistic: "The Comprehensive bill is very much talked on. The most eminent Presbyterians and Independants have been consulted with all about it by the Lord Keeper who is very desirous it should passe" (f. 62).

On February 6, 1668,[14] the eighth session reconvened after the Christmas recess. At this point, the *Diary* of John Milward becomes part of the record. Again, as he had for the July intercession, the king postponed coming in person, supposedly waiting for a fuller House. So, writes Milward:

> We only passed one vote this day, viz: that the House should receive no new business before the House was called, that so the House may be full before any new business be debated. . . . *This vote was passed to prevent the bringing in the bill of comprehension*, which will be brought in and countenanced by very great persons. (p. 179; italics added)

The plan to bring in the bill in a thin House was foiled by this procedural vote; and the following Monday, when the House reassembled, the Anglican conservative party majority moved immediately that "the King be petitioned to send out his proclamations to restrain the disorderly and tumultuous meeting of dissenters to the act of uniformity and . . . to put the laws in execution against conventicles" (p. 180).[15] Milward, a personal friend of

Sheldon, already knew a good deal about the bill, and understood the procedural move.

On February 11, after the king had delivered his speech, Starkey has a
fuller account:

> The Commons before they did rise [on February 6] voted that no new
> matter be ofered the house till it be called over which is to be on Thursday,
> yett as soone as they mett on Monday they tooke notice of the rumor about
> towne of a Comprehensive Bill, and liberty of Conscience, and before the
> King made his speech, though Sr. Tho. Littleton and others earnestly
> desired they would forbeare the question till they had heard what the King
> would say to them, they would not agree to it, but voted that the house do
> speedily desire [i.e. petition] the King that he would forthwith publish his
> proclamation for the effectuall execution of the Lawes for Conformity and
> suppressing seditious Conventicles, after which they went and heard the
> Kings speech, of which I have sent you a Copy. (f. 66)[16]

Timing, as they say, is everything.

The initiative thus passed to the anti-comprehensionists, going against the
king's expressed desires. The king's speech had two parts; the first requested
a Supply, the second succinctly asked parliament to consider some means of
making Dissenters more comfortable. Specifically the king said (in Starkey's
transcription): "I do recommend it to you to consider of a way to bring the
minds of my Protestant subjects at home to better Union and composure in
matter of Religion that they may the more willingly submitt to the Government
and more chearfully contribute to the support of it" (f. 67). Thus toleration and
taxes were subtly linked. The king's speech was promptly printed, and regarded
as highly significant.

The Commons were not at all inclined to hurry their consideration of
the speech, with its troublesome linkage of Supply and comprehension. They
began by discussing the miscarriages of the war, and on February 14 or 15
Andrew Marvell made his celebrated attack on Secretary Arlington for
providing inadequate intelligence. On the 17th, as Arlington himself reported
in correspondence: "This day [Marvell] hath given me cause to forgive him,
by being the first man, in the midst of this enquiry, [who] moved the taking
into Consideration of his Majesty's Speech." This could be interpreted, as it
obviously was by Arlington, as a gesture of support for the court; but in hindsight we can recognize it as an attempt to get onto the floor the "latter part"
of the speech, with its expression of the king's desire for some toleration. On
February 19 the debate finally began, and Milward quickly displays both the
divisions in the House and his own views:

Sir Charles Wheeler[17] first spake to it, and began an unexpected and indeed unnecessary and generally unpleasing speech against the church government and all the abuses thereof: "And although," said he, "I cannot speak against the doctrine of the church and . . . the Bishops are as learned and as pious men as any are in the Christian world," yet he impertinently spoke against their courts and judicatures and against archdeacons and their courts and the exorbitances of them and against lay chancellors and their courts, and against excommunications. Such an invective speech was not expected from [him], especially at this time, he being accounted by some good men a severe son of the Church; but it appeared to be in favour of the Presbyterians and sectaries and that party in the House, for when he was taken down in his speech, as not speaking directly to the question in hand; many of that party justified him in that speech contrary to the general sense of the house. (p. 191)

On February 28, Milward reported, "we had a stout debate upon several complaints against the insolence of sectaries in several counties" (p. 201), based on reports brought in by several members, Sir James Thynne, Randolph Egerton, Robert Coke, and Sir Thomas Meres. This effectively set up the case *against* any toleration. It having been agreed to return to this issue on March 4, on that day there was a five-hour debate on "abuses committed by sectaries," leading to an Address to the king to issue a proclamation to put the penal laws against Nonconformists into better effect. This, says Milward, "was mainly opposed by the undertakers, but in the end it [was] voted" (p. 206).

As well as Starkey, who shows his excitement if not his hand, and Milward, who is gravely evaluative, we can now follow the records of Anchitell Grey, who had begun taking his shorthand notes of debates. Melward's summary account contrasts strongly with Grey's, which excerpts speeches in favor of the Address by only Sir Edmund Wyndham and Sir John Berkenhead, whereas Edward Seymour, John Swinfen, Edmund Waller, Sir Walter Yonge, Sir Robert Howard, and Hugh Boscawen all opposed it. It is hard to tell where Thomas Clifford stands from his remarks about "the great zealots of the Roman church," but his aphorism (and Grey loves aphorisms) leads me to think he was opposed to the Address: "We have a fire in the middle of the room, let us not kick it about to set all on fire."

The House returned to "the latter part of the king's speech" on March 11, 1668. This extensive debate was heavily reported by Milward, who gave summaries of no fewer than forty-one speeches, with by far the greatest coverage going to Sir John Berkenhead's absolute anti-tolerationist position. The importance of this debate for Milward produced a different mode of reporting, which in its naming of individual speakers and summaries of their speeches more resembles that of Grey. As Witcombe summarizes the affair, this was an "unequivocal defeat" for the king. On his side, or at least on the tolerationist side, "were Littleton, Seymour, Clifford, Birch, Swinfen. . . . Against them, and against the King's known wishes, were such loyal cavaliers as Henry Coventry, Giles Strangeways, and Sir John Berkenhead, together with Sir Thomas Meres and a significantly large number of 'backwoodsmen', whose names do not appear in the records of any other debates" (p. 82). In other words, this was the debate that drew out even the most reticent of speakers.

If we follow Milward, the opening gambit on the tolerationists' side was the king's declaration of indulgence for tender consciences at Breda, which Littleton and others pressed to be read aloud in the House. "He made," wrote Milward, "a very long and impertinent speech and indeed such a one as I never heard him speak; he extravagantly ran into foreign nations and heretical opinions tolerated in Poland, and concluded . . . that the restraint of conscience in England was the occasion of the late war" (p. 216). Sir Walter Yonge, a member of the Country party, "spoke very much for an indulgence but very impertinently and very little to the purpose" (p. 218). On the other side, Sir John Berkenhead "made a long and most excellent speech" refuting the arguments from Poland and Holland, and disputed Littleton's account of the reign of James I. And as for the argument that it was restraint of conscience that had caused the Civil War, he reminded his hearers of how those who were now Dissenters took the covenant "with hands lifted up to heaven to extirpate prelacy." "We may well be cautious that we be not again cheated and destroyed by indulging their conscience into a new rebellion" (p. 220). Then Sir William Morrice, under-secretary of state, moved to adjourn the debate for a month, perhaps because it was not yet clear where the balance of opinion lay.

Andrew Marvell, writing to Hull the next day, had a different, more constructive take on where things now stood:

> Yesterday was the debate concerning the latter part of the Kings speech wherein they seemed inclinable to abate the renunciation of the Covenant the Assent & Consent, to the dispensing with Ceremonyes the reforming the Bishops Courts the taking away of Pluralityes the rectifying of Excommunications, the punishing of scandalous Clergy men & severall things of this nature, but [were not] able to mature these deliberations at present. (P&L, 2:69)

His optimism was misplaced. For Grey tells us that when, on March 13, the House debated a motion to renew the act against conventicles, due to lapse at the end of 1668, it was observed that considering the "latter part of the King's Speech" and renewing the Conventicles Act seemed "to cross" each other diametrically. This did not prevent the House from eagerly pursuing the penal route.

At this point Milward returns to summary mode:

> Many spoke effectually for it [the bill], as Colonel [Samuel] Sandys, Colonel [Giles] Strangways excellently, cousin Milward, Sir John Denham, Sir Thomas Meers, Sir Robert Holt[e] and others. Against it there spake Sir Thomas Littleton, Mr. Swinfen, Mr. Marvell, Sir Robert Carr, Mr. Jones,[18] and others, but to little purpose, for it was carried with a multitude of voices in the affirmative, *of which I was one.* (p. 225)

This is our only source for the information that Andrew Marvell spoke against the renewal of the Conventicle Act;[19] the same is also true of Milward's report that on March 30 Marvell was apparently the only speaker to oppose the bill when it was brought in (p. 238).

On April 15, Milward tells us that he attended the committee charged with drafting the new act. On April 25, Marvell reported to Hull that the act was engrossed and "will I believe pass our House next week" (*P&L*, 2:74). On April 28, Milward reported that the engrossed act had been read in the House: "many impertinent speeches were made against [it] by the sectaries and those that affect the Presbyterians, and several provisoes were tendered to be added on purpose to clog the bill that it might not pass in the House of Lords" (p. 282). On May 2, it did indeed run into opposition there. Starkey reported that "upon a speech of the Earle of Angleseye they have laid it aside without appoynting a certaine day for the reading of it" (f. 95). On May 9, the king advised parliament to adjourn until August 11. It was called back in August, and again in March 1669, only, as Witcombe puts it, to be sent straight home again (p. 92).

Earlier, however, the Commons had returned, on April 8, to "the later part of the King's speech," a debate that had been strategically postponed for another month. The question now at issue was whether to move an Address to the king to take the matter into his own hands (since, it was implied, he had made his wishes known and the Commons were at loggerheads). At this point an important discovery by Nicholas von Maltzahn brings Wharton back into the picture, now directly allied with Andrew Marvell. Among the Wharton Papers, in Marvell's hand, is the draft of an "Addresse from the House of Peeres to the King to make use of his prerogative in Ecclesiastical Affayres for the better composure and union of the mindes of his protestant subjects in the intervall of the present adjournment." The Address is dated May 9, 1668, the day the king proposed the adjournment. There is a logical problem with the title of the draft, however, since once the adjournment was in process the Lords could vote on nothing—unless Marvell and Wharton imagined that the Address could actually have been voted on in the Lords *on* the 9th, before the adjournment took force. In fact, Marvell informed his constituents that same day that the Commons adjourned promptly when so ordered, "but the Lords sat on & sentencd Sr Samual Barnardiston upon his knees" and devised other penalties to drive home their point about their privileges (*P&L*, 2:76).

The original proposal in the Commons—to ask the king to take the matter into his own hands—was finally brought to a vote, and defeated 176 to 70, with Milward noting triumphantly of the majority (for which he mistakenly wrote 167): "*I was one.*" John Starkey, on April 9, sent Aston a less personal but in some ways more persuasive account of the same debate:

> Yesterday the Commons according to former order tooke into debate the latter part of the kings speech, and having the whole day to send the business of liberty of Conscience too and fro, and could not come to any resolve, they adjourned the further debate of it till wensday next, but they are so divided some for bringing in the presbyterians only, others for a generall toleration, and the major part against both that tis most likely a bill against conventicles will sooner pass, then any thing for Indulgence. (f. 91)

That was the end of the move towards toleration or comprehension until 1672, when the king did indeed take matters into his own hands by publishing his second Declaration of Indulgence. But on November 18, 1668, John Starkey reported to Aston that John Wilkins had been consecrated bishop of Chester, an eminent sign of his being in favor with the king. This is one of Starkey's gems. He made a good speech, Starkey wrote, "at which was the Duke of Buckingham, the Lord Arlington, Lord Keeper, &c. The Consecration was performed by the Bishop of Duresme [Durham, i.e. John Cosin] and others but the Archbishop and Bishop of London [Humphrey Henchman] stood behind the Curtaine all the time of the Ceremony" (f. 119). Thus the divisions in the regime were registered in their own amusing and theatrical way—Starkey using a phrase that, metaphorically and in other contexts, would denote insider or privileged knowledge, but that here designates, literally, the location of the losers.

"The Price of Money": The Conventicles Act of 1670

The adjournment until August 11 gradually stretched out until parliament was recalled on October 19, 1669. Then a new Conventicles Act received a first reading on November 4, and after a long debate was committed on

November 12; but on December 11, probably because it had only voted the king a Supply of £400,000, parliament was prorogued again, not to meet until February 14, 1670. Thus the anti-conventicle legislation remained in limbo. On June 19, Starkey reported that the Nonconformists had been making good use of their temporary liberty, and that "Mr. Baxter of Kidderminster" had been committed for six months to the new prison at Clerkenwell. On June 29, being brought before the Court of Common Pleas, he was discharged on the insufficiency of the warrant. On July 13, 1669, Starkey reported that a standing committee of the Privy Council had been inquiring into whether the previous act was still in force or not. Its members were Sheldon, Henchman, Manchester, John Egerton, earl of Bridgewater, and William, earl of Craven. On August 26, Starkey reported that "Dr. [Samuel] Annesley an eminent presbyterian, who kept a great Conventicle, was fixed on upon the Oxford Act and committed by 2 Justices, but the king hath by a speciall order discharged him" (f. 144).

When parliament reconvened, then, for its tenth session, on February 14, 1670, the supporters of uniformity were prepared to give something to get something. As a result they put the matter of the king's Supply on the front burner, and eighty "country gentlemen" walked out of the House in protest, among whom may have been Anchitell Grey, whose reports cease until March 1. On February 27, as part of the implied deal, Sir John Bramston brought in a new Conventicles Bill. On March 10, Marvell wrote an unusually long letter to Mayor Tripp of the Hull Corporation, informing him that the bill had passed in the Commons on Monday 9, by a vote of 138 to 78. Most unusually, Marvell specifies in his letter the terms of the bill. It makes dark reading:

> That the Act of 35 of Eliz: is still in force. And for further remedy because seditious Sectaryes, under pretense of tender consciences do contrive insurrections at their meetings. That from the 3d of Aprill next if any person of 16 years or upward shall be present at any meeting under pretense of religion in other manner then allowd by the liturgy & practise of the Church of England at which meeting . . . if in an house there shall be 5 persons or more then those of the houshold, or if in an house field or place where no family inhabits then where any 5 persons or more are assembled, any one or more justices of the Country liberty or division or the chiefe magistrate of the place are injoyned either by confession of the party or oath of witnesses or by notorious evidence or circumstance, or, in default of evidence, unlesse the offender can by two witnesses upon oath prove that he came on other lawfull businesse, to make a record of such offense under his or their hands & seals & this record shall be in law a full & perfect conviction & thereupon he or they shall fine the person 5 shillings which conviction to be certifyed at next quarter Sessions. The next offense as

before but the fine 10 shillings or (*or as I remember at the Justices discretion a months imprisonment*) & so as oft as he offends. Fines to by levyed by distresse & sale or in case of his poverty, then upon the goods & chatells of any other person convicted of the same conventicle. . . . Every one that preached there being convicted in the way before to be fined for the first 50 li, but if a stranger or fled or poore it shall be levyd on the goods of anyone or more persons that were there & distributed as before. And upon a second preching 100 li. & levyed in same manner &c. upon one or more if he be a stranger or &c. . . . nor any proceedings thereupon shall be revers'd or avoyded by reason of any default in forme or lack of forme or other defect whatsoever. (*P&L*, 2:101–02; italics added)

One wonders what John Milward, still alive but no longer a diarist, would have thought of the Commons' achievement. Marvell's letter is particularly valuable in recording the state of the bill before it was amended and softened by the Lords.

On March 21, 1670, Marvell wrote, in a personal letter to his nephew, William Popple, that "the terrible Bill against Conventicles is sent up to the lords":

They are making mighty Alterations in the Conventicle Bill, (which, as we sent up, is the Quintessence of arbitrary Malice,) and sit whole days, and yet proceed but by Inches. . . . So the Fate of the Bill is uncertain, but must probably pass, being the Price of Money. The King told some eminent Citizens, who applyed to him against it, that they must address themselves to the Houses, that he must not disoblige his Friends; and if it had been in the Power of their Friends, he had gone without Money. (*P&L*, 2:314–15)

This sardonic comment was, believe it or not, inserted by the editor of Grey's *Debates* as an explanatory footnote to the act (1:228).

That the "Friends" of the Dissenters to whom the king refers included several members of the House of Lords has already been established; but their records also show extensive, painstaking amendments to the Conventicles Bill. These amendments reduced the penalties by more than a half, and abolished the clause that Marvell thought he remembered, a month's imprisonment at the justice's discretion. They limited the monetary liability to £10 for attendance at a conventicle, provided for appeals for fines above 10 shillings, gave one-third of the fines so collected to the poor, and restricted the offense to indoor meetings. They tried to raise the defining figure for a conventicle from five persons to ten, but this was rejected by the Commons. They also limited the duration of the act (22 Car. II, c. IX) to three years from June 24, 1670.[20] How much would we love to have a record of *those* debates!

"Better Than Going to a Play": The King in the House of Lords

In default of debates, we have gossip. On March 26, 1670, John Starkey reported that the Lords

> have proceeded further in the bill against Conventicles, which they alter as they goe. They were on it yesterday, when unexpectedly the king came and tooke his place amongst them. He told them he came not to disturb them but to claime an ancient right that his ancestors had of sitting amongst them and hearing their debates. (f. 173)

This remarkable event has not previously been connected to the toleration issue, but it looks as though the king very much wanted to hear who said what on the subject of the Conventicles Bill, as well as on Lord Roos's suit for divorce, which Charles favored, perhaps because he was interested in a divorce for himself. In the margin of the same newsletter Starkey reported something equally remarkable: "Dr. Manton's meeting was disturbed on Sunday last, he bound to appear at sessions of court. The names of those there were taken, among whom were the Lord Wharton, Mr. Hamden a member of the Commons, and many others of quality." This flagrant expression of defiance by Manton and his aristocratic supporters led to Manton being arrested under the Five-Mile Act and imprisoned for six months in the Gatehouse.

It is another sign of the shared interests of Marvell and Starkey, which perhaps resulted in them sharing information, that the former also reported the unprecedented appearance of the king in the Lords, drawing from it alarming constitutional meaning. Needless to say, this letter of Marvell's dated April 14, 1670, too, was not to Hull, but to William Popple, and hence rather colorful: "It is true that this hath been done long ago, but it is now so old, that it is new, and so disused that at any other, but so bewitched a Time, as this, it would have been looked upon as an high Usurpation, and Breach of Privilege" (*P&L*, 2:316). Marvell saw the Lords' failure to protest, and indeed the continuation of this practice, as setting a new precedent: "So this Matter, of such Importance on all great Occasions, seems riveted to them, and Us, for the future, and to all Posterity." He speculates that the king's intentions were to reduce the influence in the Lords of the duke of York, whereas it was probably partly to remind the Lords of Charles's interest in toleration. But the gravity of the innovation is barely deflected by the king's own joke: he "says it is better than going to a Play" (2:317).

On March 26, the Lords passed the Conventicles Act, but seventeen members of the House entered a formal dissent. They included Wharton, Manchester, Anglesey, Halifax, Lucas, and Holles. On April 11, parliament was adjourned, to reconvene on October 24.

This was a low period in the fortunes of the Opposition. In the Commons, several of its most important speakers deserted to the Court party: Seymour, Temple, Howard, Clifford, Osborne, and, alas, Littleton (bought out temporarily, though he would soon return). Witcombe entitles this session "The Dominance of the Court," and stresses how much money Charles was able to extract from a now pliable Commons. "One rather less pleasing feature, so far at least as Charles was concerned, was the cavaliers' insistence on the other side of their bargain—the right to enforce by penal sanctions adherence to the anglican church" (p. 120). In early December, they brought in "an additional Act to prevent Conventicles," the previous one having been deemed ineffective. But the temper of the House was changing. This new bill went side by side with appeals to the king to hinder the "growth of popery." On March 28, 1671, Starkey reported:

> The Lords have read the bill against Papists the 2nd time and committed it, tis thought that that shall dye in the Lords house and the Conventicles bill in the Commons who at the reading of it upon the report from the Committee did not like it at all so that it was near throwing out, but by 4 voices it was carryed to be committed. (f. 216)

The bill passed the Commons on April 5, 1671, by a much narrower margin than its predecessor, 74 to 53, in a much thinner House.[21] As Witcombe observes (p. 121), this was the last legislation of the Long Parliament in favor of persecuting Protestants. Thereafter the target would become exclusively the Roman Catholics, especially those in office. However, neither of the two church bills finally made it through. After another quarrel between the two Houses, on either April 22 (Marvell) or 24 (Witcombe), parliament was prorogued until February 4, 1673.

"Tender Consciences": The Declaration of Indulgence, 1672

On March 15, 1672, the king made a pre-emptive strike in favor of his own religious policy. While parliament was prorogued, he issued another Declaration of Indulgence. By this time Starkey's newsletters had ceased, and the parliamentary diarists were silent. One person who was not silent was Andrew Marvell, who, having earlier maneuvered to give the king his full prerogative in matters ecclesiastical, could not now fail to support him. He was incited to engage in controversy by one of Gilbert Sheldon's creatures, Samuel Parker, who had himself joined in the attack on the Dissenters in his 1669 *Discourse of Ecclesiastical Politie* and its vitriolic sequels. The result was the two parts of Marvell's *Rehearsal Transpros'd*, which were published with the support of Anglesey, Shaftesbury, and eventually, after he had read the first part, the king himself. The chief difficulty for Marvell was not the various attempts to get the work suppressed, but the fact that the second part was written *after* the king had been forced by the Commons, who reconvened on February 4, 1673, to rescind the Declaration of Indulgence.

For a modern reader to understand the Declaration, and how the Commons responded, it will be helpful to have to hand what Charles actually declared. He began by stressing the amount of disciplinary action he had taken heretofore:

> Our care and endeavours for the preservation of the rights and interests of the Church have been sufficiently manifested to the world by the whole course of our government since our happy restoration, and by the many and frequent ways of coercion that we have used for reducing all erring or dissenting persons, and for composing the unhappy differences in matters of religion which we found among our subjects upon our return.

He then made the point that, given the "sad experience of twelve years," force does not seem to have worked; and that therefore he has resorted to his prerogative in ecclesiastical affairs to bring about a change of direction. That change had already been suggested in the "latter part" of his speech in February 1668, but here the advantages are fleshed out:

> As well for the quieting the minds of our good subjects . . . for inviting strangers in this conjuncture to come and live under us, and for the better encouragement of all to a cheerful following of their trades and callings . . . as also for preventing for the future the danger that might otherwise arise from private meetings and seditious conventicles.

He then explained carefully what the Declaration did not require or permit. There were to be no changes in the "doctrine, discipline, and government" of the Church of England "as now it stands established by law"; nobody of differing views would be exempt from paying their tithes; and nobody could hold a benefice "who is not exactly conformable," the last point seeming to put an end to the various plans for comprehension. What the Declaration would have done was to suspend "the execution of all . . . penal laws in matters ecclesiastical." Not abrogate those laws, but suspend their execution indefinitely. To the ends proposed in the opening paragraph, and especially to avoid the need for conventicles, the king also declared that there would be "a sufficient number of places . . . for the use of such as do not conform to the Church of England . . . to meet and assemble to their public worship," provided the place and the preacher had been approved. This provision did *not*, however, extend to Roman Catholics, who would be allowed to worship only in their private houses. The Declaration ended by wielding the stick as well as holding out the carrot:

> If . . . any of our subjects shall presume to abuse this liberty and shall preach seditiously, or to the derogation of the doctrine, discipline or government of the Established Church, or shall meet in places not allowed by us, we do hereby give them warning . . . that we will proceed against them with all imaginable severity; and we will let them see we can be as severe to punish such offenders, when so justly provoked, as we are indulgent to truly tender consciences.

For some mysterious reason, there is at this point a year's gap in Marvell's letters to Hull, so we have no account from him of what happened in February 1673, when parliament reassembled in the wake of the Declaration. One would have thought he would have been active in the Commons in defense of the policy he himself had privately supported: that is, having the king use his prerogative in ecclesiastical matters to bypass partisan struggles in the Houses. We know he was in his seat in the Commons on February 7, when he was named to the committee of elections and privileges at an unusually important moment for the committee because the very first business of the new session was to protest the fact that in the intersession Shaftesbury, as chancellor, had issued writs for empty seats and arranged for by-elections. Marvell was named to two more committees on February 27 and 28. Yet he apparently kept a very low profile when on February 8 the House began to debate the Declaration, which members immediately saw could not be allowed to stand. The letters from Hull about this debate, of all debates, are missing. Indeed, we cannot know whether they were ever even written.

One might assume that the Commons, or at least a majority in that House, were angry about the Declaration because it undid all their efforts against nonconformity. But reference to Grey's *Debates* suggests a more complex story. On February 10, after that part of the king's speech that related to the Declaration had been read aloud, and "after a silence some time," Sir Thomas Meres, who had been one of the strongest supporters of the Conventicles Bill, began to speak with a certain caution:

> In this affair we are like waters, the deeper the silenter; it is of great weight— He would have us leave the Laws as we find them, to our posterity—In the

country, upon the first putting out the Declaration, he has conferred with books, and learned persons in the Laws, and finds that a general suspension of the penal Statutes is against Law; if we are mistaken, let us hear it clearly proved—Speaks only to method; if no man has anything to say against it, there is an end, and let us go to the question.

Then Edmund Waller spoke in favor of the Declaration; if we follow Grey, his speech was scarcely coherent, throwing out precedents in all directions, but Sir Edward Dering heard it as "a long, premeditated speech, concerning the power of the King in ecclesiastical matters [and] the usefulness to the people of his power and dispensing, instancing particularly in the dispensing of the keeping of Lent, which, because it pleased us, we did not complain of" (Dering 1, p. 115). Then Henry Powle opened a way out of the dilemma. It is true, as Henning reported in *House of Commons*, that he made a "long speech" showing that "the King could not dispense, much less suspend the laws in being." Grey reports him as saying: "The Consequence of this is direful; the King by this may change Religion as he pleases; we are confident of him, but knows not what [the] succession may be." But Powle began his speech by suggesting a procedural compromise: "Would comply with the King, to do in a legal way, as now the Declaration does in an illegal." He subsequently chaired the two committees that prepared Addresses against the Declaration, but he *also* chaired the committee that drew up a bill of ease for Protestant Dissenters, and was a member of the committee for preventing the growth of popery. In fact, both Powle's speech, with its gesture of alarm about the heir to the throne, and his subsequent behavior, are a sign of the turning of the tide.

Powle's statement that the Declaration was illegal, however, was too strong for most of the members. Sir Robert Howard was nervously effective in reminding his colleagues that the country was at war, and that this was no moment for constitutional challenges:

> The King says, "it is legal, and he will stick to it;" and we say, "it is not legal, and he shall not."—Is the Black Rod at the door? Shall we so hastily fall into such a vote?—Do Papists make ill use of it, or any other cause? Then address the King, but vote it not illegal—Proceed not this way to the King, else the Hollanders will rejoice.

And towards the end of the first day's debate, Sir Thomas Meres could be heard saying:

> We may, at this time, come nearer his Majesty than ever; for now the House of Commons having seen how little good force will do, it may be, the

reason of the thing will oblige us in a fair legal way of doing what the King has been designing these twelve years. This may prevent those heats that have been, more or less, about ecclesiastical affairs, almost every Session of Parliament.

"What the King has been designing these twelve years." In that pungent admission, as well as in his acknowledgement that force would do little good in the arena of conscience, Meres pointed the way forward to a new era of church policy. That it had to come initially by way of repression of Catholics was bad news for the long-term reputation of the Long Parliament.

CHAPTER 7

❖

The Sessions of 1675

The Commons Fight Back

As the disputes over church matters seemed to recede in importance, and the Third Dutch War succeeded the Second, both king and parliament were able, or forced, to assess what the Restoration had accomplished. It was not a pretty sight, either fiscally or in terms of international relations. The fourteenth and fifteenth sessions mark the real beginning of the rule of Danby as treasurer, "rule" indicating a degree of centralization of power in his hands that had not been available even to Clarendon; and highly centralized power does not often lead to public trust. The Commons emerged from the frustrations of 1673–74—their inability to prevent the Modena marriage high among them—with bad feelings, which during the spring session were expressed in a failed attempt by the Opposition to impeach Danby. Increasingly during these sessions they learned how the rules of the game were stacked against them. They had been tricked into a war, alongside France, against the Dutch, and though Charles had signed a peace with the Dutch it was evident he was still collaborating with Louis XIV, not least in supplying him with troops. They could refuse to vote the king money, but then the navy would deteriorate. National security trumped all other issues. They could send the king formal Addresses asking for the removal of his ministers or a change in his foreign policy, but when the Addresses were ignored or circumvented there was absolutely nothing they could do about it. When the attempt to impeach Danby failed, Oppositional energies were redirected into hostility towards France.

As part of his new supremacy, Danby embarked on a daring campaign to consolidate the king's power and his own by a rearrangement of interests in the country. As Andrew Browning put it: "his aim . . . was a firm alliance of Anglicans and Royalists against Catholics, Dissenters, and all opponents of the prerogative"[1]—especially, perhaps, the latter contingent, always difficult to identify, and likely to multiply if one took the wrong tack. To this end he had planned to recall parliament in early 1675, but to hobble it by bringing in a new Test, or loyalty oath, for members of both Houses, which we now refer to as the Non-Resisting Bill, but which was designed to quash almost any initiative for change in church or state. Chapter 5 has already revealed the fate of this bill in the Lords, as recorded for posterity in the *Letter from a Person of Quality*; and the concerted opposition to it there was a proving ground for the Whig lords who would soon become huge thorns in the government's side.

But to evaluate the tone of this session in the Commons, we will set side by side the voices of Sir Edward Dering and Andrew Marvell, already paired in my Introduction. Dering at this stage was a loyal member of the Court party in parliament, in the confidence of Danby, and was evidently charged with a certain amount of strategic responsibility in the House. His *Diary* for the spring session of 1675[2] is much more revealing of his politics than the earlier section, from 1670 to 1673, edited by Henning. He left us not only records of debates and summaries of his own speeches, but also glimpses of behind-the-scenes caucuses which explain much of what happened in the House. Marvell, whose performances on the floor were both much rarer and more enigmatic than Dering's, nevertheless left us a record of what he thought and felt about this session. His appropriately cautious constituency letters to Hull are in absolute contrast to one flamingly candid letter to his nephew William Popple; and in his *Account of the Growth of Popery and Arbitrary Government* he would satirize the lord keeper's speech at the April 1675 opening. Though it would be misleading to call Marvell a member of the Opposition (since his contempt for the Commons rivaled his disgust at the court), he offers a fine counterpoint to Dering. Both give us an insight into what lay behind resolutions and debates, "behind the curtain" of the blander public record. And beside them both we can set, as a control, the multivocal record of Grey's *Debates*, impersonal only because uninterpreted by the compiler.

The spring session of 1675, the fourteenth session, had been called on the secret understanding, agreed on in council, that the king would ask for no money, but rather would ingratiate himself with the Commons in preparation for making large demands in October. Ingratiation was in order. The session followed a recess of fourteen months. The short thirteenth session had been marked by attempts to impeach Lauderdale, Buckingham, and Arlington—the remaining members of the Cabal, now that Shaftesbury had been dismissed from the chancellorship and had gone over to the Opposition at the end of 1673. By the spring of 1675 Buckingham had done likewise. Arlington had defended himself so ably that the case against him expired. Lauderdale seemed untouchable. The Commons had also shown their new temper by introducing a Habeas Corpus Bill, and by calling for the disbanding of the army on rumors that peace with the Dutch was imminent. They were in exactly the same mood when they reconvened on April 13.

The editor of Grey's *Debates* (since Grey was not in his seat for the first week of this session) provided a summary of the king's speech:

> That he would leave nothing undone that might show the world his zeal for the Protestant religion, as established in the Church of England, from which he would never depart, recommended to them the condition of the fleet, and above all, such a temper and moderation, as might disappoint the expectations of those, who could hope only by violent and irregular motions to prevent the bringing of the session to a happy conclusion.

Heneage Finch, who had replaced Bridgeman as lord keeper, then delivered a speech, as James Ralph commented later in his *History of England*, of "no less than 16 folio pages, every one of which is garnished with the flowers of rhetoric, and withal so void of matter, as scarce to afford pretence or excuse for an extract" (1:251). The speech was not so entirely void of matter as Ralph thought, however, since its emphasis on control of dissent anticipated Danby's Non-Resisting Bill in the Lords while at the same time advocating that the Commons remain passive, except for funding the fleet. Latin quotations were supposed to deliver this gag message with the weary authority of the very distant past:

> there are Two Symptoms which are dangerous in every State, and of which the Historian hath long since given us Warning. One is, when Men do *Quieta movere*, when they stir those Things or Questions which are and ought to be in Peace. . . . Another is, *Cum Res parvae magnis Motibus aguntur*, when Things that are not of the greatest Moment, are agitated with the greatest Heat.[3]

Marvell reported to Hull only that the Speaker had failed to give an account of Finch's speech to the Commons, but that he would send it when printed (*P&L*, 2:145). However, when the *Account* appeared in early 1678 it contained an attack on Finch's speech, which it now saw as a preparation for Danby's Non-Resisting Bill, introduced in the Lords on May 17, and actively supported then by Finch. And therefore, wrote Marvell:

> My Lord Keeper did by his patronizing this Oath, too grossely prevaricate, against two very good State Maximes, in his Harangue to the Parliament, for which he had consulted not the Astrologer, but the Historian, advising them first, That they should not *Quieta movere*. . . . And secondly, that they should not *Res parvas magnis motibus agere*. That is, said he againe, *when as much weight is laid upon a new and not always necessary Proposition, as if the whole summe of affaires depended upon it.*

> And this Oath [Danby's Test], it seems, was the little thing he meant of, being forsooth but a *Moderate Security to the Church and Crown*, as he called it, but which he and his party *layd so much weight on, as if the whole sum of Affairs did depend upon it.*
>
> But as to the *Quieta movere*, or stirring of those things or Questions which are and ought to be in Peace, was not this so, of [having to abjure] taking Armes against the King upon any pretence whatsoever. . . . Had not the three Acts of Corporations, of Militia, and the Five Miles, sufficiently quieted it? (pp. 282–83)

In this rather difficult passage, Marvell conflates the speech on April 13 with that delivered by Finch in the Lords in support of Danby's Test; makes fun of his Latinity; and points out the absolute contradiction between recommending quiet to the Commons and supporting a major change in the status quo by way of the proposed Test. Note his dry use of "forsooth" to imply that Finch's statement of the Test's insignificance was a manifest untruth. We will shortly meet this ironic locution again.

That Finch's speech on April 13 was a miscalculation seems clear from what followed. In default of a written text, the Speaker suggested that members who were present could inform the House of its content, and so they must have done, because the Commons were not pleased. Grey's editor merely reported, from the Commons Journal, that it was resolved, *nemine contradicente,*

> That the humble and hearty thanks of this House be returned to his Majesty, for his gracious promises and assurances expressed in his speech, to preserve and maintain us in the established religion, and our properties according to law; and for his calling us together at this time for that purpose.

In fact, this was one of those occasions on which the required formality of thanking the king for his speech was hotly contested, as Dering reported in detail. Sir Thomas Meres moved to proceed to name committees, "as was usuall in beginnings of parliament," but Sir Baynam Throckmorton said "there was something first to be done, which was to give his Majestie thanks for his gracious speech." Secretary Henry Coventry seconded the motion, but it was opposed by Sacheverell, Cavendish, Russell, Powle, Waller, Sir John Coventry, Malet, Garrway, and Sir William Hickman. Dering summarized their reasons:

1. It did justify the ministers in all they had done since our last addresse if we gave thanks now,

2. that they did not desire the severe execucion of the lawes against papists which is the chief part of the speech, Sir John Mallett,[4]
3. that it would preclude all debate concerning the altering or amending the laws for the execution [of] those laws which are [in force].

Since there was nothing in the king's brief speech to arouse such a response, the complaints must be against Finch's more complex performance, which spoke much of enforcing the laws against both papists and Protestant Dissenters. "Happy is that Government when Men complain of the strict Execution of the Laws," Finch had said, not quite what all would have used as a definition of happiness (p. 129). The Commons did not yet know what was pending in the Lords, the introduction of Danby's Test, but they clearly sensed that Finch's speech was intended to hamstring them.

There ensued, according to Dering, a debate that was almost three hours long. After a division on the motion to adjourn the debate, which was lost by 91 to 180, they arrived at the carefully worded motion for thanks cited above. The last clause, which is double-edged ("for calling us together at this time for this purpose"), was added by Sir Robert Howard, who at this point was working fairly steadily against the court. There was trouble also in the Lords. As Marvell reported to Hull on the 15th: "Some of the Lords have enterd their Protests against the Generall Thanks of their House having rather desired that they should have been limited much after the same manner as by the House of Commons" (*P&L*, 2:146).

The following day, the Country party leaders returned to the aggravations of the previous session. Re. the king's worsening habit of proroguing at will, Sacheverell produced records from the reigns of Richard II, Edward II, and Henry IV that seemed to supply precedents against such behavior. Then they returned to the subject of Lauderdale, who "was still there," even though they had asked the king for his removal, "and [had] since [been] made a peer of England, and £3,000 per annum pencion bestowed upon him." Dering reports himself as speaking not in defense of Lauderdale but, "now he is hear," in favor of bringing him to defend himself. After a brief gap in Dering's manuscript (there is no report of debates on Thursday, April 15), we find ourselves at a meeting at Hampden House, Danby's residence, where Danby's parliamentary friends discussed the strategy for Friday's meeting—something must have happened on Thursday to indicate that the wrath of the House was about to descend on Danby too:

After this informacion finding nothing in all this which could justly render my Lord Treasurer obnoxious to any censure in parliament we agreed to divert it if we could, and that the best way of diverting it was to ingage the house in other businesse; that the best businesse to be gone upon for the Kingdom and the likeliest also to ingage the house warmely in it, was matter of religion. . . . I concurrd with it, so that we did not interest the nonconformists in the matter. . . . This being resolved, it was concluded Sir Joseph Tredinham should begin the motion and I should second it, and *the rest should then keep it up till the day was spent.* (pp. 61–62; italics added)

And on Friday, April 16, accordingly, Tredenham proposed a motion that the House should respond to the king's invitation to consider the security of the Protestant religion, and Dering seconded it. If it looks as if religion were back on the front burner now as a diversionary tactic, read closely: "I confined my mocion" Dering said of himself, "to poperie . . . and [said] that it was my desire chiefly to prevent the grouth of them for the future rather than to punish them that are allready so" (p. 62; italics added). This was well received. But at this point Sir Charles Wheeler (a notable loose cannon) "stood up and made a speech of an hour long of great circumference of discourse, offering us many things which he thought necessarie to be considered in matter of religion, and at last mencioned the case of our [next] King's marriage and the educacion of the children as protestants." This more provocative suggestion was taken up "and prest hard" by Clarges, Littleton, and Powle, until Wheeler, who saw himself about to be nominated to draw up a bill to this last purpose, panicked and wondered why they should begin with what he had mentioned in last place, and for which he had no legislative plans. So the debate foundered, and the day passed, as Danby's group had intended, with nothing concluded.

Just how successful Danby's supporters had been can be judged by Marvell's next letter to Hull:

The House of Commons hath this two days been in a Committee of the whole House concerning Religion. The occasion of which rose from the motion of a member of the House concerning the growth of Popery; for giving ease to Protestant Dissenters, and other good things of the same Tendency. (*P&L*, 2:146)

Marvell at least had been successfully "diverted." Dering, that same day, recorded another meeting at Hampden House, where Danby told them he would be there every evening by 8 p.m. "while the parliament did sit," the other members of the group being Peregrine Bertie, Sir John Bramston, Sir Humphrey Winch, Thomas Cholmondely, Charles Cheyne, Sir William Alington and Sir Richard Wiseman (who compiled lists for Danby of court supporters).

"Those Cucumbers": Court Caucusing

Marvell's last letter had also mentioned that "on Munday is appointed a Bill to be brought in against levying mony without or beyond the Consent of Parlt." This sounds innocuous enough. In fact, it was a direct challenge to Danby's fiscal administration, and Dering's caucus read it as such. On Sunday night they met again and agreed

> that if the bill for making levying of money otherwise than by act of parliament to be treason should be brought in the next day, as we expected, it would not be safe to endeavour to throw it out the first reading: which is hard for any bill, but more hard for a bill which bore the pretence of the publique good, and which had the last session made it up to ingrossment, but rather to speake only to the weightinesse and importance of it, and to get what time we could for a second reading.
>
> And if the mocion of recalling the King's forces out of France should be started, that it would not be possible to over beare it, or resist it, and therefore better to let it passe. (pp. 63–64)

Accordingly, on Monday, April 19, with Grey back in his seat, the House gave the Habeas Corpus bill (dropped by prorogation) another first reading, then turned to this money bill, introduced by Sacheverell, which was quietly voted a second reading.[5] The rest of the day, as Dering had predicted, was spent in a vehement debate on recalling the English forces in the French service. This was initiated by "a set speech" by Littleton on the growth of the French king's power, and Dering reported both the weak demurrals of Secretaries Coventry and Williamson and the effective riposte of Sir William Coventry. So an Address to the king was voted "for the speedy Recalling of all his Subjects out of the French King's Service; and for hindering any more from going over into that Service for the future." The only text that we have is the above, from the Commons Journal. Dering does not include one, Marvell did not send one to Hull. On April 22, however, Dering did report Charles's reply, delivered in person to the Commons, who had trudged to attend him at Whitehall: "The matter was of too great Importance for a present Answer but that he would consider of it and returne them an Answer." It would take a second Address to the same purpose to get the promised answer, on May 8, and then it was highly unsatisfactory.

But we must not jump ahead. For on Monday, April 26, Dering reported that the House returned to the second reading of the "treason to levy money" bill, which was committed. "The objections against this bill are many and great and unanswerable," wrote Dering, "and it was much wondered that it past so easily to the commitment, and nothing said against it":

But the truth was that at a meeting the night before between Sir Charles
Wheeler, Sir Richard Wiseman, Sir Philip Musgrave, Sir Joseph Tredinham
and myselfe and some others, I were of opinion that we should let it passe
in that manner.

1. For it is agreed by all of us that this is a very ill bill and can never be
   made good.
2. That it was to no purpose *to dresse those cucumbers that we resolved to throw out
   of doores.*
3. That the worst time to attempt throwing out a bill of four times we have
   to offer at it, is when it comes to be committed, because every thing is said
   against any part of it, is an argument for the committing it not for rejecting
   it, for if the scope of it be good, every part of it may then be allowed.
4. That if we should speak against the penalties of high treason in it, and
   they should then change it for a praemunire, it would reconcile many to
   the bill, who are now frighted at the name of high treason, and yet the
   bill would still be a very ill bill.
5. That if we set to it now one effect must follow, either to heat the other
   partie or to discourage our owne, as we did or did not carry the question, both which were inconvenient, especially considering that the
   Question about getting money for increase of the Navy was to come on
   the very next day to which it was fit to reserve our forces entire. (p. 70;
   italics added)

Dressing soggy cucumbers only makes them soggier. This maxim helps to
explain why Dering was so effective in these behind-the-scenes negotiations,
as indeed he also was in the House, if we can judge by how often he managed
to modify a position or improve a bill not dangerous to his master, such as
when he got the grand committee on religion to abandon the idea of a volun-
tary register for Roman Catholics (p. 67). His advice about tactics and timing
speaks volumes about parliamentary procedure and the sophisticated use that
was already being made of it.

Tactics and timing, however, could not hold off the inevitable. No sooner
was this bill committed than William Russell rose to deliver a speech against
Danby, saying that he thought impeachment was warranted; Sir Samuel
Barnardiston produced a paper with five articles of high crimes and misde-
meanors; and Powle stood up and "desired the house to proceed upon them
to impeach my Lord Treasurer, for he was ready to prove the articles" (p. 70).
It seems clear that some Opposition leaders had been having behind-the-
scenes meetings of their own. After some debate, wrote Dering, the treasurer's
friends carried the point that the accusers must produce their proofs in the

House. And then they adjourned to Wallingford House to hear how Danby intended to answer the charges. Marvell, in the meantime, sent the articles to Hull on the 27th, urging them to be very prudent about communicating them to others, since they concerned "very great persons and the successe yet uncertain" (*P&L*, 2:150). On Monday, May 3, Dering reported the conclusion of the impeachment hearings, which was that the articles were either trivial, personal, or not a basis for impeachment:

> After which Sir Joseph Tredinham made a speech of the honour and integritie of my Lord Treasurer, and moved that we should declare it so by a publique vote, but it was not seconded and fell flat in the house. Nor did I thinke it was seasonably moved, it being much that he came off so well, though very just I thinke he should do so, but it was not to be hoped that an impeachment should end in panegyrick. (p. 77)

This is quintessential Dering: moderate, fair, and even epigrammatic.

The exoneration of Danby at this first attempt to impeach him is something of a mystery. The attackers made the mistake of starting with two of the weakest articles: Danby's use of patents and his interference in the marriage of Sir Robert Viner's daughter. Browning believed that the failure of these first two conditioned the Opposition for their defeat, as he also believed that Arlington's jealousy was the prime cause of the attack, for which there seems little evidence.[6] Grey's *Debates* for May 3 is unusually full, and covers the discussion of the rest of the seven articles, one of which was the disappearance of £2,000,000, said to have been spent on the navy and secret service but without being properly accounted for, another the Stop of the Exchequer, another "procuring great gifts and grants from the Crown." These were neither trivial charges nor based merely on hearsay. In respect of the missing money, although the Country party leaders spoke fiercely for their right to see the account books, they do not seem to have been sent for. In respect of the Stop of the Exchequer, they could not prove that Danby was responsible, and Sir Richard Temple, now working for the court, declared: "This Lord Treasurer has paid the interest to the creditors, and, as much as in him lies, has endeavoured to rectify the errors of his predecessor." In respect of the "gifts and grants from the Crown," Sir Charles Wheeler made a speech that was extraordinary in more ways than one. He "is sometimes at the Lord Treasurer's [as we learned from Dering, in caucus] and sees his chargeable way of living, and 'tis for the King's honour":

> We sometimes admire the great way of living of foreign great officers of state, and four or five thousand pound, in a bargain, is no great gift to him.

Do you consider nothing but the bare gift? His father was sequestered, and sold one thousand pound per. ann. upon account of his loyalty; and this Lord Treasurer is 10,000 l. the worse, and is this gift so great a matter? Is there no consideration to his Lady, whose Grandfather lost his life for the late King's interest, and the late Lord Lindsey his son, who bestrid his father when he was hurt and fought with a pike in his hand to get him quarter . . . ? (Grey)

These appeals to cavalier sentiment were successful, and Danby's pension (of £3,200 per annum) was voted unimpeachable.

No trace of the content of the debates of May 3 appeared in Marvell's letter to Hull, where he simply reported the acquittal. However, that was not his last word on the matter. In his personal letter to William Popple about this session, written in late July, he presented the impeachment attempt as (almost) the last in a series of violent moves by the Commons to take back the initiative. In this letter Marvell begins with information about what must by now have been common knowledge: what lay behind Danby's Test—meetings between Danby, Lauderdale, and the duke of York in league with the bishops in the Lords to create a new "Episcopal Cavalier Party." He knew that the strategy had been to recall parliament, by proclamation, in March, no more than the required month in advance, and thereby to forestall Oppositional preparations. We have seen part of this letter before, on the issue of giving thanks for the royal speech, but that was merely the prelude to a series of adversarial motions:

And the King should ask, *forsooth*, no Mony, but only mention the building and refitting of Ships. And thus the Parliament meets, and the King tells them 'tis only to see what farther is wanted for Religion and Property. The Commons were very difficultly brought to give him Thanks for his gracious Expressions. Strait they poured in Bills for *Habeas Corpus* against Imprisonment beyond Sea; Treason to levy money without, or longer than, Consent of Parliament; and that it should be lawful to resist . . . [the] New Test, and Way of Proceeding, for speedyer Conviction of Papists; and, which is worse, for appropriating the King's Customs to the Use of the Navy; and, worse of all, voted one Morning to proceed on no more Bills before the Recess . . . Address upon Address against Lauderdale. Articles of Impeachment against the Treasurer, but which were blown off at last by great bribing. Several Addresses for recalling Forces out of the French service. (*P&L*, 2:341–42; italics added.)

The king should ask, "*forsooth*," no money; and he got none! He could even be said to have lost some, by the appropriation of the customs, normally part of his own revenue, for the navy. And whereas Dering had reported the exoneration

of Danby with satisfaction, as an act of justice, Marvell undermines the procedure by the scorn of his charge that it was "blown off at last by great bribing."
When Grey's *Debates* was published in 1763, the editor added an evaluative
footnote:

> Whether the charge against the Lord Treasurer was held frivolous or mali-
> cious, whether sufficient proof was wanting to make it good, or whether he
> had more friends in the House than his Royal Master, on examining the
> foundation, the whole building fell to the ground. It must be owned our
> lights fail us in this matter. Bishop Burnet contents himself with saying,
> "The majority were for him." Marvell is express, That he got off by high
> bribing. Nothing is easier to be said, nothing is harder to be proved. *Ralph.*

Thus the editor not only consulted Burnet's *History of His own Time* for guidance
in this matter, but also sought out the personal correspondence of Andrew
Marvell, some of which had been published in 1726 in Thomas Cooke's edition
of his poems.

Marvell, it might seem, thereby provided the last word, however modified
by Ralph's caveat. And Dering's accounts of the meetings in the treasurer's
house can certainly help to explain why the impeachment debates went the
way they did. Browning's account of them is too dismissive, especially his
claim that Danby "had no need to rely on . . . personal friends" (p. 156) for
his defense.[7] It is true that members who had previously taken Oppositionist
positions, like Garroway and Temple, supported him. Sir William Coventry
declared that there was nothing illegal about the patent, and so helped bring
about the collapse of the first article. On the other hand, we might take seriously the suggestion by the editor of Grey's *Debates* that Danby might have
had "more friends in the House than his Royal Master." This would not be
true on the occasion of the second attempt to impeach him in 1678.

France

"We truckle to France in all things"—Marvell to Popple, 1671

The last item in Marvell's satirical history of the fourteenth session in his letter
to Popple, however, was not about Danby's unimpeachability but rather the
"Several Addresses for recalling our Forces out of the French Service." The
compiling of these Addresses and the king's delayed or evasive answers created
a new source of anger in the Commons, which would eventually erupt into
the full-blown attack of the 1677 session. The first Address was, as mentioned
above, voted on Monday, April 19, after an inflammatory speech by Sir Thomas

Littleton, who led the Francophobic charge throughout. On April 21, Charles had replied "that the matter was of too great Importance for a present Answer but that he would consider of it and returne them an Answer." When this failed to materialize, on May 5 the House voted a second Address to the same effect. On the 7th, they were asked to attend the king at Whitehall with the Address, and Charles said he would send them an answer in writing. Here is part of his response, delivered to the Commons on May 8:

> That such [troops] of his subjects as were in the Most Christian King's service, before the last treaty [made] with the States General of the United Provinces, and were not, by that, to be recalled, as they are at present become inconsiderable in their numbers his Majesty conceiveth that they cannot be recalled without derogation to his honour and dignity. . . . But as to the prohibiting the going over of any more, his Majesty will renew his Proclamation, and use all other effectual means both to forbid and hinder it.

Marvell decoded this almost unintelligible message for his constituents that same day, to the effect that English troops who were already in France when the treaty with Holland was signed were not required by that treaty to be withdrawn, and in any case there were hardly any there! Nothing was said about those who been sent subsequently. Debate on this devious answer began in the Commons on Monday, May 10, and quickly moved to a grand committee. It is clear that members saw in the answer the king's reluctance to do anything to annoy Louis XIV; referring to Louis as "the most Christian king" annoyed certain members of the House. Littleton observed that the previous proclamation had been completely ineffective, that eight thousand Englishmen at least were fighting on the French side, including the duke of Monmouth's regiment. He wanted to be informed whether the treaty with Holland left Charles free "to keep these men actually in that King's service." Powle pointed out: "To the first part of your Address you have a denial; to the second you have no Answer at all. There are several forces gone over *since* the Address." Sir William Coventry did "not conceive it possible to have these forces back, or prevent others going over, . . . before Holland have peace with France." Secretary Coventry said shrewdly that soldiers will follow the money, "the eagles will go where the carcass is." The use of the king's "honour" as a big gun was both supported and protested against. Sir Edward Dering characteristically recommended an adjournment to let tempers cool.[8]

All this information comes from Grey, who tells us the question was then put "Whether a farther Address should be made to the king for recall of his subjects now in the service of the French King." At this point something so dramatic happened that Grey, Dering, and Marvell all reported it in detail.

Even those readers who are not interested in parliamentary procedure may want to follow it.

Given the way the votes had gone on the Danby impeachment, the last thing the court might have expected was a tie on this issue—or what seemed at first to be one. Dering's account of the vote is the clearest:

> The committee divided, the Yeas on the right hand, the Noes on the left. Sir Trevor Williams teller for the Yeas and Sir Gilbert Talbot for the Noes, and the numbers happened to be equall, viz., 135 on each side. The Noes called to report. The Yeas called to tell again, saying that one member, viz., Mr. Cofferer was told twice. Sir Gilbert Talbot refused to tell again, it being the rule when the tellers disagreed, to tell again, but not when they agreed, though others did call to tell again. (pp. 81–82)[9]

In the event of a tie the Speaker may usually cast the deciding vote, but this was an occasion when one party denied that it actually was a tie. The Opposition members demanded a recount, which, they believed, would give them a majority of one. At this point, mayhem broke out. Sir John Cavendish seems to have been the first aggressor, in attempting to make Sir John Hanmer change his mind. According to Dering, Cavendish spat at Hanmer, and Hanmer spat back. According to Grey, "Others said, that Lord Cavendish spit in Sir John Hanmer's face, but that was only eagerness of speech, and so some might accidentally fly from him!" A couple of men had their hands on their swords. Marvell, for Popple's amusement, exaggerates: "Every man's hand on his hilt." Grey (who liked a scuffle) has the fullest account of the disorder:

> Gentlemen rising from their places and mingling in the pit; hot and provoking discourses and gestures passed on both sides, especially between Lord Cavendish and Sir John Hanmer . . . Mr. Stockdale, and some others, setting their feet upon the mace, which lay below the table, as is the usual place at Grant Committees. This disorder continuing near half an hour, the standers by, on the upper benches, expecting very fatal consequences, especially when the young gallants, as Mr. Thynne, Mr. Newport, and several others, leaped over the seats to join Lord Cavendish. But the Speaker, very opportunely and prudently, rising from his seat near the Bar, in a resolute and slow pace, made his three respects through the crowd, and took the Chair. The mace was still retained by the said gentlemen, but, at last, being forcibly laid upon the table, all the discord ceased, and the gentlemen went to their places.

And Dering, in his orderly way, may be allowed to finish the story:

> As soon as silence was made, several healing mocions were made, by Sir Thomas Lee, Sir Robert Carr, Sir Philip Warwick and others, which ended in a forme of words dictated by the Speaker, and assented to by every member standing up in his place as it came to his turne, which was that they would not send or receive any challenge nor otherways remember or resent any offence or displeasure for any thing had past that day, which they promised upon their honour. Which being done, we adjourned till next day without returning upon the dispute or so much as entering [in] our bookes the said protestacion. (p. 82)

Needless to say, the Commons Journal contains not a trace of the fracas, nor of the vote that gave rise to it.

This episode shows how the balance of voting power had shifted in the House when the issue was the French threat; it shows how intensely differences of opinion were felt; and it demonstrates why Speaker Seymour continued to hold the respect of the House, despite his evident willingness to take instructions from Whitehall. On the following day the debate was reopened as though the division had not occurred. Attention focused on whether the motion to recall the forces from France should include the word "all," a proposal that was eventually, after a debate of more than four hours, lost by one vote, 174 to 173 (Dering 2, pp. 82–83). Even then, a struggle ensued over Sir Winston Churchill's vote in favor of the inclusion of "all," since he "was on the stairs coming down from the gallery" when the Noes were counted, but his vote was permitted because "he was at the gallerie door, but could not get roome to come in there, the gallerie door being crowded."

On June 3, Marvell wrote: "The Commons have sent to desire his Majesty to issue a fuller Proclamation to recall his subjects out of the French service" (*P&L*, 2:161). A week later they were prorogued.

In the October session, the fifteenth, they were still pounding the same sand. On October 23, Marvell informed his Hull constituents: "Today the House voted that all the Kings subjects who are or shall be in the French Kings service contrary to his Majesty's Proclamation shall be deemed Contemners of his Royall authority and Enemys of the Interest of this nation. To desire the Lords concurrence herein" (*P&L*, 2:167). On November 17, the motion was engrossed. On November 22, parliament was prorogued again. Then followed the Long Prorogation, which was widely believed to have been decided upon by Charles as a compromise with Louis XIV, who could see from these Addresses that his interests could not be well served while parliament sat, and indeed wished his cousin to dissolve it altogether.

If readers have been wondering why this issue has been pursued in such relentless detail, they may translate their own feelings of frustration into a simulacrum of what was increasingly felt by members of the House of Commons, those at least who were genuinely concerned as to where the king's Francophile policies were taking the country. The longer the king prevaricated over this seemingly minor issue, the more their numbers grew and the stronger their determination became. In the next session, the very long session that followed the Long Prorogation, we will see, literally, how one thing led to another; how their failure to get the English troops recalled caused them, step by step, to ask for more aggressive measures against Louis XIV, and how each new failure led not to retreat but to another forward push.

CHAPTER 8

❖

Foreign Policy
The Sessions of 1677–78

The Sixteenth Session

Part One: February 15 to May 28, 1677

This very long chapter is all about length. The Long Prorogation was followed by the second longest session of the Long Parliament—from February 15, 1677 to May 13, 1678. The length of this session was manipulated by means of long adjournments partly in order to keep in the Tower the four Opposition lords who had protested the legality of the Long Prorogation. Indeed, when Daniel Finch sent his uncle a long relation of this session, he remarked, in connection with a small fracas between the two Houses over the wording of a bill, that

> here the providence over this nation in the imprisonment of the Lords was very great, for as they have heretofore been very dextrous in the management of Quarrels between the two houses, so most certainly they would not have lett slip this opportunity, where though the matter was of less importance to them than in the other cases, yet their right was more clear, & more easily & more inoffensively to be defended.[1]

Finch, at least, was happy to have the four lords out of the way.

But the point of this chapter is to show how it happened that the Long Parliament became obsessed with the king's foreign policy. It might be helpful, therefore, to review the history of England's foreign relations during the Restoration up to this point. To greatly oversimplify, it was dominated by two impulses, which gradually converged: trade rivalry with the Dutch republic, as the other great maritime nation, which was, however, largely Protestant; and ties with France, increasingly a Roman Catholic superpower, as the influence of Spain and the Hapsburgs declined. The king's ties with France were inevitable, given his French mother, and a beloved sister married to Louis XIV's brother,

Philippe, duc d'Orléans. Henriette-Anne remained in close touch with Charles II until her premature death immediately following her visit to England in 1670, the visit in which she served as intermediary in negotiating the secret treaty of Dover between Charles and Louis. The Second Dutch War, whose debacles (from the English perspective) led to Clarendon's downfall, and of which we have heard from his own memoir, was concluded by the treaty of Breda on July 21, 1667. That same year, while England and the Dutch were distracted, France had invaded that part of the Spanish-owned Netherlands which is today Belgium, a signal of larger imperial intentions. To protect themselves against those intentions, England and the Netherlands signed a defensive agreement against France in January 1668, which was joined in May by Sweden. This was the famous Triple Alliance, the product of Sir William Temple's negotiations.

No sooner was it signed, however, than Charles and Louis secretly agreed to embark on another war against the Dutch, from which France would gain in terms of territory, Charles in terms of a huge monetary subsidy which would allow him, it was hoped by both parties, to circumvent parliament. The war was declared on March 17, 1672, with a trumped-up list of causes, on which Marvell would pour scorn in his *Account*, and with England and France as allies against the Dutch, to which alliance Sir Henry Coventry had also secretly converted Sweden in 1671. While Louis attacked the Netherlands with alarming success (and with English troops to support him) the war went badly for England at sea. Thanks in part to *Englands Appeale*, the parliamentarians began to understand how they had been tricked, and were increasingly determined not to fund the war. By November 1673 Shaftesbury had learned of the secret clauses in the treaty of Dover, which included a commitment by Charles eventually to return the whole English flock to the Roman Catholic fold. Shaftesbury was dismissed from the chancellorship and went over to the Opposition. On February 19, peace between England and the Dutch was negotiated and signed at the treaty of Westminster. But France continued to encroach on the Netherlands, and English troops continued to be deployed in Louis' service. In the previous chapter we have seen how the Opposition group in the Commons eventually managed to vote this a major grievance of state.

In the sessions of 1677 and 1678, to which we now turn, we will hear the Commons enlarge their focus on foreign policy to the point of actually dictating to Charles how to extricate himself from his dangerous friendship with Louis XIV, first by alliances with the Dutch, both defensive and offensive. There was no doubt as to why an offensive alliance was needed. Eventually they argued themselves into a much more radical solution. England should declare war against France. The Commons were thus back in the militaristic mood into which they had been coaxed in 1664 and tricked in 1672; but now the responsibility for another hugely expensive war would, had it come about, been entirely their own The country was lucky they were outmaneuvered. This chapter follows this process in detail, and, inevitably, the ideological issue had to be filtered through the mesh of money.

For the sixteenth session, we have no fewer than five (or seven) sources of information, in different genres and differently motivated.

1. One private court correspondent, Daniel Finch, MP, who wrote a thirty-five page letter to his uncle, Sir John Finch, describing the business of the session in detail but only to the adjournment of May 28, 1677. His main motive seems to have been amusement, his style at once candid and spiced with interesting suspicions.
2. The parliamentary journal of Thomas Neale, MP, which covers the same period. Neale was apparently reporting to Danby, but his other motive was to record his own speeches! This is the least valuable source of information, except that its having been compiled is itself evidence of Danby's methods.
3. Marvell's *Account of the Growth of Popery and Arbitrary Government*, the quintessential scofflaw pamphlet, which, as discovered by Nicholas von Maltzahn, incorporates two manuscript journals which might themselves have been intended for publication. Marvell clearly separates the two sides of the debates, but names no names.
4. Marvell's official letters to his Hull constituents, which fill out our knowledge of the end of the sixteenth session, and part of the seventeenth.
5. Grey's *Debates*, which becomes greatly more expansive in its reporting for this crucial session. Without Grey's assiduous coverage, and identification of the speakers, we would not be able to observe exactly how the Commons grew into stronger positions, piling Address upon Address, and turning each frustration into new leverage.

The length of this chapter may seem oppressive, but it is necessary; first, to show how comparing differently motivated witnesses gives us a more nuanced take on the issues than the polarized Court/Opposition divide suggests; second, to reveal precisely how the Opposition position was worked out on the floor of the House, statement by statement, incrementally, rather than being agreed on behind the scenes. This is a view of a deliberative process we seldom have today, and in its own right, as a phenomenon of early modern politics, it may be therapeutic.

Let us start with Daniel Finch. Son of Heneage Finch, now, Chancellor, Daniel's allegiances to the Court party were only natural, but they were those of an intelligent and financially disinterested man. Elected in 1672–73, he first became a strong figure in the debates of 1677. It does not appear that J.P. Ferris, who wrote the article on him in the *House of Commons*, knew of his letter to his uncle describing this session; but the article presents him as opposed to France, wary of Catholics, and inclined to the toleration of Protestant Dissenters. Finch's letter differs from the other sources by discarding chronological order in favor of topics: first, major ideological bills; second, the debates on Supply; and, lastly, the struggle over foreign policy and relations with France. This makes it harder to see causation, how one thing led to another. And Finch also allowed himself some expansive digressions from his own chosen topics.

He began, it is true, at the beginning, by describing the struggle in the Lords on February 15 and 16 over the Long Prorogation, mentioning his father's speech there. The issue, he said, would have passed more calmly in the Commons had not Sir John Ernle "in mistaken zeal moved for the consideration of the King's speech, when Sir Thomas Clarges had moved before for the reading of the bill for recalling the K's subjects out of France . . . . For the reading of the bill, which was brought in and twice read before, did imply that the prorogation was good" (p. 2). This misstep allowed Cavendish and Sacheverell to raise the question as to whether the prorogation should not rather be called an adjournment. This led to a motion by Sir Thomas Lee for a debate on whether it had been an adjournment or a prorogation. Eventually the House proceeded to name committees and so the question was determined by default. This unusually messy debate was, said Finch, of advantage to the Court party,

> for so many Countrey Gentlemen began to suspect the evill Consequences of following their leaders whose counsels were such as could produce nothing but Confusion, so that this great matter which so long threatned the King's affairs and was cast as a rock upon which the King's affairs must necessarily split proved most advantageous to them. (p. 3)

Finch then proceeded to give an account of Dr. Nicholas Cary's involvement with one of the anti-prorogation pamphlets that he had carried to the press, suggesting that the total lack of support for Cary in the Commons was for fear of starting another quarrel with the Lords. Then he jumped to the two long bills sent down by the Lords about religion, which were not in fact debated until the very end of March, but which demanded several pages of Finch's attention. The second of these, "An Act for further securing the Protestant Religion" should there be a Catholic successor, Marvell had also fastened on as especially significant in the *Account*. Marvell regarded the bill as pernicious, and was pleased when it died in committee. Finch, instead, saw it as a curiosity, and offered a gossipy explanation of the bill's origins:

The Lord Chancellor and Lord Treasurer having represented to the King the necessity of doing something extraordinary to satisfy the people in matter of religion . . . the King was very sensible of it and resolved to doe any thing that might not provoke the Duke of York [,] to extinguish the fear of Popery. And the rather that he might thus prevent under attempts of a bill to disable a Papist to inheritt the Crowne an impeachment of the Duke of York which t'was whispered that the Master of the Rolls [Sir Harbottle Grimston] resolved to bring into the House of Commons. And Burnet the Preacher at the Rolls told the Duke he heard the Master of the Rolls say so, and thereupon he sent to the Master of the Rolls about it, who denied it. However these things made the King positive in his resolution & the Duke more patient of the makers of this bill than otherwise he would have bin. (p. 8)

The king discussed particulars of the bill before the session and agreed that it should be brought into parliament. "It was designed that some Country Gentlemen should propose the matter in the House of Commons, thinking they would like a child of their own body, & fearing they should be jealous against it if it came from Court" (p. 8). This latter stratagem seems to have been dropped, and the bill was sent down from the Lords.

Finch then proceeded to describe the debate in the Commons, where Grimston attacked the bill, as did Littleton, Vaughan, Birch, and Cavendish. But "in Conclusion it was carried that it should be committed by 127 to 88." And, Finch continued:

It cannot be imagined that they could have any zeal for the prerogative [as] they pretended who were many of them against the repeal of the Act for Triennial Parliaments . . . which is not only a violation of the prerogative but a kind of dethroning of the King. And yet it is possible they might doe this to gratify the Duke of York who has greatly courted the Nonconformists . . . not that they love him but they would make use of him as he would doe of them.

But another reason why they opposed both this and the other bill, may possibly be because many of them doe not intend to doe anything that may really serve the Protestant religion, that the fears of Popery may still remain for a handle of disturbance. (p. 9)

This cynical insider analysis offers a useful counterpoint, from the diametrically opposite position, to Marvell's *Account*. It helps to explain what is otherwise a rather obscure parliamentary moment which forebodes the Exclusion Crisis, but which has left little trace in the records because the bill, as Marvell told us (and Finch did not yet know this when he wrote his letter), died a quiet death in the committee of which *both* were members.

Finch also gives a clear account of what happened to the other bill sent down from the Lords at the same time:

> After it was read in the House, Mr. Sacheverell made a very furious Speech against it calling it a bill for toleration & introducing of Popery; after he had mistaken & misrepresented (I will not say willfully) several parts of it to the House; & at last Mr. Williams of Gray's Inne spoke, and said he [had] many things to say against the bill but he would fain see the man that would have the Confidence to speake for it which no man did; and upon the Question it was thrown out of the House with this Special entry of it in the Journal . . . that the substance thereof . . . appeared to be much different from the title, And thereupon the House nemine contradicente rejected the same. (p. 13)

In the *Account* Marvell matches this from the opposite side of the House, though without naming names. "As soon as it was first read a Gentleman [Sacheverell?] of great worth and apprehension spake short but roundly and thorow against it . . . a third demanded that they should stay a while to see whether there were any one so hardy as to speak a word for it" (p. 311). But Finch knew something that Marvell did not:

> My Lord Stafford was as much against it in the House of Lords but for a different reason, for he declared openly in the Hous twas a bill that in a few years would extirpate the Roman Catholick Religion out of England, & perhaps the rest of the Popish Lords thought so too, for every one of them to a man was against the bill. (p. 13)

At this point Finch backtracked to early February, to the Supply debate. On Tuesday, February 20,

> Mr. Neal moved for 600000 li. to be given to his Majesty for building of ships and was seconded by Sir William Drake; Mr. Leveson Gower (that marryed my Lord Baths daughter) moved for 800000 li. But these motions being irregular for money ought to be considered of in a Committee of the whole House & it being late, the matter of supply was ordered to be considered the next day. (p. 13)

Thus we are introduced to a figure who was compiling his own journal at this time. Thomas Neale, as Paula Watson wrote in *House of Commons*, had "reached an understanding with Danby, to whom he supplied detailed accounts of the debates." In fact, though these may have been intended partly as intelligence for Danby, Neale's main reason for keeping a parliamentary journal was evidently to showcase his own speeches. His journals survive in two halves in two separate manuscripts,[2] only the second of which has been previously identified as his. The first, however, can be recognized by its egregious self-promotion. Here is its entry about Neale's motion to take into consideration the king's speech and vote him £600,000 (f. 30): "The King's speech being read Mr. Neale stood upp and said . . . 'What more then this can be wished for. What more can be hoped for from the best of kings?' " This remark grounded a long speech of a page and a half in a larger script than the surrounding debate, which Neale renders considerably more briefly than does Grey; pausing, however, to record, presumably verbatim, his own second speech on the issue on February 21 (f. 33): "This made mee Name 600000 and makes mee to presse it."

After his brewing business had nearly gone bankrupt, Neale suddenly recovered his fortunes at this point, which tends to support the theory that he was now on Danby's payroll.[3] What Finch's relation obscures, however, and so of course does Neale's, is that this irregular procedure was clearly planned as a pre-emptive strike, to get the large figure on the table right from the start, a strategy recalling the notorious "Paston" move of 1664. As Grey shows, the Opposition fought to keep the regular rules of order, whereas the Court supporters said it was not necessary to "go by these wary steps" (Tredeenham). Vaughan remarked shrewdly on the timing:

> when we contend for money, it puts him in mind of country fellows going to foot-ball play. . . . They get up early, though possibly all the sport may end in breaking their shins, and tearing their cloaths. These early motions are as if these movers were the only givers, and that others not so forward were the deniers.

Finch noted, as Grey did not, "a very malitious passage in Sir Thomas Littleton's speech, who concluded it with praying to God that when the Ships were built, a right use might be made of them . . ." (p. 14). The next day, he cited the Opposition leaders one by one:

> Garraway desired to know whether the Supply now to be asked was intended for all his Majesty's occasions, or whether they were to expect any further demands this Session. And to this it being answered that t'was design'd for ships only: Mr. Sacheverell rose up and said that the last session they had voted 300000 li. for 20 ships, & therefore required to know why

they should now aske more money or more ships; he said he could never move more for a full exchequer for that was the . . . best expedient to have no more Parliaments: Sir Thomas Meres said the Countrey was poor & therefore he was not for giving any superfluous sum . . . he said, the money formerly given had been misapplied, & he saw little better security for the right use of this which was now asked. Col. Birch said that if the present-ness of our danger was the occasion of this great supply, why were we prorogued for 15 moneths. . . . Mr. Garraway desired, that before we built our ships the king would be pleased to name such a Lord High Admiral that we might trust. . . . I presumed to speak too, as I have done upon several other occasions this session. (p. 14)

But instead of giving his uncle the substance of his own speech as Neale would have done, Finch supplied a cogent summary of the data presented by Samuel Pepys, "A kind of succinct history of the state of our Fleet." As usual, Pepys's command of the facts and figures was persuasive, and "in conclusion it was carried by many votes (though I never saw a fuller House)" that the king should have £600,000 for ships. Finch does not here give the vote, which he greatly simplifies. Nor does the Commons Journal. In fact, as Marvell wrote to Hull,

the Debate divided it selfe betwixt 600000li & 400000li[.] And . . . about six a clock at night . . . the Question being put whether that of the 400000li should be now put; the House divided and it was carried in the negative by 199 against 165. So of Consequence the next Question for 600000li passed in the Affirmative. (*P&L*, 2:180)

This is confirmed by Neale (f. 33), who is careful to record voting figures.

The question—again—of how the money was to be raised was discussed over several days, in a debate to which Finch evidently attached singular importance, since he devoted three full pages of his letter to it.[4] On March 5, however, Marvell reported that a shift of focus had occurred. When the House moved to a grand committee to consider grievances, this allowed the topic of France to be raised. The result was the first of many Addresses to the king about foreign policy, to which Finch would not turn his attention until a later section of his letter. Instead, Finch inserted at this point an account of yet another difference between the Lords and the Commons—a minor one, as it turned out, about whether the Lords should be named as partners with the Commons in the title of a money bill. And this occasioned a digression on the behavior of Speaker Seymour, which is worth transcribing partly because of its drama, and partly because of its connection to later Speakerly transgressions:

Some opposition there seemed to be made in the House of Commons to this Amendment, but many of our grandees being gone out of towne, the votes of the House having gone against them almost in every instance this Session, and the generality of the House at this time too crying out agree, agree. The rest that remain'd despair'd of any success. . . . But of a sudden to the amazement of both partyes the Speaker, who has bin very fortunate in occasioning and advancing differences between the 2 houses, rises up & says, that though it was not orderly for him to speak, yet in a matter of so high importance as this he thought it his duty, & therefore craved leave to tell them his opinion, which was that since [time immemorial] yt was the undoubted priviledge of the House of Commons to give money, 'twas no less their right to appoint the manner & the forme. (p. 18)

Therefore he concluded that the Lords' amendment encroached on the Commons' privileges. "Hereupon in a moment the scene was changed," wrote Finch, and all the Commons voted not to agree with the Lords' amendment. He proceeded to speculate as to what had motivated Seymour:

But what should make the Speaker give up a question & thus unnecessarily hazard the king's affairs is very hard to conjecture. Some think he did it inadvertently, not thinking that so little a seed should so quickly grow up into a great tree; Others think 'twas by designe, & fancy several ends in it. Some make it to be by concert with the Court that to accommodate the difference that must arise upon it whole Clause of Accounts might be left out; & from thence maliciously infer a desire of misspending the money: but this you may judge of, when you have considered that the king is not only most impatiently desiring of a Fleet, but all about him are very sensible that without the right application of this money 'tis very improbable the Parliament will ever give him any more, a consideration much more obligatory then any Clause of Accounts. Some others fancy he [Seymour] is weary of the Speakers Chair, & would fain be a Lord, but this surely can have little weight in it, for he is more eminent in this Post then he can reasonably expect to be in any other, for he is certainly as dextrous a man as ever satt in that Chair, and I believe his usefulness there is the best security he can have for other Employments. (pp. 19–20)

And then Finch added yet another hypothesis, that Seymour's move was the result of a quarrel with Danby, a theory he dismisses, since "this could be no direct Injury to my Lord Treasurer." The whole digression seems to be some sort of guessing game he sends on to his uncle, inviting still other explanations. Marvell makes no reference in any of his letters or in the *Account* to this affair—one way of differentiating his style of secret history from that of Daniel Finch, who writing privately could afford to be interested in scandal and court intrigue. Finch gave short shrift to the legislation enacted, and calmly remarked:

> I shall trouble with no more bills of this session, not but that there were some others of importance, but because I know of no circumstance relating to them that may be of any entertainment to you, & I imagine you may have the Journall it self transmitted to you as formerly by Mr. Secretary. (p. 25)

"Any entertainment"! This speaks volumes about Finch's selection of materials, as well as to the fact that the secretary—probably Williamson—was transmitting copies of the Commons Journal on a regular basis to Sir John Finch, who had no professional need of them.

Only late in his letter did Finch turn to what was undoubtedly the defining issue of the session: "what has past in reference to the French." He did not grasp what Grey's *Debates* reveals, that it was via the debate on grievances that Sir William Coventry was able to introduce the problem of France. So let us now turn to Grey, who had different priorities. On 6 March Coventry began:

> As for "Grievances," he is not very forward to present any. But there is one, above all, that concerns us all to think of. Consider the posture we are in, in relation to France, the greatest Grievance that can be to the nation. In respect of France, all other things are trifles. . . . Would now consider, though there is a Bill for recalling the forces out of France, that that is no plaister for this sore.

And Sir Thomas Clarges recommended putting aside the complaints about the Chancery judges "till this be off your hands. This 'Grievance' of France is a matter of great consequence, that if there be no tendency of redressing it this day, we are lost." Thus the frustrations of the 1675 sessions, and their impotent Addresses on the subject of recalling the English forces in French service, returned to the forefront.

From this point on, the Commons were focused on how to get the king, if not to agree with them, then at least to understand that the Supply he requested would be conditional on a shift away from his pro-France policy. Various Addresses were suggested; and by the end of the day it was resolved that a committee be appointed to "prepare an Address to represent to his Majesty the danger of the power of France and to desire his Majesty, by such Alliances as he shall think fit, to secure his Kingdom, and quiet the fears of his people, and for the preservation and securing of the Spanish Netherlands."

By the end of the session, "such Alliances as he shall think fit" will have been abandoned in favor of a highly specific alliance with the Dutch; and even that, when produced, will be rejected as inadequate.

This evolution of the Commons' position is, as I have said, unintelligible from Finch's letter. It is much clarified, however, by Marvell's *Account*, which in turn was taken, largely verbatim, from a remarkable manuscript, BL Add. MS. 35865, which has two titles: "Journall touching the Engageing the King to joyne with the Confederates in a Warr against France," and "Proceedings of the Parliament against the growing Power of France."[5] The word "Journall" implies a private diary, but "Proceedings" suggests precisely that which was illegal, to publish parliamentary proceedings; and in fact the elegant presentation of this manuscript, with ruled margins and subtitles, strongly suggests an intention to publish. As pure information, its two great values are in keeping a clear chronology, and in giving the gist of the debates, though without naming the speakers. Marvell's recension is almost, but not quite, verbatim, and deliberately obscures the fact that in this session the Addresses to the king came from both Houses in collaboration.

If we interlineate the manuscript's story of the debates with Grey's testimony and occasional comments from Finch, we will have a much better sense of what happened, which can further be clarified by giving it the shape of a calendar:

March 6   Resolution to entrust a committee with drawing up the Address.

March 10   Text of Address read in Commons; sent up for Lords' concurrence.

March 12   Debate on Supply—continuance of excise on ale and beer for three years, resolved in favor, 189 to 156.

March 13   William Coventry reported that the Lords agreed in principle with the Address, but wanted the addition of "Sicily" as territory to be preserved (also see Finch, pp. 30–31).

March 14   Debate on Lords' amendment, which was rejected.

March 15   After a conference, the Lords withdrew their amendment, and the Address was presented to the king on the 16th.

March 16 [Grey has 17]   The king replied, via the Speaker, "That his Majesty was of the Opinion of his two Houses of Parliament, That the Preservation of Flanders was of great consequence; and that he would use all means in his power for the Safety of his Kingdoms."

Debate on the king's answer was put off by the discussion of Sir John Harrington's petition, and then by the first reading of the bill for further securing the Protestant religion.

March 26 The Commons discussed the king's answer, and debated whether to send a second, clearer Address, assuring the king of their support if, in following their advice, he was led into war. Courtiers opposed another Address, but the motion to draw it up passed.

March 30 Text of Address (included in the *Account*) debated in the Commons; motion for its recommittal lost 131 to 122, i.e. text agreed to. Presented to the king.[6]

The Commons received no answer to this second Address, so that, the *Account* continued, filling out its source with interpretation, "it became doubtful, whether the Money-Bill[s] would be accepted or no, and if the Commons made any difficulty in passing them, unless they were first secured against the French Interest, it seemed that the supply would be rejected by the Conspirators good will" (p. 330). There is nothing in Grey, however, to suggest that the money bills were in danger of not proceeding through their final stages.

April 11 The king's answer delivered: "His Majesty having considered your last Address, and finding some late alteration in affairs abroad, thinks it necessary to put you in mind, That the only way to prevent the dangers which may arise to these Kingdoms, must be by putting his Majesty timely in a Condition to make such fitting preparation."

    To this end, the king proposed they meet after a short Easter adjournment "to ripen this matter." (Grey cites Stockdale: "That is, in plain English, to grant Money.")

We could use some plain English by now. Charles's oblique reference to "some late alteration in affairs abroad" was queried, and the *Account* claims it was glossed by Secretary Coventry as referring to the military successes of the French in taking Cambrai and St. Omer (p. 332). More to the point, the king's proposal that they return to finish up business after only a short Easter recess, when the House had been expecting to start a longer recess on Saturday 14th, threatened them with having to do business with only a very thin attendance. And since the two money bills were effectively finished, the king's deliberately evasive request for assistance in the light of "alterations" implied a request for still *more* money. The Opposition were, naturally, opposed. The result of the debates on April 11 and 12 (for which one can also consult the second part of Thomas Neale's journal in Egerton 3345) was merely an additional clause to the bill for continuing the excise on ale and beer. This would allow the king to borrow £200,000, which should see him through any immediate exigencies.

April 13 Sir John Trevor reported the text of this third Address to the House, and the Commons presented it to the king at Whitehall.

April 16   Secretary Williamson delivered the king's answer, of which the central point was that being allowed to borrow £200,000 was useless. "He must tell them plainly, that without the sum of *Six hundred thousand pounds*, or Credit for such a sum, upon new *Fonds* [i.e. from new taxes], it will not be possible for him to speak, or act those things which should answer the ends of their severall Addresses." That same day the Commons composed an answer, reported by Sir William Coventry (text in *Account*, Grey), to the effect that "many of our Members (being upon an expectation of an Adjournment before Easter) are gone into their Several Countries, [so that] we cannot think it Parliamentary in their absence to take upon us the granting of money."

April 17   Parliament adjourned until May 21.

May 21   Parliament convened. The king made no speech, but sent a message by Secretary Coventry requesting they "forthwith" consider his last message "because he did intend there should be a Recess very quickly." This was presumably intended to impart a sense of urgency.

Daniel Finch noted "a very great assembly, as great, I guesse, as the time before," but misreported what followed:

> So soon as they mett they laid aside all maner of business, not suffering so much as their Committee of Priviledges to sitt, that they the sooner dispatch that great affair for which they mett, so very intent they were upon it, but hoping that the house might be yet fuller, but rather that they might have time to discourse with one another they adjourned the debate of his Majesties last message till Wednesday. (p. 35)

In fact, there was considerable debate on the 21st, most of it focusing on Secretary Coventry's claim that there had not been time to complete the alliances demanded by the Commons, a way of trying to force a new Supply without informing them what it was intended to support.

At this point Marvell's *Account* switches to another source for which we have two manuscript witnesses. Both bear the title "Private Debates" (BL Add. MS. 72603, ff. 48–59, and BL Stowe MS. 182, ff. 56–66), a title that must be deliberately oxymoronic, and one of which, Stowe 182, has the same appearance as the previous source of being prepared for publication. It was, in fact, later published in relation to the War of the Spanish Succession, as *Private Debates in the House of Commons, In the Year 1677, In Relation to a War with France, and an Alliance with Holland* (London, 1702). But this version of the debate on May 21 is astonishingly close to that recorded in Grey. It was said by Sir William Coventry and Sir Thomas Meres that the Triple League—that ideal bastion of a wise foreign policy—had been made in five or six days, whereas six weeks had passed during the adjournment, ten weeks since they first addressed for those alliances. The Court spokesmen said the alliances could not be announced lest they alarm the French! The Opposition agreed that they had come to hear not only that alliances had been made, but that they were "proportionable" to what the Commons had requested. Thus the gauntlet was thrown down.

May 23   The king sent for the Commons to Whitehall and made a speech, asking them to trust "the Word of a King." Charles insisted he had not "lost a day . . . in doing all I could for your defence," but repeated that he could neither "Speak nor Act" without a large new Supply.

The subsequent debate in the Commons is fascinating, especially if one compares the "bipartisan" reporting of Marvell's *Account*, where both sides are eloquently represented, *as* sides, with the seemingly random to-and-fro movement of Grey. The *Account*, for instance, cites one speaker (identified by von Maltzahn as Sir John Ernle) as making a major and colorful speech for the Court ("We know the King would strip himself to his shirt rather then hazard the Nation," p. 348) which finds no equivalent in Grey. But we need Grey for the trenchant summary by Sir Thomas Meres of the current standoff: "The House has already declared how Money may be had; 'by declaring Alliances' . . . we have been answered twice, 'No; Alliances cannot be declared till we give Money.'"

We also need Grey for the information as to how the next step forward in the Commons' demands came about, how the stakes were raised. Once they moved into a "Grand Committee on the King's Speech" Sir Eliab Harvey apparently spoke first, and moved that "we may enter into an Alliance, *offensive and defensive*, with the State of Holland." (Italics added.) Sir John Hotham added that this should be "against the King of France." Startled, Secretary Coventry remarked: "He hears a Proposition made, that he never heard before." But before the end of the day the House resolved to draw up Address No. 5, to that very effect, including alliances with "the Confederates," not to be named for fear of confusing matters, but offering "speedy and cheerful supplyes, *from time to time*, for supporting and maintaining such Alliances." The *Account* states that "there were but two negative Voices to it" (p. 354). Grey stated that the only negative vote was by Secretary Williamson.

May 25   Sir John Trevor reported the text of the Address to the House. After another vast debate, it was agreed to and sent up to the king[7]

As before, it is well worth comparing the *Account*'s version of this debate with that recorded by Grey. What is striking about Marvell, or rather his source in "Private Debates," is the formality, even the elegance of the remarks on both sides of the House. Court speakers stressed that the Commons' position encroached upon the king's prerogative. "The Antient Land-mark, the Boundaries between King and People must not be removed: This power is one of the few things reserved entirely to the Crown" (p. 360). The Opposition replied that they only offered advice, which was no more than the councilors had been doing all along. "This rate of discourse would make the *Kings Prerogative* consist merely in not being advised by his Parliament (of all People)" (pp. 360–61).

In Grey's *Debates*, however, while the speeches, especially of the ministers, are reported at considerable length, what stands out are the stage directions. "Several called out, 'Agree, agree.' " "There was a great cry, 'Agree, agree.' " "There was another great cry, 'Agree, agree.' " On the third such outcry, Sir Jonathan Trelawney objected: "To cry, 'Agree, agree,' savours to him like Club-Law." But Sir Thomas Meres wondered how one could so delineate something that had been voted on seventeen times, "and but a few Negatives to it." Meanwhile, Thomas Neale recorded in full his own long speech against the Address (BL Egerton 3345, f. 65), and recorded the vote (as to whether to leave in the phrase "offensive and defensive") as 182 in favor, 142 against.

May 26 (Saturday)   The Commons attended the king at Whitehall and presented their Address. The king replied "that it was long and of great importance, that he would consider of it, and give them an Answer as soon as he could."

May 28 (Monday)   The Commons were summoned to Whitehall, where the king delivered his speech of intense reprimand (already cited in Chapter 5), and ordered them to adjourn to July 16, 1677.

This was the most dramatic moment of the session. Finch, Marvell (who now speaks for himself in the *Account*, his source having run out), and Grey all give different versions, each of which we need. Finch was helpfully suspicious:

And then of course they should have adjourned, but Mr. Powell, who either had Intelligence of what the king was to say, or having heard several of the Court urge in debate that their intermeddling thus with Peace & War was against the king's Prerogative, had prepared a speech and many Precedents to shew that what the House had now done was no Invasion of the Prerogative. But the Speaker would not hear him, but to the Indignation of some members adjourned the House. And possibly there might have been some design to have done something after the signification of the King's pleasure for the adjournment, & to have necessitated a Prorogation which in Consequence could have released the Lords out of the Tower where they still lye: but this is but Surmise. (pp. 36–37)

Marvell, who saw this moment as the definitive one in and of the Long Parliament, gave a very different verdict, stressing the constitutional implications:

Upon hearing of this Speech read, the House is said to have been greatly appalled, both in that they were so severely Checked in his Majesties name, from whom they had been used to receive so constant Testimonies of his Royal Bounty and Affection . . . as also, because there are so many Old and fresh Presidents of the same Nature. . . . And several of them offering therefore modestly to have spoken, they were interrupted continually by the Speaker, contesting that after the Kings pleasure signified for Adjournment, there was no further liberty of speaking. (p. 368)

Having pointed out that it was always the privilege of the House to adjourn *themselves*, Marvell concluded: "Nevertheless, . . . the Speaker had the confidence, without any Question put, and of his own motion, to pronounce the House Adjourned . . . and stept down in the middle of the floor, all the House being astonished at so unheard of a violation of their inherent Privilege and Constitution" (pp. 368–69). Whereupon Marvell expressed dismay that the king's speech should appear in the next day's *Gazette*, while the nation knew nothing of what the Commons had actually requested in their various Addresses. If we put together Marvell's and Finch's testimonies, it looks very likely that Seymour had been instructed by Charles to make sure no egregious rebellion took place in the House, lest he be forced for form's sake to translate the adjournment into a prorogation, which would have released the Opposition lords. Seymour would repeat this tactic three times more before the session was over, and his behavior itself became a political issue.

In Grey's *Debates*, the theatrical aspect of this moment is accented with athleticism. "The Speaker adjourned the House . . . and suddenly sprung out of the Chair. . . . Many called him again to the Chair, some cried 'Stop the Mace upon the Table.' . . . But the Speaker was soon surrounded by several of his party, and the Mace secured, and he went away with it, . . . but not without reproachful speeches." When the House met again, on January 28, these reproaches still hung in the air. William Williams complained that "by skipping out of the Chair" Seymour had gagged parliament.

We will continue the story of the long sixteenth session by following Grey's *Debates*. But since we are about to lose both Finch and Marvell's *Account*, it would be well to summarize their contributions. Finch took the position of a loyal member of the Court party who believed, as he wrote in old age for his children, in the "landmarks" that divided the royal prerogative and the liberties of the people (*House of Commons*, 2:313). His loyalty, however, at least on the evidence of this letter, written when he was only thirty, was complicated by a rich and recurring pleasure in conspiracy theory. He ended his letter to his uncle with this remarkable speculation:

> To conclude: the Parliament was afraid to trust their money upon uncertainties & the King was as unwilling to have it least he might be further oblig'd to oppose France. Although my Lord Treasurer pretends this was his designe by these proceedings yet it appears to be very improbable from what has bin said before. He understands and loves his interest too Well at Court to attempt such a thing. But on the other side there was no necessity & therefore he was very unwise to play these tricks for every body sees through them & they have quite destroyed the good temper of the house of Commons. (p. 37)

Marvell, as we know, also nursed a conspiracy theory, but a much larger one, announced at the opening of the *Account* and repeated at its closing: "Thus far hath the Conspiracy against our Religion and Government been laid open" (pp. 373–74). He makes it clear that his objective has been, not only to denounce, but to provide a wake-up call, though his own metaphor is, again, theatrical: "It is now come to the fourth Act, and the next Scene that opens may be Rome or Paris, yet men sit by, like idle Spectators, and still give money towards their own *Tragedy*" (p. 375).

The other distinctive feature of Marvell's account is his negative attitude to the very House ("or Barn") of Commons whose doings he follows so assiduously, whose debates he records respectfully. He gave the members credit for rejecting the two obnoxious bills on religion, but that was all. He exhibited shock at the unwarranted scolding they received in the royal speech of May 28, but he delivered his own scolding on account of their weakness and venality. This had begun to be repaired in the later part of the session, he admitted:

> But on the other side, that poor desire of perpetuating themselves . . . renders them so abject, that they are become a meer property to the Conspiratours, and must, in order to their Continuance, do and suffer such things, so much below and contrary to the spirit of the Nation, that any honest man would swear that they were no more an English House of Parliament. (p. 370)

He blamed them, unfairly, for the incarceration of the four Opposition lords. It may be that this alignment with Shaftesbury, Buckingham, Wharton, and

Salisbury, as against his fellow-Commons members, was itself a tactical move designed to play out in Act Five. But Marvell was distinctly unfair to the Opposition leaders in the Commons, who became gradually bolder, and considerably bolder than he claimed. In what follows we will trace the next step in the Commons' defiance of Charles II, the next raising of the bargaining stakes. In Marvell's constituency letters to Hull before his death in the summer of 1678, there is at least a tacit acknowledgment that this occurred.

Part Two: January 28 to May 13, 1678
The Drums Beat for War

Adjournments followed adjournment. Proceedings properly began only on Monday, January 28, when Charles delivered a speech that, at first hearing, might seem a positive response to some, if not all, of parliament's Addresses about foreign policy hitherto. It is interesting to compare the actual speech, recorded both in the Lords Journal and in *A Collection* (pp. 141–42), which contains one of the king's favorite locutions ("it shall not be My Fault") and emits a tone of general self-congratulation, with the summary provided by Grey, which omits the rhetoric and gets straight to the point:

> He had made such alliances with Holland, as were for the preservation of Flanders, and which with due assistance could not fail of that end; . . . had used all possible means, by a mediation, to have procured an honourable and safe Peace for Christendom; . . . Declared, That since a Peace by fair means was no longer to be had, *it should not be his fault* if it was not obtained by force; and that he had recalled his Troops from France: Intimated, that though the Dutch should do their parts, ninety capital ships would be necessary, and thirty or forty thousand land-forces. . . . Made a merit of forwarding the new ships which he said had cost above 1000,000 li. more than the Act allowed . . . signified that he should not be able to maintain his constant necessary estab-lishment, unless the new imposition upon Wines, &c. were continued to him: Put the Commons in mind . . . of their promises . . . and that he expected a plentiful Supply, suitable to such great occasions. (Italics added)

What Grey's summary does *not* include is the implied threat at the end: "These Considerations are of the greatest Importance that ever concerned this Kingdom: And therefore I would have you enter immediately upon them, without suffering any other Business whatsoever to divert you from bringing them to good Resolutions."

Debate began immediately on the need for immediate action! Goring, Holte and O'Brien urged speed, the latter adding: "considering it is post night, I would lose no time." Here Grey included a splendid aside: "Some said aloud, 'What! The French Post?' " Sir William Coventry, Lee, and Birch proposed waiting a few days till members had had a chance to read the king's speech. A vote was taken for a compromise—one day's delay—and passed *nemine contradicente*. But immediately Sacheverell rose to introduce a remora— a formal written protest against the Speaker's behavior in forcing the adjournments when members had offered to speak. That produced a heated debate as to whether the protest should be read in the House, and if so, when. Eventually debate on "the paper" was postponed till Thursday.

The question of timing—why so much hurry after so much delay?—had now been raised. As the editor of Grey's *Debates* observed in a footnote:

> It appears ... from Sir William Temple, that the true reason of this Adjournment was to have time to receive the report of the league with Holland, which was signed January 16, but being properly defensive, to prevent the King of France from pursuing his Conquests in the Netherlands, it was very far from answering the desires of the Parliament. The King believed, nevertheless, that the league would be capable to impose upon them; and therefore deferred their meeting to receive the news of its conclusion.[8]

So the post was an issue! It would not take the Opposition long to suspect that they were, indeed, being imposed upon.

In the Dark

For this section of the session, though Marvell's constituency letters continue, we must largely depend upon Anchitell Grey, who rose to the occasion magnificently, producing a very expansive and coherent account.[9] Whereas his earlier records of debates had often seemed little more than a collection of sentence fragments, Grey now produces complete sentences, which still sound like real utterances. We have no way of knowing whether his selection of speeches, which heavily favors the Opposition, has changed the proportions of the debate, but his sense of the importance of particular locutions is remarkable. In particular, over and over the Opposition complained that they were still "in the dark" as to what treaty, or treaties, had been made, and Grey included each instance, as might seem repetitive or, dramatically speaking, choric.

On Tuesday, January 29, the secretaries of state, the king's mouthpieces, began by introducing the news of Spain's inability to confederate. But the real debate opened with a great speech by Sir William Coventry, who must have used Monday evening to good effect for its preparation, and may well have supplied Grey with a copy. Spain's inability to assist was not the issue. The issue was France's immense strength. He thought no alliance of any force unless it replicated the Pyrenean Treaty of 1660. Coventry did not imagine the French would attempt to invade England, being an island, so why the need for so much naval strength for defense? The point was to hinder French trade universally. "That makes me startle and wonder (I crave pardon for saying so) at that expression in the King's Speech, where he proposes 'a war with France,' and yet a continuation of the imposts on wines" (which of course were French). As to the claimed state of emergency, he turned to anecdote:

> When I was a boy, I remember to have heard that Hobson, the famous carrier of Cambridge, being overtaken on the road by some gentlemen galloping hard on, and he going his own pace, saye he, "Gentlemen, if you'll not ride softly, I shall be at my journey's end before you; for you'll either tire your horses, or break your necks."

The campaign against France was going to last for a while. But Coventry suspected worse motives than ill-judged speed:

> Those that have been partial to France, see that he must be cut short, if we go on; and therefore they put the King upon making such great demands, in his Speech, as will not probably be closed by this House, and so we must go into the French Alliance again.

He thereby established the premise that not only were Charles's demands unreasonable and unnecessary, but that the Commons should deny them.

Secretary Coventry complained: "I hear arguments against the Treaty the King has made, and all this while the Treaty is not known, I am not at liberty to tell you what the Treaty is." He thereby provoked a long series of complaints that the Commons were to be asked to respond favorably to the making of a treaty whose contents were kept from them. And the conclusion of this day's debate was a resolution to draw up an Address "that his Majesty will be pleased to admit no Treaty of Peace, but such a one as leaves the French king in no better state and condition to offend his neighbors, than he is left by the Pyrenean Treaty." On January 31, the Address was reported and debated. Powle correctly observed that "This Address will carry the thing farther on, than other Addresses have done." A clause was added prohibiting trade with France; and the usual promises of financial support were made. On February 4, the royal answer was read by Secretary Coventry. It was long, and sharp, recorded fully in Grey (as also in *A Collection*, pp. 144–45). "He is not a little surprised to find so much inserted [in the Address] of what should not be, and so little of what should." It came only from the Commons, whereas it should have come from both Houses in concurrence. In the king's answer to the Address of May 20 last year, "he told you how highly he was offended at that great Invasion of His Prerogative: But you take no Notice of it; but, on the Contrary, add to your former ill Conduct new Invasions." The Commons propose a worldwide embargo on French shipping "without either having provided, or so much as considered how to provide, One Ship, One Regiment, or one Penny, towards justifying it." And, in conclusion, "The Right of making and managing War and Peace is in his Majesty: And, if you think He will depart from any Part of That Right, you are mistaken."

What followed was predictable. The courtiers argued for an immediate Supply. Secretary Coventry said, after threatening more bad news from Europe: "One cheerful Vote will end all this." Powle said: "We are told that 'here is a League offensive and defensive made with Holland for the preservation of Flanders'. And Money is called for to maintain that Treaty, and we know not one word of it. Must we be kept in the dark!" Secretary Coventry replied, disastrously: "There may be things in the Treaty not fit to be communicated to five hundred men." Cavendish responded: "I think it very fit to be communicated to five hundred that must give Supply to maintain it. By the great delay of Counsels, we are kept in a dark mist." Sir Thomas Meres said: "We said, in our Address to the King, 'No, [Supply] unless Alliances are imparted to us.' Else we must stick upon hearsay, or what the Alliances are, till they be imparted to us, and we better informed. I would willingly hear a new thing said." Sacheverell summed up a long speech by saying that he would never "give a penny of money till the Treaties are produced." Sir Edward Bayntun, an elderly Country member from Wiltshire with a history of opposition, complained that "we are in the dark, as much as when we came out of the Country," that is, came up for the new session. While there was a clear majority, 193 to 151, to move into a grand committee on Supply, debate there followed the lines already laid down.

On Wednesday, February 6, however, the Opposition leaders tried a new tack. Sacheverell announced that he was giving up on his determination to see what alliances had been made, and was prepared to grant a Supply proportionate to what the king would need, "in case, he go into a War." Sir Thomas Lee picked up the thread:

England has once paid 1,800,000 l. for a fleet, when no fleet was set out. Therefore I move for a proportion requisite; but not for it, till they are actually at sea; lest, by the temptation of so much money, we have again no fleet at all. If we consider such a sum for the whole, that the King may actually enter into War, I am for it.

Sir Thomas Clarges was willing to "give something, but not till War be declared." Secretary Coventry was lured by these suspicions that Charles did not truly intend a war to lie: "I know nothing towards a Peace." Nevertheless, they resolved that the ninety ships requested were "necessary for the support of his Majesty's present Alliances." Thomas Neale picked up the thread again only now, to record a very long speech of his own in favor of ninety ships, and gave the supporting vote as 178 to 146.[10] On Thursday, February 7, Secretary Coventry was provoked into another lie, though this one was vicarious. "But if Peace is concluded, that is the jealousy—I have it from the King, who certainly should know, and he says nothing is more false, nor is there consultation towards it." The next day, when they were debating the land army, John Malet took the next step: "To take away fears and jealousies, I would have this army 'during an actual war with France.' " By the end of the day, the words "during an actual War against France" and "for a month" had been added to the motion. The vote on the need for ninety ships went through easily, 125 to 102, on February 14, and later that day thirty thousand land forces were agreed to, 147 to 131, in principle, provided they were sent to Flanders. But when the time came actually to vote a sum, there was a long pause. Garroway (who seemed at this point to be returning to his Oppositional mode) said: "If the danger be so great now, Gentlemen should have told us of it sooner, and we would have named a sum. . . . If 250,000 l. be too little if we have a War, if it be Peace it is every penny too much." He proposed £500,000. Several others proposed merely as much, for the moment, as would send the fleet to sea. But apparently, since Secretary Coventry referred back to it, Charles Bertie, Danby's brother-in-law, had moved for £1,000,000. Other figures of £600,000 and £800,000 were proposed, but Speaker Seymour declared that "the greatest consent has been to a Million," a statement for which there is no evidence in the debates as Grey recorded them. Nevertheless, when, according to procedure, the House voted first on the lesser sums, they were both defeated. Hence the million pounds was approved. There is no trace of this contretemps in the Journal. On February 16, Roger Morrice's *Entring Book* contains an incoherent account of the procedure, the sums proposed, and the divisions, but states: "If the Court had seen Reason to have Insisted upon 2 Millions they might as well have had it as one." Eventually a poll tax became the preferred solution as to how to raise such a vast sum. The Opposition managed to get a prohibition against importing French goods annexed to it. This was on February 27.

At this point the news from Europe, though mighty unreliable in its details, was certainly grim in its broad outlines, in that Louis XIV had attacked both Ypres and Ghent in Flanders, and terrified the Dutch. On March 14, the Commons turned into a grand committee to consider the state of the nation.

At this point Sir Gilbert Gerard broke a four-year silence[11] by rising to open the debate with a powerful speech and a new proposal, one that raised the stakes once more:

> The King has had unhappy Counsels. I will not exasperate matters, nor ravel into Counsels. I will only say that, if the advice of the Parliament had been taken, we had not been in this situation. . . . I will not sit down therefore without a motion, viz. "That we may humbly move his Majesty to declare War against the French King," the consequence whereof will be the bringing in our allies; and we will venture our hearts and lives, and our purses will be open like Englishmen.

Secretary Coventry complained that this would cause Louis XIV to attack English merchant ships, a point repeated later by Sir John Ernle; but Gerard's mention of "unhappy Counsels" had set the stage for a discussion of precisely what those counsels had been, and from whom they had come. Williamson unintentionally stoked that fire by saying: "I am not conscious to my self of giving ill Counsels." This complicated the focus of debate.

In the grand committee Powle referred to the fact that "there are Copies and Prints abroad of the Treaties" that have been concealed from parliament, from which he deduced that the French would be left in possession of Burgundy, Franche-Comté, Sicily, and Lorraine. The secretaries refused to say whether this was so. Powle replied: "These Treaties are public to all the world, and I know not why they should be a secret to us." Sir Thomas Clarges picked up the theme of ill counsels again, and suggested the ministers had been bribed by France. He then raised the stakes once more: "That we address the King to declare War with France, and that he call back his Ambassador from France, and remand the French Ambassador." Williamson, beginning to see where things were heading, declared himself in favor of such an Address, provided that it was presented hand in hand with the Supply. The Address was formulated and its language debated. Meres proposed that the offer of monetary support should read: "That *from time to time*, we will supply the King for prosecuting this War [italics added]," a crucial phrase rendering the king still dependent on parliament for funds as the war proceeded, rather than handing him the million pounds in a lump sum. Cavendish, Holman, and Harbord insisted that it should include a recommendation to recall the ambassadors from France and Nijmegen. Several Opposition members wanted to add a sentence asking the king to remove those counselors who were responsible for the king's angry answer of last May. This implied that Charles was not himself the author! But when the House divided on this last issue, it was defeated 135 to 130, and the Address went forward without reference to ill counsel. The next day, it was eventually resolved to seek the concurrence of the Lords, a move that K.D. Haley attributed to Danby, desperately playing for time.[12]

On March 19, several amendments came down from the Lords, of which the most important was to remove the word "immediately" (as in "immediately to proclaim, and enter into an actual War") and to replace it with "with all expedition that can possibly consist with the safety of your Majesty's affairs." This of course would have opened portals to delay for all sorts of reasons, not least the claim that war could not be declared before money had been supplied. The House divided on this amendment from the Lords, and rejected it, 155 to 112. And the rest of the amendments, including the omission of the "whole Clause or recalling the Embassadors & ceasing the Mediation," were equally rejected. Marvell carefully reported this to his Hull constituents that same day (*P&L*, 2:226). On Tuesday, March 26, the Commons addressed for a short recess, and the king appointed them to adjourn until April 11. When they returned, Seymour's illness, real or strategic, required a replacement Speaker, and Sir Robert Sawyer took the chair. But on Monday the king required them to adjourn themselves again, until Monday, April 29; the reason given being that "the affairs concerning the Alliances were not yet so ripe, or fit to be imparted to the Parliament, as it was expected they might have been upon this last Adjournment." Immediately, in order to score the point with the new Speaker that it was the members, not he, who adjourned the House, several motions were made, and then a debate on the reasons behind the adjournment was begun, only to be cut short by news that the Lords had risen.

This further adjournment, and the reason given, did not please the Opposition. Sir John Coventry, the hero of the Nose, said boldly: "These kind of Adjournments are very strange things, and this proceeds from your Counsels to raise men against Magna Charta, and set up Popery. If the King thinks we are not fit to serve him, I desire he may be moved for a new Parliament, and new Counsellors." When the House reconvened on April 29 it was greeted with a speech by Chancellor Finch, which purported to explain why no declaration of war against France had been made, claiming that the bent of all the Addresses had been for alliances, and putting the blame on the prince of Orange and the desire of the States General for a peace. Finch offered now to communicate to parliament the terms of the league he had made with Holland (the one signed on January 16), but expressed his fear lest the Dutch sign a separate peace with France on whatever terms they could. So *now* the king, they were told, was asking for their advice! In the debate that followed, it was clear that the Opposition were not deceived. Sir Thomas Clarges said: "all our Addresses to the king have been made for a War; and, in the Chancellor's Speech, we hear of nothing but Peace." Garroway said: "I would see the Treaties, that the World may see how we are abused." Sir John Hotham said significantly: "I would see all the Treaties, *for I believe there is more than one* [italics added]," indicating the general suspicion that Lord Feversham had been treating with Louis to very different ends. Sir Thomas Meres said:

> we told you all along we went blindfold, and stumbled in the dark. . . . When they would not let us see this Treaty, it seems, our advice was not worth taking. The thing was only for Money. . . . We see it; now we see it plainly, that these Alliances are a sort of riddle and aenigma.

Even Sir John Ernle said they should ask to see the treaties.

At this point, the editor of Grey's *Debates* becomes extremely active. First, he inserts an interpretive footnote on what lay behind the chancellor's speech—a shift, he infers, in the king's position:

> No doubt, if ever his Majesty was in earnest provoked against France, it was now; when they not only belied him in their Declaration, all over Europe, but trifled with him in his Money Treaty. We are therefore to give so much the more attention to the scope of the Lord Chancellor's Speech, which is very imperfectly touched on by Mr. Echard, and totally suppressed by Rapin and any other Historian. It is remarkable too, that Mr. North, when correcting the omissions of Bishop Kennet, either overlooked or had no intelligence of this remarkable speech. *Ralph*.

He then helps his readers to observe another change in the temper of the House by inserting an explanation of what happened next:

> The House then resumed the consideration of the state of the Kingdom, with regard to Popery, and received and approved an Address to be offered at a Conference with the Lords, to induce them to co-operate . . . which ended with these remarkable words:
>
> And that this may be done with all expedition; because the Commons cannot think it suitable to their trust, to consent to lay another charge upon the people, how urgent so-ever the occasion be that require it, till their minds be satisfied, that all care and diligence has been taken to secure the Kingdom, and prevent the dangers that may arise from the prevalency and countenance that is given to that party.

"This remarkable Speech . . . these remarkable words." This is a form of historiographical highlighting easy to overlook, but crucial to our understanding. And, finally, another footnote: "Sir William Temple charges Sir Thomas

Clarges with having been the Author of 'this peevish Vote,' as he calls it, in spite to my Lord Treasurer. He adds, 'Tis certain no Vote could ever have passed more unhappily, or in such a counter season.' "

Thanks to the "peevish vote," Charles lost his temper and his resolve. "He reproached me," wrote Temple, "with my popular notions" (p. 446), and the brief moment of opportunity to declare war against France was lost. "The turn that the King gave to all this was, that, since the Dutch would have a peace upon the French terms, and France offered money for his consent to what he could not help, he did not know why he should not get the money" (p. 447).

We might not have recognized this as yet another turning-point downwards without the editor's interventions. But he and Temple between them may have skewed the question of motive and increased the sense of bad luck and bad timing. In fact, the Address to the Lords, with the last clause included, was approved by a large majority, 129 to 89.

Between April 29 and May 13, when Charles brought this long sixteenth session to an end by prorogation, there were seven agonizing days of debate in the Commons, much of which can now be predicted. On May 2, the term "jealousy" flew in all directions. Then the treaties were read, and the chancellor's speech was reread. On May 4, the Commons agreed, by 166 to 150 votes,[13] to a new Address (the sixth), in which they asked the king to enter into alliances with the Emperor, the king of Spain and Holland, in order to carry on "the present War against the French King," and advised against any separate treaty with Louis. To this Charles replied on May 6 that, having been apprized of their votes, he "was very much surprised, both with the matter and the Form of them," and in any case refused to answer until he had had advice from both Houses. On May 7, the Commons debated whether to attempt to bring the Lords in on the Address, and decided that it would be futile and constitutionally unnecessary. Indeed, Addresses in general seemed futile. As Clarges put it: "the effects of all our Addresses have been to heighten what we addressed against." The only solution was "to go to the root," and remove those counselors who were responsible for the "resenting speech" of May 28 last year. The result was a motion, which passed 154 to 139, "That an Address be presented to his Majesty to remove *from his Presence and Councils* those Counsellors who advised" the offensive royal answers. The italicized phrase in Grey was excluded from the Journal, as the editor pointed out in a footnote. The Opposition then proposed to specify Lauderdale as one who especially needed removal, and eventually, by 137 to 92, it was resolved to draw up an Address to that purpose. But when it came back for debate, it ran into difficulty, and was finally tacked on to the end of Address No. 7, thereby also failing to register in the Journal.

On Friday, May 10, there was a long debate on the text of the new Advice that asked the king to "to remove those Counsellors, who advised the Answers to our Addresses of the 16th of May, and the 31st of January." The piling on of Addresses was clearly seen by the House to be futile, if not rebarbative, but what other weapons did they have? As usual, Sir Joseph Williamson raised difficulties, finally driving Grey to exasperation: "And so Williamson talked on, much at the rate of his former Speeches on the like occasion, to trifle away time, *that the House might be wearied out, and grow thin.*" This unusual moment of editorializing on the part of Grey points to the uncomfortable role that the two secretaries of state played during this session, attempting to justify royal behavior that was manifestly obstructive and deceitful. The stage direction acquires more force when Grey begins his report on Saturday, May 11, thus: "*Early, when the House was thin, by surprize,* Mr. Secretary Williamson moved the House to supply the King with Money, Ships, &c. on a verbal Message from his Majesty." This reprise of the tactics of the early-morning surprise motion for Supply, from Sir Robert Paston to Thomas Neale, did not improve Williamson's standing in the House.[14] By mid-November he would be in the Tower and, though he was immediately released by the king, his career would be at an end.

When the Speaker reported the substance of the king's verbal message to this effect, it read: "that, by reason of the Expence and Charge his Majesty has been at, for equipping and furnishing the Navy, and raising Soldiers, & [he desires] that the House would [immediately] enter into consideration of a Supply for him; for his Majesty must either disband the men, or pay them." The editor put square brackets round "immediately": though it does not appear in the manuscript, it was obviously spoken, as is proved by the reaction. Powle said:

> There is one word in the King's Message which I take notice of, the word "immediately." . . . I think that word "immediately" over-rules the Debate, and invades the Privileges of this House. I am sorry those about the King will impose these things upon his Majesty. It will be time to take . . . into Debate, when our Grievances are redressed, and our Address answered. And then, giving Money ought to be last thing. . . . Why was the Army so hastily raised?

This focus on a particular word—the same word the Commons had insisted should be included in the Address of March 19—was effective. Although some of the Country members, including Sir William Coventry, were opposed to a plain negative, it being an insult to Charles and an encouragement to Louis, Edward Vaughan was probably part of a very slight majority when he gave his analysis of where they now stood: "If all the delusions of the last Session were forgotten, then this might have been moved; but now we have the same stories repeated, and more would rejoice against giving Money than for it; because they would heighten still the King's displeasure against us." That same afternoon the House attended the king at Whitehall with the Address. Here is Charles's answer: "The Address is so extravagant, that I am not willing speedily to give it the Answer it deserves."[15] And, on Monday 13, he prorogued parliament, though not without informing the Lords that he was by no means displeased with *their* "dutiful behaviour."

The Seventeenth Session

May 23 to July 15, 1678: "Immediately" Again

On May 23, Andrew Marvell wrote to his constituents about the opening of the new session, promising them copies of the king's and the chancellor's speeches. "What I remarke," he wrote, "in the House is that it is much fuller then ordinary and more are still upon the Road and there seems a more then usuall concernment among all men as if some great and I hope good thing were to be expected. God in his mercy direct all to the best" (*P&L*, 2:234–35). This is Marvell in his dutiful mode. At that very time, copies of his *Account of the Growth of Popery and Arbitrary Government*, which offered no hope at all, were being circulated and large government efforts were being made to suppress it, as he informed Popple in quite a different tone on June 10 (*P&L*, 2:357).

On June 1, his letter to Hull recorded some of the disastrous effects on the temper of the House that were produced by the chancellor's speech, when members finally got hold of its text as spoken, and discovered that they were being blamed for bringing on the very inadequate peace that they feared. Worse, they discovered that some of the hostile things he had said, as that their votes had been "a republican defamation of the King and the House of Lords," had been omitted from the subsequently printed version.

In fact, both the king's and the chancellor's speeches evince a desire to bully rather than to negotiate. Charles declared a resolution to "save Flanders, either by a War, or a Peace," thus leaving the parliamentarians still "in the dark," as they complained in every debate, as to what was intended. He asked them to consider whether disbanding the army or keeping it on standby was the better policy. He asked for a regular Supply ("a Branch of my Revenue . . . is now expiring"), and for the repayment of the £200,000 they had allowed him to borrow; and he ended by attacking "tacking," that is, the Commons' previous strategy of attaching a clause prohibiting French goods to the poll bill. "If several Matters shall ever again [be] tacked together in one Bill, That

Bill shall certainly be lost, let the Importance of it be never so great" (*Collection*, pp. 159–60). In 1705, the radical printer John Darby Jr. printed this last paragraph, along with Finch's more elaborate attack on tacking, in a pamphlet designed to bring the issue up to date for the reign of Queen Anne.[16]

The Commons were not encouraged by these two speeches to do what was asked of them. First, they argued about whether to resolve that they were innocent of Finch's charges, without mentioning Finch! Then, on May 25, they took up the king's invitation to consider what to do with the army, and formulated a motion that if the king wished to use the newly raised forces "in a war against the French king, this House will support him in it; If not, this House will proceed immediately to disbanding the Army." It was Littleton who had added "immediately," which occasioned, ironically, another debate on the word. Sir John Trevor threw back the arguments that had been used against Charles's "immediately," that "it takes away the freedom of Debate here, the essence of parliament, and I would not take it away in another place." Powle replied: "This is the only word that can give you light into this matter. If the King does it not 'immediately,' I conclude the King cannot do it at all." And Sir Robert Sawyer, newly knighted, spoke with aphoristic common sense: "I would not divide the House upon the word 'immediately.' It will imply as much as not to assist the King, if he does it not 'immediately.' Unanimity is worth a thousand immediatelies.' "

Then, on June 3, 4, and 5, for which Grey's records are missing, the Commons again took up the disbanding issue. On June 7, Secretary Coventry read them a message from the king, trying to head off the Disbanding Bill on the grounds that they should wait to see what came of the temporary "Cessation in Flanders." The Commons responded by reading the Disbanding Bill a second time! When the bill was formulated, with "immediately" replaced by "the speedy disbanding," the House voted £200,000 to pay off the soldiers, though which troops this referred to required much discussion. The bill was finally sent up to the Lords on June 14, but was delayed by amendments there, and eventually cut off by the prorogation. They also resolved, that after Tuesday, June 18, when they would begin to debate that part of the king's speech that related to a further Supply, they would make no new motion for Supply before the recess.

On June 18, however or consequently, the Commons were summoned to the Lords, where the king made an unexpected speech in evident defiance of this decision. Marvell commented on the king's timing and, implicitly, his insolence:

> Today being the last on which any new motion could be made for supply his Majesty commanded the House to wait on him in the House of Lords

when he spoke long to them but it hath been impossible for me to send you a Copy of the Speech, the House having sate all day till seven in the Evening. But the most remarkable point was that his Majesty desired beside these supplyes already in Prospect, to be further furnished with an additionall Revenue for his Life of 3000000 li a yeare, on which condition he would appropriate 500,000 li a year to the Navy.

Marvell reported that they "voted *without trying the Division* that they would not go into Committee of the House for raising a Revenue of 3000000li a yeare for his Majesty's life" (italics added) and that they defeated, 202 to 145, a proposal to compensate the king for losses he was said to have suffered from the prohibition of French goods (*P&L*, 2:241–42).

This gives only a bare summary of what took place back in the Commons on the 18th, when Opposition members had been outraged, and made a long day of it. This from Sir John Knight:

Consider the poverty of the nation, and fall of rents; it is impossible we should grant what is desired. Here are Pensions . . . upon the Revenue, and we must still supply it. I would have an Act of Parliament to annul them all. At this rate we shall be Normans, and wear wooden shoes. I move, therefore, "That there be no farther addition to the Crown Revenue, but that the Revenue may be better managed." Which will sufficiently do the business of the Crown, without addition.

Henry Booth, elected for Cheshire in March, picked up the same theme, and mentioned the "great expences in lodging at Whitehall (the Dutchess of Portsmouth)." By the end of the day the flurry of indignation about pensioners of the government had produced an abortive motion for an inquiry into corruption, which disintegrated when so many Country party members left before the relevant committee had been appointed that this merely procedural motion failed, 100 to 86. So much for Marvell's optimistic prospect of a full and focused session.

We might infer that Anchitell Grey was also growing frustrated. He missed several days of reporting, including July 4, 5, 6, 9, 11, 12, and 13. On July 6, Marvell reported that an insignificant division about imposts on wines was lost 78 to 61 "(so thin is the House)." On July 15, the session was prorogued, ending with whimpers. The editor of Grey's *Debates* inserted a footnote, taken from Rapin: "Thus ended the seventeenth Session of this Parliament; and thus England saw herself engaged in an expence of 6000,000 l. to pay an Army and Fleet, which certainly had not been prepared to make War with France, or for the security of England." It is helpful, therefore, to remember

Gilbert Burnet's assessment of how there occurred yet another turn of the tide. During August the Peace of Nijmegen was signed greatly to the advantage of Louis XIV, who retained almost all the territories he had invaded. And so, wrote Burnet,

> the party against the court gave all for lost. . . . And many did so despair of being able to balance [Danby's] numbers, that they resolved to come up no more, and reckoned that all opposition would be fruitless, and serve only to expose themselves to the fury of the court. But of a sudden an unlooked for accident changed all their measures. (2:144)

That unlooked-for accident was the first rumor of the Popish Plot, which, in fulfilling their conspiracy theories, gave the Opposition ammunition. When Montagu's letters incriminated Danby in Charles's financial collusion with Louis XIV, all the fulminations against evil councilors appeared to have been justified. This implies a shift in the balance of power; but the next chapter, and the final session of the Long Parliament, will finish the story, and reveal just how clever Charles II had learned to be.

CHAPTER 9

❖

The Eighteenth Session
Plots and Dissolution

A t the end of his account of the seventeenth session, Anchitell Grey noted not only the prorogation announced on Monday, July 15, 1678, but also the following three prorogations: from August 1, to August 29, to October 1, and "from thence to October 21." By the time parliament finally convened, Titus Oates had already spread his lies about what came to be known as the Popish Plot, supposedly a Catholic conspiracy to assassinate the king, which led to the trials and executions of Catholic peers and priests, and to the Whig determination to prevent the duke of York's succession. Precisely because this deplorable but sensational affair has fascinated modern historians,[1] attention has been deflected from what else concerned the Commons in this brief two-month session: Coleman's letters; Montagu's letters (which led to the impeachment of Danby); and the various attempts to disband the army. This last issue was mentioned by Spurr without much emphasis, but for the Commons the continuance of the army despite their Addresses and their act, and Charles's remarkable veto of their new Militia Bill on November 30, 1678, were the threads that connected all the sessions since 1674.

In fact, what this last session shows is the Commons' ability to piece together into a single damning fabric the discoveries of real, though entirely different, conspiracies made by Coleman's and Montagu's letters, which for them confirmed the testimony of Oates and Bedloe, though in fact they pointed in different directions. Some members of the Commons may have been foolishly gullible. Others, under Shaftesbury's influence, may have exploited the supposed crisis as a convenient weapon in their own campaign to reduce the influence of Catholicism at court. But since 1674 the Commons had, as a group, increasingly come to believe that they were being deliberately deceived by "the government" or "the court" or "the ministers," whichever fiction most conveniently concealed their growing suspicion of the king himself. It was the earlier history of the Long Parliament that made the

Popish Plot an obsession in the House, however illogical it might seem that the plotter-in-chief was now supposed to be the chief victim intended.

The other great event of the session was the famous "proviso" division. On October 28, the Commons had sent up to the Lords a bill "for the more effectual preserving the King's person and government by disabling papists from sitting in either house of parliament." On November 21, the Lords, who had been dragging their feet, finally sent the bill back with a proviso exempting the duke of York from taking the two oaths of allegiance and the Test, and therefore from expulsion from their House. As Gilbert Burnet put it, "contrary to all mens expectations, it passed in the House of Commons," specifically by 158 votes to 156. Sir John Reresby, as he tells us himself, voted for it (p. 160). Had he not, it would have been a tied vote, and the outcome of the efforts towards altering the succession might have been different. As Roger Morrice observed presciently, in almost his only comment on the event: "This was the first division, and the measure surely of all others."

For this session we have Grey's reports, which are superb. The Newdigate newsletter writer (or writers) adds very little—and of course tells nothing of the debates. Roger Morrice's *Entring Book*, which is much less informative about parliament at this (for him) early stage than for the Exclusion Crisis, fills in one gap when Grey was absent for several days. Marvell has been dead since August. If Dering was still taking notes, they have not survived, though we have two drafts of a speech on the Plot that he prepared for delivery on November 16, and did in fact deliver, at least in part. In fairness, we might begin with these, since they eloquently convey the difficulties, emotional and technical, that members of the Court party now found themselves facing. In addition, comparing the drafts with what Grey reported has the double value of setting in contrast what got thought and what got said, or at least what was heard.

The first of Dering's two drafts is a complaint about the delaying tactics of the Lords, and the consequent lapse in the Commons' response to the Plot. His frustration is audible:

> We have voted some time since, and that unanimously, none dissenting, that there is a damnable and hellish plot, those I thinke are the words, against his Majestie's person and government [and our religion] and we have desired the Lords concurrence. . . . His Majestie also was graciously pleased on Saturday last [9 Nov.] to quicken us to it and to promise his concurrence. Monday was [solemnlie] appointed for it, and I believe the papists apprehended that day with some terror and apprehencion. . . . That day is past and 3 dayes more and nothing done in it, not so much as another day appointed for it, and it is visible that the papists do lift up their

heads [and make that argument that we do not believe what we say] and the protestants hang downe thereupon.

Are we colder than we were? I hope not.

Are we safer than we were? I thinke not.[2] (italics added)

On his second attempt, Dering framed this quite reasonable appeal for action in more apocalyptic and anti-papist language:

If there be any who thinke it impossible to prevent the danger which hangeth over our heads, and by a single thread [which if it be not cut out, must wear out],[3] that all remedies are vain, and therefore we have nothing to do but to digg our owne graves and ly downe in them, let those men consider that it was never thought the part of a good citizen desperare de Republica. . . .[4]

I thinke that more loudly we express ourselves against poperie, the safer we are. If the death of one man [Sir Edmund Berry Godfrey] terrify us, two or 3 more such strokes will do their worke. . . . But if we proceed to express our resentment [of] that terrible fact as we ought to do, the terror will reflect back upon themselves. (p. 186)

The classical allusion, already recycled for the 1675 parliament by Heneage Finch, placed the current crisis in a venerable Ciceronian tradition, but to use the word "Republica" now might possibly carry a different valence. An even odder classical reference was the old metaphor of the sword of Damocles hanging overhead by a single thread, another Ciceronian allusion, but one that here took on a fresh twist, requiring deletion; for what did it imply? Was the single thread the life of Charles II? Or that of the duke of York? When Grey reported this speech as actually delivered on November 16, either Dering had much condensed it or Grey did that work for him. Grey's version registers both the frustration and the prophetic gloom, but it badly misrepresents the important rhetorical questions italicized above, substituting "bolder" for "colder" and thereby making it a nonsense:

It is now fourteen days since we voted, that there was Plot and Conspiracy of the Papists, &c. and the Lords promised their concurrence for preservation of the King's Person, &c. Nothing yet is done in it; nor is the King's Speech considered, though we sat upon an unusual day (Sunday). Are we bolder than we were, or safer? I think not. The people will think of the danger, according as we apply remedies to it. I declare, if nothing be done this Session for the Protestant Religion, . . . nothing remains but to make our graves, and lie down in them.

The last phrases evidently rang in Grey's ears, but as so heard they are no longer a rebuke to the timid, but an invitation to despair. By the end of the day, however, the Commons had agreed to send the Lords a message requesting "speedy proceeding on the Bill before you." When, on November 21, the Lords finally sent the bill back with their proviso of exemption for James, Dering joined the chorus of court supporters. Grey reports the speeches of twenty-two people in favor of the proviso, and remarks: "Those against the Proviso sat silent." (Later Waller, Meres, and, surprisingly, Robert Sawyer, whose allegiances shifted at this point, spoke against it.) The courtiers were as emotional as James himself had been in the Lords. Sir William Killigrew was recorded as saying: "I dread taking the Duke from the King— (*and weeps.*)", another of Grey's stage directions. The earl of Ancram said: "The Duke is the King's only Brother, the Son of that Martyr who died for his religion." But Dering's argument was pragmatic: without the proviso, he argued, the king might veto the bill. Should it pass, "You have then but one Popish Peer in the Lords House, (if the Duke be one)," and the chance of other bills against popery would be improved.

The Coleman Letters

But starting with Dering's speeches has broken the chronology. On the same day that the bill disallowing Catholics to sit in parliament was sent up to the Lords, Monday, October 28, Sir Robert Southwell reported to the House the discovery of Coleman's letters, and the Commons appointed a committee to translate them from French. On that committee were both Dering and Grey himself. It is a sign of the importance of these letters in shaping what followed that when Grey's *Debates* was published in 1763 its compiler was identified on the title-page as not only MP for Derby for thirty years, but as he who "deciphered Coleman's Letters for the use of the House."

Edward Coleman (or Colman) was a courtier who became a Roman Catholic in the early 1660s, and in the early 1670s became closely associated with the duke of York. In 1673, James appointed him as secretary to his new duchess, Mary of Modena. From this point onwards he carried on what, according to Andrew Barclay in the *Dictionary of National Biography*, was "arguably an independent foreign policy" on behalf of James, with whose views on religion and toleration he was in tune. He cultivated several members of the French court, especially the royal confessors, Jean Ferrier and François de la Chaise. The object was to obtain subsidies from Louis XIV in order to reduce Charles II's dependence on parliament, which the French king knew to be increasingly concerned with "the growth of popery" in England. Danby disliked Coleman, and managed to get him removed from his secretarial position in late 1676; but Coleman continued to communicate with Barillon, the French ambassador, and received from him money intended to be used to bribe members of the Commons. It was thanks to Titus Oates, who implicated Coleman in his fantasy plot, that the "real" secret negotiations between Coleman and France were discovered. On September 29, 1678, his house was therefore raided and a cache of letters found. This was the discovery reported by Southwell to the Commons, a month later, on October 28. The day before, Sir Edmund Berry Godfrey had warned Coleman of Oates's accusations.

This scenario, as outlined in the *Dictionary of National Biography*, explains a letter written by Sir Henry Coventry, as secretary of state, to the king, who was racing at Newmarket, on October 4. Coventry reports that some of Coleman's letters have been read in council. They contain "little as to the present question" (presumably the plot to kill the king), "but so much presumption" in treating with Louis's confessors and ministers "for the altering of Religion and Government" in England that Coventry is astounded. Coleman has written discreditable things about Charles, James, and various ministers:

> Nay undertaking for a Sum of money to Govern your Majesty as to the calling or not calling your Parliament, and in making a Manifesto for your Majesty to Justify the Dissolution of that Parliament, That I believe that never any age produced a man placed in no higher Post than he is, nor of so indifferent quality, that he had the confidence to adventure on so many . . . Extravagant Crimes at one time, nor so little Care as to have such papers to be seized after so fair a warning.[5]

Such was the gist of Coleman's letters as Coventry thought the king ought to hear it; but it is interesting to observe the note of governmental annoyance that the man had been such a fool as to let written evidence be found. This muddied the waters considerably, not least by seeming to incriminate the duke of York.

On October 29, the catalogue of the letters which, according to Southwell, were about forty or fifty in number, was read, and the texts of those dated 1674, which, Grey *himself* reported, "contained several passages for promoting the Catholic cause, and endeavours to dissolve this Parliament at any rate, with frequent touches at the Duke's desire of it at any rate." Unsurprisingly, news of this scheme to procure a dissolution from abroad infuriated the Commons (although they certainly knew that Shaftesbury and Buckingham had attempted to achieve that in 1675). A Commons committee was appointed to interrogate Coleman in Newgate prison, and Sacheverell reported on the 30th that

Coleman denied absolutely any plot against the king's life, but admitted the design to get parliament dissolved "for liberty of conscience." Coleman was reported to have said: "Not three men in the world knew of this design, but the Duke of York knew of it . . . and why this dissolving of the Parliament would not be ungrateful to the King he had his private reasons." On November 4, the Speaker, who had been sent to interrogate Coleman once more, reported that Coleman now claimed that he began the correspondence with the duke's knowledge, but that its continuance was known to nobody. He also confessed the amount of the French bribes paid or promised "could he keep off the war with France" (Grey). That same day (and this acquires more significance as we proceed) Russell moved to address the king to remove the duke from his presence and councils. He was seconded by Henry Booth, who had just entered the House in a by-election in March, and also in his own parliamentary journal recorded his own long speech on that occasion.[6] This inflammatory proposal was adjourned until Friday, November 8.

On Wednesday, November 6, there was a strong debate about getting the most incriminating of Coleman's letters into print, so that the world at large would be convinced of the existence of the Plot. On the 8th, Sir John Coventry called for the official business of the day, the debate on removing the duke, to be resumed, but it was not. The Commons did, however, arrive at a long and urgent Address requesting greater security measures. And then, on Saturday the 9th, the king in person delivered a response to their Address that could be read either as conciliatory or as throwing down the gauntlet. After its courtesies and thanks for their care of him, it contained this unmistakable warning;

> I am come to assure you, That whatsoever reasonable Bills you shall present to be passed into Laws, to make you safe in the Reign of my Successor, so as they tend not to impeach the Right of Succession, nor the Descent of the Crown in the true Line; and so as they restrain not my Power, nor the just Rights of any Protestant Successor, shall find from Me a ready Concurrence. (1772, p. 156)

Considering what has been said above about the king's speeches, and his psychostrategical approach to managing his parliament, one must wonder what he thought he was doing. Certainly he placed on the agenda, for the first time, by specifically putting it under embargo, the issue of the succession. Was this a mistake? Or was it an insidious form of provocation? What provoked him to clarify the issue in this way? When the House began to complain, on Monday the 11th, that the Lords were delaying action on their bill to prevent Catholics sitting in parliament, Sir Thomas Meres remarked:

"The Bill went fairly on with the Lords till Friday last, and you know what we did that day." As glossed by Grey, this referred to the motion by Russell and Booth to remove the duke from the king's presence and councils. If the Lords had perceived where things were leading, Charles certainly had too. That Saturday, Thomas Bennet, who was emerging as an even more extreme member of the Opposition than Sacheverell, noted that the debate on the duke's removal had been adjourned again, until Monday the 18th. But on that day it was diverted by news of "supernumary" horses possessed by Catholic families, and the discovery that Secretary Williamson had been countersigning military commissions for Catholic officers, in defiance of parliament's legislation. On the 21st, the bill to test for the religion of members of either House finally came down from the Lords, and the debate on the proviso exempting James effectively subsumed and disposed of the Russell/Booth/Coventry/Bennet initiative. Indeed, some of the arguments from Court party supporters about why literally alienating the duke could be counterproductive—for example, by driving him into the arms of Louis XIV—sound extremely sensible today.

Thus the discovery of Coleman's letters, more than Oates's "revelations," led directly to the standoff over the succession that would consume the next three parliaments. During the debate on the proviso, Grey tells us, "*Several cried out, 'Coleman's Letters, Coleman's Letters.'* " And more fuel would be added to the fire with the discovery of the Montague/Danby letters, which showed that Coleman was not the only person intriguing for French money to render parliament superfluous. For all Danby's own anti-French, anti-Catholic persuasions, in 1677 he had let himself be the broker, and in writing, of a deal whereby in exchange for a French subsidy Charles would agree to be neutral rather than hostile towards Louis's military imperialism.

The Montagu/Danby Letters

To deal with the Montagu/Danby letters now also involves a breach of narrative chronology, since military matters—the issue of Williamson's imprisonment, the Militia Bill, its veto by the king, and the disbanding debate—came to the fore at the end of November and continued through the dissolution. It was not until December 19 that the story of Montagu's letters broke in the Commons; but the story is so excellent it needs to be kept in one piece.

There were a dozen Montagues with parliamentary profiles, including Edward Montagu, first earl of Sandwich, a prime agent of the Restoration. Another, Robert Montagu, was the third earl of Manchester. Ralph Montagu was Robert's cousin, and started his career as a quintessential Restoration courtier. Master of the horse to Queen Catherine, he was appointed ambassador to France at the time of the Treaty of Dover, although, as E.R.E. Edwards wrote for *House of Commons*, he knew nothing of its secret clauses. When he was disappointed in his hopes of succeeding Arlington as secretary of state, he returned to France, and Danby entrusted him in 1676 with the role of secret negotiator between Charles and Louis. As Edwards also colorfully wrote, Montagu "was irresistible to women, and in the spring of 1678 his leisure was abundantly occupied in satisfying the demands of his wife, the ravenous Duchess of Cleveland, and her teen-age daughter, Lady Sussex." The king, possessively if not morally outraged, dismissed him from his position, and Danby prevented him from buying the other secretaryship from Henry Coventry, so Montagu had nothing to do on his return to the country (which was unauthorized) but to exact his revenge. He got himself elected member for Northampton in November, which provided him with parliamentary immunity, and waited. Danby, naturally, was worried, and arranged for him to be accused from abroad of holding private conferences in France with the pope's nuncio. On December 19, Sir John Ernle reported to the Commons that the king, having been so informed, had ordered Montagu's papers to be seized. Needless to say, Montagu had carefully secreted the incriminating letters to and from Danby; he produced them for the House, and the Speaker read two of them, dated January 16, 1677 and March 25, 1678, aloud.

Here is Grey's report:

The principal matter therein is contained in these words: "In case the conditions of Peace shall be accepted, the King expects to have six millions of livres [3,000,000 l.] yearly, for three years, from the time that this agreement shall be signed between his Majesty and the King of France; because it will be two or three years before he can hope to find his Parliament in humour to give him supplies, after your having made any Peace with France. *Subscribed* "Danby."

"To the Secretary [i.e. Coventry] you must not mention one syllable of the money. And the editor added [At the bottom of this Letter were these words: "This Letter is writ by my Order. C.R."]

There must have been a long silence after this was read aloud. Then Bennet broke it:

I wonder the House sits so silent when they see themselves sold for six millions of livres to the French. Some things come home to Treason in construction. ... Now we see who has played all this game; who has repeated all the sharp Answers to our Addresses, and raised an Army for no War. You know now who passes by the Secretaries of State. I would impeach the Treasurer of High Treason.

Sir Henry Capel complained about the spate of prorogations and adjournments, and said that Montagu's letters confirmed Coleman's. Vaughan differentiated between the two plots: "The Papists would have a Dissolution of the Parliament, and these men make it useless." It was resolved, 179 to 116, to draw up articles of impeachment against Danby. On Saturday, December 21, Danby's friends attempted to get the articles of impeachment recommitted, and failed, by a vote of 179 to 135. The first article began: "That he has traitorously assumed to himself Regal Power"; and when it was debated whether the word "traitorous" should stand there, the House divided. "Sir John Lowther and the Compiler were tellers for the Yea's, 179, Lord Latimer and Mr. Coke for the No's, 144." The Journal incorrectly listed "Mr. [Richard] May" instead of Grey as teller, thereby confusing Arthur Onslow, who thought that this meant that May had had a hand in compiling the *Debates*. Sir John Reresby gives an unusually full account of the debate, including the text of the six articles, remarking: "I spoke twice in this debate this day" (pp. 162–66).

The articles of impeachment were sent up to the Lords, with a request to put Danby into safe custody. After he had defended himself with vigor before them, however, the Lords declined either to imprison him or to bar him from his seat. January 3 was set as the date when he would answer the articles of impeachment, but on December 30 the king prorogued parliament, with a very odd speech in which he complained (yet again) of having been misused. On January 24, the Long Parliament would be dissolved by proclamation. Having lost the services of Williamson, Charles had no mind to continue this parliament without Danby. In January, Montagu, deprived of his parliamentary protection and expecting a dissolution, decided that it would be only prudent to leave the country. As Reresby reported: "he was soon after discovered in a disguise at Dover, going for France" (p. 167).

Control of the Military

But there were other reasons for the king's decision to get rid of this parliament than his willingness to protect his chief minister. Around the affair of the Montagu/Danby letters sits the thorny frame of the struggle between the Commons and the king over control of the army, which had begun as soon as the Commons saw that all hopes for a war with France were lost. Following this issue requires us to backtrack somewhat. Once again, it was the king who also in a sense made it an issue. On May 23, at the opening of the seventeenth session, he had delivered a speech announcing that "Things [have] driven violently on towards a Peace," but that given the uncertainty he would like to keep up his army and navy for some time, "till a peace were concluded." Nevertheless, he *invited* the Commons to consider "Whether to provide for their Subsistence so long, or for their Disbanding sooner" (*Collection* 1776, p. 149). By the end of the day on the 27th, the Commons had sent the king a vote "that if his Majesty pleases to enter into a War against the French King," they would be ready to support him in that war, "but if otherwise they will proceed to the consideration of providing for the [speedy] disbanding of the Army." Charles promptly replied that, since peace was not yet certain, he did not think it prudent to dismiss either fleet or army, and so he asked for a Supply for their subsistence! On May 30, Grey's *Debates* indicates that all speakers except the secretaries and Pepys were for disbanding the land forces raised since September 29 last: that is, those raised specifically for a war against France. The intention was clear but the devil was in the detail. On May 31, they agreed "That a Supply be granted to the King towards the paying and disbanding" of all those forces. While they were still working out how to pay for the disbanding, Charles sent a message via the Speaker to the effect that he was "every day more and more confirmed in his first opinion" that the forces should be kept up, at least until the ceasefire agreed to with respect to Flanders came into effect. Sacheverell complained that "the same argument may be used, one, two, or three months hence. . . . At a month's end you may be told, that the Cessation will be for three months more." But eventually they agreed, on June 11, by a vote of 172 to 166, "That the time shall be enlarged for disbanding the Forces now beyond the sea, not exceeding the 17th of July." The tax bill passed on June 15 was entitled "An Act for granting a Supply to his Majesty, for enabling him to pay and disband the Forces." That same day, as mentioned above (p. 206) the Commons resolved, by 163 to 154, to receive no new motion for Supply before the recess. Astonishingly, on June 18, the king delivered a speech anticipating the recess in which he demanded an entirely new Supply, £3,000,000 a year in perpetuity, a flagrant piece of royal insolence. A motion to go into grand committee to consider this outrageous request failed, *without a division*.

On July 15, the money bill was passed, and parliament was prorogued until August 1. As we saw at the beginning of this chapter, however, the eighteenth session was not actually to start until October 21, on which day Charles calmly informed both Houses that "he had been obliged to keep up his troops" and "that both the honour and interest of the nation were so far improved by it, that, he was confident, no man would repine at it, or think the money, raised for their disbanding, to have been ill employed in their continuance"! The gist of the speech appears in Grey's *Debates*, although Grey himself would not return to his seat until October 28, by which time everyone's attention was focused on the Popish Plot.

It would take until November 18 for the attention of the Commons to come back to the army, and then it would be by way of the need, it was thought, to get the militia prepared for a Catholic uprising. Sir Gilbert Gerard moved an Address to the king, "that he command at least half the Militia of England to be in readiness," and Bennet made the connection between this and past frustrations: "Let the Militia be in order, and then consider of dismissing the Army." This provided considerable discussion as to whether the law regarding the militia, revised in 1662, would permit this. And this in turn gave rise to the complaint that Williamson had been countersigning military commissions for Catholics, without reading them first! Lord Cavendish pushed home the advantage: "I am of opinion, that a standing Army, in time of Peace, whether the Officers be Popish or Protestant, is illegal." Powle and Thomas Papillon repeated the ominous phrase "a standing Army." Williamson was sent to the Tower, but the king immediately released him. The stakes were being raised by the day. On November 19, while the House fumed about Williamson's release, Cavendish spoke again, to some purpose: "I do not like any compounding motion. If you address the King to remove these Commissions, we, in effect, authorize the rest; nor do we express any care to disband the rest." On November 22, after the Opposition failed to vote down the proviso exempting the duke of York from the oaths and Test, Powle delivered a rather incoherent speech making both the failure to disband and the new commissions all part of a great plot. On the 25th, the king actually asked for a Supply for disbanding the forces in Flanders without delay. On the 26th, the Commons passed a bill for raising the militia.

The new Militia Bill revealed the military paradox. The Commons wanted security, but the last thing they wanted was that dreaded entity, "a standing army" in peacetime. This recalled the difficulties experienced in passing the original Restoration Militia Bill of 1662, ironically based on an ordinance of the Protectorate. As ably described by Paul Seaward, even in that optimistic phase the militia was seen as the hedge against a standing army.[7] Now the Commons *believed* they had passed an act for disbanding the army, and that it had been overridden by the king. A long debate on disbanding took place on November 27, when there seems to have been remarkable unanimity. Sir Nicholas Carew warned: "As you consider how [the forces] were raised, by Vote of this House; so consider how you were induced to it, by fine words." Williams said: "We should be circumspect to fall into the same trap twice." Colonel Titus advised: "Before we enquire why this Army was not disbanded, according to Law, I would first disband them. Enquire how we got the disease, but get a remedy for it first." Boscawen said: "If you go the same way you went before, to disband this Army, you cannot but expect the same effect." Colonel Birch proposed an expedient: to pass an act for raising £200,000 to disband them, but to pay it into the Chamber of London, the city treasury, rather than the Exchequer. Swinfen feared that unless they were disbanded during the session, it would not happen at all. So instead of another bill to supply the king for the purposes of disbanding, the House resolved, *nemine contradicente*, "that all the Forces which have been raised since September 29, 1677, and all others [that since that time have been brought over from beyond the seas from foreign service] be forthwith disbanded." "Forthwith" was not as problematic a term as "immediately," but, as we shall see, fixing its precise meaning would itself cause delay. Charles's response was to say he must first consult with the Lords—despite the fact that they too had passed the Militia Bill without reserve on the 27th. The king must have been hoping for a different result. On November 30, he summoned the Commons to attend him in the Lords, and, after the passing of the bill for disabling Catholics from sitting in either House, he said:

> That, as to the Bill for raising the Militia, he did not pass it, because it put the Militia out of his power for a time. For though it were but for half an hour, it was the same thing; for the right of the Militia being in the Crown, he would not consent to any Act that might put it out, though but for half an hour.

If they gave him the money to do it, however, he would only raise as much of the militia as was necessary for security.

This was the only veto of a public bill that Charles allowed himself during the entire reign. Its significance was lost on nobody—not least by its exclusion from the Commons Journal. The Lords Journal contains an even more imperious version.[8] It was not printed. In Morrice's *Entring Book*, significantly, a page was left blank for "His Majestie's Speech November 30th 1678," but Morrice obviously never got his hands on a copy.

On Monday, December 2, the Commons debated the veto, and generally denied that the Militia Bill in any way invaded the royal prerogative, though Sir John Berkenhead made an unfortunate analogy to 1641: "It is a wonderful thing," said Dering, "that the disbanding of the Army should not be done, when an Act was solemnly passed for that purpose; but more a wonder now, when the king has invited us to do it, and we desire it: And yet to be let fall!" This gives us some sense of where once unquestioning courtiers now stood. Two days later, the king made a concession of sorts, which only made matters worse. Secretary Coventry delivered the following message:

> His Majesty, to prevent all misunderstandings that may arise from his not passing the [late] Bill of the Militia, is pleased to declare, that he will readily assent to any Bill of that kind, which shall be tendered to him, . . .

so as the whole power of calling, continuing, or not continuing [of them] together . . . be left to his Majesty.

This appeared to be an invitation to bring in a new bill to the same effect, which was against the standing orders of the House. The Opposition leaders saw this as a royal attempt to save face, or to get them to admit, by amending the bill, that in its original form it had invaded the prerogative. Sacheverell said that he would "rather let them see the shame of what they have done, than patch up their defect in another Bill."

On Friday, December 6, Birch offered to report from the committee for disbanding the army, and Powle said sharply: "There are two ways of disbanding the Army; by Money, and no Money. If they have none, they will disband themselves. I would give no Money, under any colour whatsoever, till you have assurance that the Army will be disbanded." "And the House adjourned abruptly," added Grey. On December 7, returning to the problem of military commissions issued to Catholics, the Commons resolved "That [a Clause be brought in, that] if any Papist convict shall take a Commission, or appear in arms, he shall be pursued, apprehended, and prosecuted as a Felon." On Monday, December 9, they returned to the task of drafting a Disbanding Bill, which included a clause that all funds should be paid, not into the Exchequer, but into the Chamber of London.

At this crucial moment, Anchitell Grey left his seat for ten days, not to return until December 19, by which time the scandal of the Montagu/Danby letters had broken. From the official Journals of both Houses, however, we can still piece together what happened. It was quite remarkable. The Disbanding Bill, which included Birch's expedient for securing the funds by paying them into the Chamber of London, was sent up to the Lords on December 16. The Lords, who were themselves eager to have the soldiers at home disbanded before others returned from Flanders, at first made rapid progress. The Newdigate writer reported for December 17 that "The Lords proceed so fast in the Bill for disbanding the Army that this day they gave it a 2d Reading." However, the proviso as to where the funds were to be located caused a slight panic. They consulted lawyers. On December 20, the earl of Aylesbury reported a long list of amendments, the most important of which was to insist that the funds be paid, as usual, into the Exchequer. But according to Morrice's *Entring Book*, if we can trust his date, already on the 17th "The Lords have put out of the Bill that Clause about depositing the Money in the Chamber of London. . . . They put it to the Question 43 Contents, 30 Non contents. This yields much matter of discourse."

On the 20th, the House accepted the amendments, including, as Morrice put it, "that great alteracion mencioned," and ordered a third reading, but twenty peers entered a formal protest: "*Dissentientibus:* Buckingham, Winchester, Leycester, Kent, Essex, Shaftesbury, Clare Grey, Bedford, Halifax, T. Leigh, C. Cornwallis, Delamer, P. Wharton, Grey Werke, Howard, J. Lovelace, Poulett, Chandos, Holles, Rockingham." Most of these had also protested in 1675, over Danby's Test Act. The significance of this would become clear when, on December 23, the Lords reviewed the articles of Danby's impeachment sent up from the Commons, and eventually voted not to expel him from their House. In this case eighteen peers protested against the decision, thirteen of them from the previous list of dissenters.

Thus the stage was set for the last great confrontation between the Houses, in this case one in which the procedural issue (whether the Lords had the right to alter a money bill) was subsumed into a larger constitutional and legal one. When, on the 23rd, the Commons returned their answer, insisting on the place of deposit and that they themselves should appoint commissioners to distribute the money, they made no bones about their reasons:

> That the Commons having the last Session granted a Sum of Money for the Disbanding of the Army, and instructed it in the Exchequer, the Money had been issued for the Continuance of the Army, without ever disbanding one Man, as far as they can understand. And the Commons cannot think it safe, to trust the Money into the Exchequer again; it remaining in the Managery of the same persons.

Who managed the Exchequer? Danby, of course; and the second of the impeachment articles against him accused him of deliberately acquiring money for disbanding under false pretenses, when in fact he was intending to set up a standing army. When, on the 26th, the Lords, having heard the Commons' objections, voted to insist upon the "Amendment . . . which relates to the Payment of the Money into the Exchequer" twenty-one peers protested. The bill was erased by the prorogation on the 30th. In his prorogation speech, Charles promised to proceed immediately with the disbanding.

After all this, a moment of humor would have been welcome. On December 21, when the Commons first considered the Lords' amendments, it was noticed they had referred to Colonel Birch as John Birch, Esq. Birch took the opportunity to complain that *he* had therefore been disbanded, as well as to summarize his loyalist military career. The Lords corrected this mistake!

The Dissolution

Thus the eighteenth session finally disintegrated over its efforts not only to impeach Danby for high treason but also to take back control of the military.

On Monday, December 30, the king prorogued parliament until February 4, 1679. It was to have been further prorogued until February 25. On January 23, the Newdigate writer informed his client that, given the focus on this issue in the Privy Council, people were beginning to hope that the proclamation for this further prorogation "will be stopt before it Come to the presse." And he added: "Tis not Convenient to Expresse what the discourses of people are concerning the prorogation." On January 25, he reported that, after another Privy Council debate, the proclamation was indeed stopped, "soe that now it is Concluded the parliament shall sitt the 4th ffebry." But on the 27th, he of course knew that this was not to happen, a dissolution having been proclaimed instead. "This startles people much many of the Members are hasting out of towne." In other words, the alarmed Opposition members were making themselves scarce. But, Newdigate was informed, "that which troubles people most at this juncture of time is the K of France his greate preparations to hasten out his fleet before the End of the Next Moneth." And, on February 15, the newsletter contains a very full description of a flamboyant medal that Louis XIV had ordered to be cast, celebrating the conclusion of his war with the Dutch in ominously triumphalist terms:

> The French King hath Caused to be formed A large Meddall of Gold wherein he stands Enamelled In the rayes of the sunn Environed with Clouds, thunder the Lightning darting from him on every side which dissipates it selfe Into these words Ortus Est Sol. The states that opposed him are Represented by A Hydra with 7 heads with A lyon & an Eagle with these words Congregata sunt Adversus me, underneath in the ocean & and on the further shoare meaning England there is A lyon dormant [the king] & A dogg [parliament] with these words probaverunt Et Viderunt & there is scattered all over the Meddall branches of Olives & round about this Haughty Expression Venite et Videte opera domini qui posuit prodigia super Terram Auferento bello. ["Come and see the works of the Lord what desolations he has wrought with war upon the earth," Psalm 46:8.]

No such medal has survived, possibly because, as Mark Jones explained, the canon of French imperial medals was continuously revised to take account of later events and, in cooler moments, to avoid insulting foreign powers.[9] But its careful description here matched Sir Edward Dering's analysis of the international situation, as described in my Introduction, and confirmed the Francophobic conspiracy theory of Andrew Marvell, whose *Account of the Growth of Popery and Arbitrary Government* was reissued in folio late in 1679, recommended on its title-page "to the Reading of all English Protestants."

What really caused the dissolution? The story told in this chapter is some-what different from the standard narrative, whereby the Whigs in their joyous embrace of the Popish Plot overreached themselves, as they would continue to do in the next three short parliaments. What I have tried to show is that there was, after all, a Plot, though not the one described by Titus Oates, and that it was not the Whig leaders in the Lords who were running the show, but the Opposition members in the Commons who, frustrated by the king's provoking moves, began to think their way towards new expedients. Where there is a stalemate, something new must be tried. There was no rhetoric in favor of limiting the king's prerogative; far from it. There was certainly no revolutionary rhetoric. But having put together their case, they managed to touch a bigger nerve than had been irritated by anything they had done, or refused to do, in the previous eighteen years.

There were other theories as to why the prorogation turned into a disso-lution. Gilbert Burnet had his own secret historian's theory of how this occurred:

> After the prorogation, the earl of Danby saw the king's affairs and the state of the nation required a speedy session. He saw little hope of recovering himself with that parliament, in which so great a majority were already so deeply engaged. So he entered into a treaty with some of the country party for a new parliament. He undertook to get the duke to be sent out of the way against the time of its meeting. Lord Hollis, Littleton, Boscawen, and Ham[p]den were spoke to. They were all so apprehensive of the continu-ance of that parliament, and that another set of ministers would be able to manage them as the court pleased, that they did undertake to save him, if he could bring these things about. But it was understood that he must quit his post, and withdraw from affairs. (2:177)

Such negotiations were also known, though in less detail, to Sir John Reresby, who reported them in his *Memoirs* as being instigated not by Danby but by some of the Opposition leaders. He was at least partially in Danby's confidence:

> My Lord Treasurer sent for me, and tould me the King had declared that he would desolve that Parlement . . . the way they found out for it (as was credibly reported) was to persuade the Treasurer to obteane it of the King, promissing him if it succeeded ther should be noe further prossecution against him in the next Parlement. But they deceived him, as appeared afterwards. (p. 168)

This account of the matter was accepted by Andrew Browning in his biography of Danby. Browning also explained why Shaftesbury was not party to the negotiations, though he later claimed credit for them.[10]

There is a variant account of how the dissolution was negotiated, derived from some shorthand notes by Roger Morrice retained in the *Entring Book*, whereby Boscawen and Hampden were not involved, and the intermediary between Danby and the leaders of the Opposition was Sir John Baber, who was also being paid by Barillon. In Morrice's account, Danby himself "came one evening at night late in a sedan privately to give my Lord Holles a visit," and in subsequent negotiations the king promised to disband the army and summon a new parliament, and agreed not to have any parliament "continue less than six months nor longer than three years." Charles, however, outwitted all the negotiators. He kept changing his mind, and on the 23rd told Baber to tell Holles and Littleton of the forthcoming proclamation to dissolve. When it appeared, it contained neither of the clauses on which the Opposition leaders had counted, so that it was they, not Danby, who were deceived.

That Burnet's version, wherein Danby was the initiator of the dissolution to save his own skin, might after all be closer to the truth is suggested by a rather remarkable document in a volume of the Leeds Papers, materials collected by Danby in preparation for his impeachment, many written in his own hand.[11] One is a letter of intelligence to Danby from Thomas Knox, dated January 23, 1679, which passes on information gathered by James Netterville, an Irish Roman Catholic informant. Among this information (which includes the rumor that Shaftesbury had a printing press in his house) is the following threatening news:

> That being two nights agoe with Sir Robert Payton Sir Thomas Player and Mr. Jincks, they told him they were endeavouring to call a Common hall, which is called the three Estates of the Citty, consisting of the Lord Mayor and court of Alderman, Common Councell men, and Liverymen which all may amount to 5000 persons, theire designe by soe doeing is, that they sitting whilst the Parliament sitts, may keepe a true Correspondence with the factions there, and that there are severall Addresses and Petitions already fram'd and prepar'd, to bee presented to the King and Parliament, which he himselfe has seene *and which tend extreamly to your Lordships Prejudice*, as allsoe several premeditated and malitious speeches which are to be spoake by the factions in that assembly [italics added].[12]

If Danby received this news on January 23, the day that Baber informed Holles that the king had made up his mind to the dissolution, the timing, and the appearance of the proclamation on January 24, after so much apparent hesitation on Charles's part, suggest that Danby might have put last-minute pressure on his master in order to save his own skin.

There were, however, other comments on the dissolution, some of which we now classify as literature, but they too can serve as historical witnesses. In November 1681, John Dryden published his poem *Absalom and Achitophel*, which, though directed more immediately to the dissolution of the third and fourth parliaments of Charles II, and the king's Declaration of April 8 defending that policy, nevertheless looks back at the history of the Long Parliament. Dryden's Achitophel, a Shaftesbury figure, explains to Absalom, the poet's version of Monmouth, how the parliamentary strategy has been to emasculate the king by control of the purse strings:

> The Thrifty Sanhedrin shall keep him poor;
> And every Sheckle which he can receive,
> Shall cost a Limb of his Prerogative. (ll. 390–92)

And at the poem's end the reinvigorated King David asserts his right to do without parliaments:

> Votes shall no more Establish'd Pow'r controul,
> Such Votes as make a Part exceed the Whole. (ll. 993–94)

By such an assertion of unlimited power, Dryden concludes: "Once more the Godlike David was *Restor'd*/And willing Nations knew their Lawfull Lord" (ll. 1030–131; italics added). This virtually declares the failure of the Restoration (such a loaded term) hitherto, and implies the incompatibility of monarchy with parliamentary government. So Dryden correctly predicted what has been called the Tory Reaction.

There were, of course, less complacent interpretations by the Whig satirists, as witness the various volumes of *Poems on Affairs of State* that began to appear in 1689, as well as private manuscript collections. Sir Samuel Danvers of Cudworth, who died in 1683, collected several satires on the earlier prorogation of October 1674 and one on "The Dissolution," which was later published as "On the Dissolution of the Club of Voters, Anno 1678" in *Poems of Affairs of State: the Second Part*:

> When K . . . by evil Counsels' lead,
> Crushes the Trunk to raise the Head,
> And does the Members fiercely sever,
> To make them calmly lye together.
>
> . . .

Thinks on new ways for new supplies,
And damns the Parliament as Spies;
Prorogues and then dissolves their Heats,
And gives no time to try Court cheats,
. . .
When K . . . to Commons makes fine Speeches,
And draws his Reason from his breeches,
. . .
And Dissolution may be said
The Effect of Staggers in the Head.[13]

This is clever stuff, punning on the word "dissolution," wittily reworking the old fable of the Body and the Members, which had been used as a powerful royalist metaphor for the doings of the first Long Parliament, and circulating the rumor that the real mover behind the dissolution was not Danby but the duchess of Portsmouth, who had supposedly gotten the king drunk and staged an orgy for him as an incentive—one kind of dissolution in exchange for another.

A better satire developing this hypothesis was included in the same collection: "The Royal Buss," subsequently published in the 1703 volume of *Poems on Affairs of State*. Probably written in 1675, it was flexible enough to apply to both moments, 1675 and 1678. It is better not only as a satire, but also as a retrospective history of the later days of the Long Parliament. Here is most of the poem, as it appeared in the Danvers manuscript prior, probably, to 1681:

Whilst Parliament too frequent gave
and Courtiers could but ask & have
Whilst they were making English french
and Mony vote to keep the Wench
And the Booffoons & Pimps to pay
a Devil a bit Prorogued were they
. . .
But when the Parliament would no more
Raise Taxes to maintain the Whore
When they would not abide the awe
Of standing force instead of Law
When Law Religion Propertye
They'd fence against Will & Popery,
When they provide that all shall be
From Slavery and oppression free

That a Writ of habeas Corpus come
and none in Prison be undone

. . .

That peace with Holland should be made
When Warr had spoyld our Men & Trade
That Treason it should be for any
without Parliament to raise a Penny[14]

. . .

That when an end to this was Gave
a yearely Parliament we should have
According to the antient Lawe
that mighty Knaves might be in awe

. . .

Then Carwell that incestuous Punk
Made the most gracious Sover[eign] drunk
And drunk she let him give the Busse
Which all the kingdom's bound to curse
And forced thus with Wine & Whore
He kikt the Parliament out of dore.[15]

This poem, it seems, is confirmation both of the agenda that Thomas Knox reported to Danby, whereby the first item of business for the March session would have been an improved Habeas Corpus Bill, and of the negotiations that Roger Morrice reported between Danby and Holles, whereby a dissolution was conditional upon a promise for yearly parliaments thereafter. That is, it draws the two reputed causes, the political and the sexual, together; an explanation so nuanced (and corroborative) that perhaps we can trust it.

Roger Morrice hated the Long Parliament and rejoiced at its dissolution, apparently because he still saw its record in terms of the Act of Uniformity, and believed that "the hierarchy," that is, the Anglican church, was in control to the end. This chapter should put his extreme views in perspective, not least because the greatest period of persecution of Dissenters followed the dissolution of the Oxford parliament, when those who shared the views of John Dryden had the upper hand. It is well worth contrasting Morrice with Sir Edward Dering, whose dark retrospective of the period from 1670 to 1681 was set out in my Introduction, and whose gradually shifting loyalties and concerns are, in their own way, impartial witness to how the Opposition formed, and what it had to put up with.

To conclude with two more retrospective assessments: both Archdeacon Echard and James Ralph thought fit to provide a character sketch of the Long

Parliament after its decease. Together with the above-cited satires, their epitaphs provide the balance promised in my Introduction, if not between a revisionist and a post-revisionist history, then between a moderately conservative view and a Whiggish fantasy. Each in his way tackled, in order to dispose of, the opprobrious term "Pensionary Parliament." Thus Echard:

> Thus ended the famous Long Parliament . . . which had been continu'd, by Eighteen Prorogations, and several Adjournments, for Seventeen Years, Eight Months, and Seventeen Days. For above two Thirds of which Time, the King had liv'd with so entire Agreement with it, insomuch that both the Protestant and Popish Dissenters had us'd their utmost Efforts for its Dissolution. . . . From whence we have less reason to believe those Corruptions charg'd upon them [the Commons] by Enemies on both sides.

Echard then cited Danby's *Memoirs* to the effect that the term "Pensionary Parliament" seemed counterindicative when "I who was call'd the Promoter and Pay-Master of those Pensions, had not Power to preserve my self from being impeach'd of Treason by those Pensioners." And, wrote Echard: "We shall conclude with observing that during that Time they were under the least Temptations of Bribery, they were most Loyal and Complying with the King; but when they were under the Greatest, they were most Opposing and Contradicting."[16]

James Ralph, on the other hand, in his farewell "Sketch of its Character," gave a darker account of the Long Parliament's shift in temper. After describing the early goodwill between king and parliament as if it were a love-match, and noting how much power the Commons had put into the king's hands at that stage (control of the militia, repeal of the Triennial Act), he turned to the later years:

> Henceforward their Intercourse was mutually mercenary; the King chaf-fer'd for a Supply, and the Party Leaders set their Prices: But tho' willing to be bought, they were afraid to trust him with the Purchase-Mony. Hence the very Means of Corruption fail'd; and they began to dread the Power they had bestow'd. Hence all their subsequent endeavours were to undo their own Work, and reduce their Monarch once more to the Servant of the Commonwealth; not, however, from honest Motives, or by Honest Means, but by any Means indiscriminately; and as our *own Barbarians* on the Sea-Coasts, hang out Lights in tempestuous Times, to mislead the Mariner, that they may pray [sic] on the Wreck.

This deeply cynical summary results from Ralph's intense dislike of Shaftesbury, Buckingham, and some of the other leaders of the Opposition; but no sooner is his cynicism expressed than his idealism recovers:

> Good often rises out of Evil: Had not the King slighted the Parliament, and had not they shown a proper Resentment, the Constitution had been long ago at an End: Tho' their Opposition was, in many instances, Extravagant, and always partook of the Leaven of Faction, it serv'd to awe the Throne and keep the Flame of Liberty alive among the People.[17]

PART FOUR

THE EIGHTEENTH CENTURY

❖

CHAPTER 10

How We Got Parliamentary History

The last two chapters increasingly depended for their information on Grey's *Debates*, a large-scale work that we have long taken for granted as one of those semi-official kinds of archive, such as the eighteenth-century *History and Proceedings of the House of Commons*, now often simply referred to as "Chandler," or its early nineteenth-century successor, *Cobbett's Parliamentary History*. This process of institutionalization, which tends to ignore how and why such works were produced, has accelerated in the new world of digitalization, by which both "Grey" and "Chandler" have been promoted to resources anyone can use with ease and impunity. This chapter aims to reverse that process, by focusing on the eighteenth-century men, historians and publishers, who brought into existence a new genre of history—parliamentary history—to which they were attracted for primarily political reasons. In the process we will arrive at an answer to the questions implied whenever mention has been made of the editor of Grey's *Debates*. Who was that editor, and why does it matter?

Eighteenth-century historians and readers were intensely interested in the Restoration era, up to and including the Glorious Revolution. This was hardly surprising, given that the premise implied by the very term "Restoration" was that England's legitimate rulers were the Stuarts, a premise that the Glorious Revolution denied but that remained unsettled so long as there were Stuarts in France. There was a strong eighteenth-century market for memoirs and collections of correspondence, in particular from the reign of Charles II. The first of these actually preceded the turn of the century: the appearance of Sir William Temple's *Memoirs* in 1691, produced with the help of Temple's secretary, Jonathan Swift. This generated a riposte in the form of an edition of Arlington's letters, produced in 1701 by Thomas Bebington and dedicated to the duke of Grafton, with the explicit purpose of vindicating Arlington's memory and showing that he, not Temple, was the chief architect of the Triple League. The preceding year, however, something quite different had appeared, with not quite so explicit a motive: a text of *The Proceedings of the*

House of Commons touching the Impeachment of . . . Clarendon (1700), mentioned above as being one of the first instances of detailed reporting of debates, made in shorthand in 1667, and kept safely in manuscript until this moment. Newly alive in the context of the attempted impeachment of the Junto lords in February 1701 but brewing since Lord Somers was dismissed from the lord chancellorship in April 1700, the pamphlet, which concealed its place of origin and was quickly reissued (i.e. swiftly sold out), carried a preface with strong Whig overtones, though it is not quite clear whether it was intended to help or harass the Junto lords, given the potential ironic reading of the context:

> We live now (God be thanked) in a time when we need not fear Encroachments on our Just Liberties and properties; are we not Blest with a King who hath no Design to Enslave or Burthen his People? Have we not Ministers that act with Uprightness and Integrity? . . . What Courtiers do we now find breaking their Promises, or giving oyly Words instead of just performances?

The editor claims that it was published

> not to reflect on the Memory of any, but at the desire of some very Judicious Persons, who thought it pitty a Collection so fill'd with Law and solid Sense shou'd be kept secret . . . several of our greatest Men have highly valued it in Manuscript, and I doubt not but all who read it, will think it fit, not only for a Lawyer's, but every English Gentleman's study.

And then, in 1702, there appeared another similar item resurrected from the scribal past, *Private Debates in the House of Commons In the Year 1677. In Relation to a War with France.* Without mention of any provenance, and with heavy emphasis on the need *now* for the war against France that parliament had been unable to bring about in 1677, this pamphlet put into print one of Marvell's two manuscript sources for his *Account of the Growth of Popery and Arbitrary Government.* In this case the role of the Junto lords in supporting and financing William's war policy would seem to have been, by analogy, vindicated, as their impeachments were rejected by the House of Lords when the Commons failed to make their case.

Archdeacon Echard

Such materials would be grist to the mill of Archdeacon Echard, the first eighteenth-century historian to produce a sequential history of the Restoration era, one in which parliamentary history not only played a central role but also helped to explain how William III came to be king of England. Laurence Echard seems to have been quite a character. Born in 1672, he died in 1730, and so, though we think of him as an eighteenth-century historian, he was in fact sixteen at the time of the Glorious Revolution. He was clearly a prodigy: as R.T. Ridley observes in the *Dictionary of National Biography*, Echard had while still a student at Cambridge "produced an astonishing list of publications," including translations of both Plautus and Terence and a major history of Rome. These early works were frequently republished. Not so his history of England, which appeared in three volumes. In the first volume (1707) he began way back—"the first entrance of Julius Caesar"—but proceeded as far as the relatively recent reign of James I. It took two more volumes, which appeared in 1718, to continue the story through to the Glorious Revolution. By this time Echard had taken orders, becoming in 1712 archdeacon of Stow. In 1702, he had published a considerable *Ecclesiastical History*, which he dedicated to Queen Anne.

The *History of England*, however, was entirely secular, and has been praised as the first "complete" history produced by a single author. Its predecessor was the self-asserted *Compleat History of England* (1706), a compilation made by White Kennett of Milton's *History of England* and Arthur Wilson's *History of King James I*, with a third volume by Kennett himself bringing the story up through William and Mary. The third volume of Echard's *History* was dedicated to George I, and signaled several new departures. As Ridley reports, permission for the royal dedication had been obtained by Archbishop William Wake and Joseph Addison, an interesting pair of patrons. Addison was himself always a sturdy Whig: in 1706, he had accompanied Halifax to Hanover to negotiate the Elector's succession to the English throne, and in 1715 was appointed secretary to the lords justices, the regents who handled George I's arrival. In 1715–16, the first Jacobite rising was easily quashed, and the restoration of the Whigs to power seemed secure. But a new history of England that revealed the role of parliament in battling the Stuarts, appearing in 1718 with a dedication to the new king, was particularly timely.

As a source of parliamentary history, Echard's work is innovative to a degree hitherto unnoticed. The most important of his innovations was the careful chronology he provided for the sessions of the Stuart parliaments. Chronology was an integral part of his story, which, despite the attacks on Echard by John Oldmixon, was far from being a Tory story. Echard not only consulted the Journals of the Lords and Commons for this calendar, but counted the number of days in each session and each recess, thereby revealing with shameful clarity exactly how Charles II manipulated his parliament. Concerning the eighth session, which began on October 10, 1667, and was prorogued in May of that year until October 19, 1669, Echard explained that parliament had sat for (only) nearly three months, and that this was followed by a recess of "one year and five months plus ten days." Vis-à-vis the tenth session, which convened on February 14, 1670, and became mired in a dispute between Lords and Commons on the right of the former to interfere in money bills, Echard reported: "Before they could finish their Arguments, or put any Period to this great Controversy, on the 22nd of April, his Majesty, who had been us'd to cut those Knots that were not easily unty'd, came to the House of Peers, in order to a prorogation" (p. 275).

The prorogation was to last initially until April 16, then until October 30, and eventually until February 4, 1673. "And thus ended," Echard commented, "the tenth session of the Second and Long Parliament . . . in which Session more Mony is believed to have been granted, tho' not all at once, than in any before. After which there was the longest Recess that had been in this Reign, namely a Year, and above nine Months" (p. 276).

Echard also provided (almost) complete texts of the most significant speeches—not only those by the king himself and his chief ministers at the opening of sessions, but also the suppressed speech of Sir Orlando Bridgeman, lord keeper, at the continuation of the tenth session on October 24, 1670; the scandalous speech of Lord John Lucas in the Lords in 1671; Buckingham's speeches there on toleration in 1675 and on the illegality of the Long Prorogation on February 15, 1677; and Shaftesbury's speech against Lauderdale on March 25, 1679. Where Echard got his material is usually unstated. For 1667, he printed Albemarle's speech on the conduct of the Second Dutch War, adding: "we do not find that it was ever published before" (p. 183). For Bridgeman's speech he evidently turned to Marvell's *Account of the Growth of Popery*, though without acknowledgement. Instead, Echard remarks: "This Speech was thought fit to be suppress'd, and not suffered to be printed, nor is it in the Journals of the House of Commons; therefore it is the more necessary to have in full length here, without any Abridgement" (p. 256). But he adds an interpretation that fails to explain why Bridgeman's speech had been suppressed—it gave much too much information—but fits with his own view of the Restoration parliaments: "This plausible Speech, filled with so many Leagues and Treaties, Debts and Difficulties, had such a sensible Effect upon the House of Commons, which took all for granted, that they shew'd themselves willing to give (with both Hands)." The last phrase, "with both Hands," was also taken from Marvell's *Account* (p. 250).

As for Lord John Lucas's speech, which was illegally printed in 1673 beneath a quotation from Juvenal's First Satire, and ordered by the Lords to be burned as a libel, Echard either had access to the original pamphlet, or to a copy of *State Tracts* of 1689. Like the Bridgeman speech, Echard explains the reason for its recuperation: "The Speech shews so much of the Times, that it cannot be here omitted" (p. 267). Buckingham's speech on toleration he had found "inserted into the Commons Journals" (p. 397), from which it had evidently disappeared by the time they were printed. For the debate on Danby's Test Echard turned to the *Letter from a Person of Quality*, again either in the original or in *State Tracts*. As for Shaftesbury's speech in the Lords on March 25, 1679, attacking Lauderdale, Echard prints the full text along with a heavily loaded gloss: "This speech was supposed to have laid the Foundation for the ensuing trouble in Scotland [the uprising of 1679] and by the next Post Forty written Copies of it were transmitted to the Earl's Correspondents at Edinburgh" (pp. 528–29). *Forty written copies!* The circumstantiality of this information, which bears on the still powerful role in politics of scribal publishing, is tantalizing.[1]

Echard only includes debates when one of his scofflaw sources has preserved them for him. So his treatment of the Clarendon impeachment proceedings derives from the 1700 pamphlet; he rather deftly summarizes the debates, but oddly includes in full the remarks of Richard Coleman in defense of the position taken by the Lords. Since the speaker's name was, typically for debates, abbreviated to "Colem," Echard made a guess at "Colembine," a name nowhere to be found in the history of the Restoration parliament! We will meet this mistake again, and its reappearance will be telling. He also included a sampling of the debates in the Oxford parliament, which he had gleaned from one of Richard Baldwin's scofflaw pamphlets on that parliament (see below). His sample ends with two of the most striking metaphors of the session:

> As to the Expedients [against absolutely excluding the Duke of York from the succession], the longer they were urged, the more they were exploded. One compared them to Cucumbers, which, after they were well dress'd, were to be thrown away. Another said, "It seems to me, as if a Man that scorch'd his Shins at the Fire, instead of removing himself further off, should send for a Mason to remove the Chimney back." (3:621–22)

We have heard about those cucumbers before, in the *Diary* of Sir Edward Dering (see p. 170 above); but the speaker here, if we check the pamphlet, was one W.H., identified by a later reader as William Harbord; the author of the second brilliant metaphor, H.B., was identified by the same manuscript annotator as Hugh Boscawen.

Echard gives brief marginal indications as to whom he consulted at the beginning of each major section of his history, but these short lists are misleading. His primary source for foreign affairs for the reign of Charles II is Sir William Temple, who has a strong profile in the whole narrative. A secondary source whom Echard refers to first as "a foreign writer," then as "the subtle Jesuit," and eventually by name in the margin is Father Joseph d'Orléans. His *History of the Revolutions in England under the family of the Stuarts*, first published in English in 1711 and then reissued in 1722, was declaratively written to support the claims of James, duke of York. Echard himself can certainly not, however, be accused of bias in favor of James or of the Catholic party. He uses Orléans for information about the suspected poisoning of the king's sister by her husband, for the story of Shaftesbury's defection from the king's party, and for various behind-the-scenes anecdotes, the raw materials of secret history. But to balance his subtle Jesuit, Echard is highly dependent on Andrew Marvell, whose name appears in the margin several times, and whose *Account of the Growth of Popery* is the basis, often verbatim, for Echard's account of the debates in 1677—the other important exception to his general practice.

Indeed, Echard's use of the Oppositional pamphlets of the era anticipates the kind of work that a modern historian of parliament must do to fill in the gaps left by the official records. Buckingham's speech against the Long Prorogation had been made available in *A Narrative of the Cause and Manner of the Imprisonment of the Lords: now Close Prisoners in the Tower of London*, an illegal pamphlet with a false "Amsterdam" imprint, in 1677. Echard also consulted *Votes and Addresses of the Honourable House of Commons assembled in Parliament, made this present year 1673, concerning Popery and other Grievances*, which had not been included in *State Tracts*. This seven-page pamphlet covers March 29 through November 4, 1673 (that is, parts of the eleventh and twelfth sessions), includes the texts of the Commons' Addresses to the king against the marriage of the duke of York to the duchess of Modena, and concludes with an account of the turmoil at the prorogation (which was designed to cut parliament out of the picture until the duke was safely married). Here is the pamphlet's version of events:

> The House of Commons having ordered an Address to be made to his Majesty, shewing that the standing Army was a Grievance, and a Burden to the Nation; and did intend that day to wait on his Majesty to present it: but his Majesty was in his Robes in the House of Peers, and the Lords hastning to Him, the Black-Rod being sent to the Commons-House to command the Speaker and the Commons to come to his Majesty to the House of Peers; but it so hapned that the Speaker and the Black-Rod met both at the Commons-House door; the Speaker being within the House, the door was commanded to be shut, and they cryed to the Chair, others said the Black-Rod was at the door to command them to wait on the King

to the House of Peers: but the Speaker was hurried to the Chair. Then
was moved,

1. That our alliance with France was a Grievance.
2. That the evil Counsel about the King was a Grievance to this Nation.
3. That the Lord Lauderdale was a grievance to this Nation, and not fit to
   be intrusted or imployed in any Office or Place of Trust, but to be
   removed.

Whereupon they cryed, *To the Question*. But the Black-Rod knocking very
earnestly at the Door, the Speaker rose out of the Chair and went away in
confusion. (p. 7)

While following this account with fidelity as to the facts, Echard considerably
increases its drama. Thus "the King unexpectedly, and of a sudden appear'd
at the House of Peers with his Robes and Crown." Black Rod was sent to
command "the Speaker and that House immediately to come up to his
Majesty." When the Speaker and Black Rod converge, "some of the Members
suddenly shut the Door, and cryed out, *To the Chair, to the Chair*, while others
cry'd, '*The Black Rod is at the Door!*' " "The Speaker was immediately hurry'd
to the Chair," the offending motions are made, "upon which there was a
General Cry, *To the Question, to the Question!*" "But the Black-Rod knocking
earnestly at the Door, the Speaker leapt out of the Chair, and the House rose
in great Confusion." The emphasis on surprise and haste, the repetition of
the cries of the Opposition members, the vision of Seymour leaping rather
than rising out of the Chair, even the exclamation marks, register this as one
of the high moments of the Long Parliament; high in the sense of memora-
bility, though low in the sense of decorum.

After Echard's third volume appeared in 1718, and John Oldmixon's ill-
considered riposte in his *Critical History of England* (1724), the eighteenth-
century taste for seventeenth-century history acquired a partisan ping-pong
character. Gilbert Burnet's *History of His own Time* appeared from 1724 to
1734, though published abroad as if anxious about its English reception;
Clarendon's *History* was reissued in 1732–33, with a riposte to Oldmixon's
slurs on its validity, and was followed by the *Memoirs* of Sir John Reresby in
1734. The first of these was recognizably Whig, the latter two obviously Tory.[2]
Though all contained valuable insider information about the Long
Parliament, none was aimed directly at the topic.

Then, in 1740, Roger North's *Examen* was posthumously published from the
manuscript he had entrusted to Jesus College, Cambridge. It viciously attacked
Kennet's *Compleat History* as a lying slur on the reputation of Charles II, and
took a few potshots at Marvell's *Account*. North included his own version of "the

Transactions between King Charles II and the (yet long) Parliament touching the actual War with France" (p. 492), which involved him rehearsing all the Addresses by the Commons and the king's responses, taking the position that Charles always spoke both truth and common sense. "His Words, however framed, carry Reason as from an Angel" (p. 492). But North restricted himself to the official parliamentary Journals.

Chandler and Co.: A Vast Scofflaw Project?

The struggle between Whig and Tory historians over the recent past was unquestionably not just professional—who had told the truth?—but also topical: that is, driven by then current events and issues. In the second parliament of George II, on May 4, 1738, the issue of the secrecy of Commons proceedings came up once more at the instance of the Speaker, Arthur Onslow, and it was resolved, *nemine contradicente,*

> That it is a high Indignity to, and a notorious Breach of the Privilege of this House, for any News-Writer, in Letters or other Papers, (as Minutes, or under any other Denomination) or for any Printer or Publisher, of any printed News Paper of any Denomination, to presume to insert in the said Letters or Papers, or to give therein any Account of the Debates, or other Proceedings of this House, or any Committee thereof, as well during the Recess, as the Sitting of Parliament; and that this House will proceed with the utmost Severity against such Offenders.

It is true that the practice now deplored was the unauthorized publication of votes and speeches in newspapers and magazines, where misrepresentation could run rampant. But William Pulteney, a supposedly patriotic Whig, harked back with nostalgia to the good old days when "this House was so jealous, so cautious of doing any thing that might look an Appeal to their Constituents, that not even the Votes were printed without Leave." How do we know this? Because in 1742, just four years later, Richard Chandler's *History and Proceedings of the House of Commons*, Volume 10, presented its Georgian readers with an extensive and presumably verbatim account of this debate! In fact, it was in 1739, that is, just one year after the House of Commons had reaffirmed that their proceedings were secret, that the plan to create the first history of the proceedings and debates of the House of Commons was conceived, and Richard Chandler, bookseller, acquired a collaborator to that end.

How far back they would go and how far forward was initially unsettled. Plan A, it appears, was to begin with the accession of George I, and the first volume to appear covered proceedings in the Commons from 1714 to 1727.

This featured the strenuous debates on the bill for, once again, repealing the Triennial Act by which a new parliament was to be elected every three years— the same act that the Commons had repealed at the behest of Charles II and reinstalled at the Glorious Revolution. This first tome was one of a three-volume series that appeared in 1741, without attribution to any publisher, under the title *The History and Proceedings of the House of Commons of Great Britain, with the speeches and debates in that House, from the death of her late Majesty Queen Anne.* The first volume also carried a dedication to Frederick, prince of Wales, dated December 31, 1740, implying that it would find a welcome among readers who, like the prince himself, were not entirely happy with George II. The next volume to appear, then designated Volume 2, has a similar dedication. It covered the first parliament of George II. (Both were subsequently renumbered as Volumes 6 and 7.) In Volume 3 (to be renumbered Volume 8) it appears that the plan has changed. It carried the following advertisement: "In the Press, and will speedily be publish'd, *The History and Proceedings of the House of Commons from the Year 1668, to the Death of Queen Anne.*" In fact, this sweep back into the past would result in three intervening volumes, the first (the new Volume 1) covering the four parliaments of Charles II from 1660 to 1685; the second (the new Volume 2) covering James II through the accession of William and Mary; the third covering the later parliaments of William and Mary, to the accession of Anne. Two more volumes would fill in the remaining gap until 1714, and the rest of George II's parliaments took the collection to twelve volumes, which appeared as a set in 1742 under the imprint of Richard Chandler. In 1743, a thirteenth volume covering George II's third parliament appeared, and, in 1744, a fourteenth volume brought the story up to the present moment. That year Richard Chandler shot himself, thereby truncating what might have been a year-by-year early Hansard.

We have come to know this agglomerative work as "Chandler," which is not quite accurate. Its genesis has been obscured by the process of digitalization, which reproduces none of the dedications to Prince Frederick, nor the advertisement revealing the change(s) of plan, and is further confused by the account of Chandler's life included in the new *Dictionary of National Biography*, which makes several misstatements. Its author asserts that Chandler took on this project "alone," whereas the British Library copy of the twelve-volume set has a dedication signed by C. Ward and R. Chandler. But the collaborator referred to above was not this signatory, Caesar Ward, but someone better fitted than either of these booksellers actually to do the work of research and compilation for the earlier period.

That somebody was the historian James Ralph, whose own Whiggish *History of England* was proceeding concurrently. Its first number was advertised in *Old England* in April 1744. But as early as May and June 1739, Ralph had informed his friend Thomas Birch of his involvement in Chandler's project;[3] and he was certainly the man for the job of recuperating the parliamentary history of the Restoration, since the bulk of his two big volumes of English history was taken up by the reigns of Charles II and James II. Although misleadingly entitled *The History of England during the reigns of King William, Queen Anne, and King George*, a title that reveals an original intention comparable to Chandler's, Ralph in fact never got to Queen Anne, and his true interest, as it developed, was in showing the causes of the Glorious Revolution in the unwillingness of the later Stuarts to govern by parliamentary means. Ralph's *History of England* was published anonymously, as was everything else he wrote.

We will return to James Ralph and his credentials shortly. But first we will focus on Chandler's *Proceedings*, and especially on the Preface which appeared at the beginning of the twelve-volume edition in 1742, and which provided a rationale for the project:

> Not to enter into the Controversy, if it will admit of one, whether the Representatives of a People are accountable to their Constituents; or *scrutinize whether it ought to be deem'd an Offence, to lay the Proceedings of our Representatives before those they represent;* this is certain, that no History, or Dissertation on State-Affairs of any Kind whatever, is . . . so serviceable, as a View of our Parliamentary Transactions. . . . For, by this Means we examine Parties by their own Light, adjust their Characters by their Actions, not their Pretensions, and enable ourselves to form a right Judgment of the Present by the Past: *Arguments appear with more Force in the Mouths of the Speakers, than in the most lively Narration.* We become acquainted with the Men, their Motives, Prejudices, Capacities and Virtues, as well as the Subjects they canvass; nay, we seem present, become Parties in the most important Debates, and have the Pleasure of approving, or opposing both Patriot and Minister in turn, as Artifice or Prejudice discovers itself in either, to the Dishonour of Truth, and the Detriment of the Commonwealth. Here, likewise, the true Grounds and Reasons of every new Law are to be found; the Necessities, real or pretended, for annual and incidental Supplies. . . . The Progress, or Redress of Grievances: And, in fine, *whatever serves to impair or preserve the Constitution.* Of this comprehensive Nature is the noble Work before us; and, consequently, how much is it to be lamented, that it was not set on foot long ago [italics added].

This manifesto challenges the belief that publishing debates "ought to be deem'd an Offence"; second, asserts the superiority of debates—that is, as near as maybe verbatim reports of what was actually said—to narrative summaries; and third, explains the political *value* of this return to the parliamentary past.

While members of both parties may behave well or ill, the point of parliamentary history as a sequence is to warn us of what "serves to impair or preserve the Constitution." This, of course, is the language of the old Whigs, but it also uses ideas of character, drama, and audience identification that we would today call literary.

Despite the official prohibitions, from the end of Anne's reign scattered reports of debates nonetheless regularly appeared in Boyer's *Political State of Great Britain* and the *London Magazine*. In the *Gentleman's Magazine*, whose publisher was Edward Cave, a new expedient was developed in 1741, when Dr. Samuel Johnson began writing his famous "Debates in the Senate of Magna Lilliputia," semi-disguised reports of the debates in the contemporary House of Lords. In all these instances, these scofflaws were assisted, according to Erskine May, by members of parliament who supplied the journalists with notes.[4] The Preface to *Proceedings*, in 1754, takes the route of direct intellectual challenge, though its author and publisher both remain anonymous.

But we need to continue with the Preface's own words, which relate to that part of *Proceedings* which covered the reign of Charles II:

> The Period from whence we set out, is that most remarkable one of the Restoration; When the Wheels of Government return'd to their antient Track; and from whence, as will appear in the Course of these Papers, they again deviated by Degrees, till the Appearance of a new System of arbitrary Power brought on the Revolution. This Interval contains one complete Section of the British Story. That from the Proclamation of William and Mary to the Death of the late Queen Anne, another. And as to the determination of the next which ensued, it must be left to some future Historian.

It appears from this that the author of this Preface was not, when he wrote it, aware that his work would eventually be attached to the front of a history of the Georgian parliaments. How the project eventually got sutured together must at this stage remain a matter of guesswork.

The Preface assures us that "No Cost or Diligence . . . has been spar'd to glean up every valuable Relique that Time has left us, either to illustrate or adorn this Collection; which we hope, we may, without Vanity, affirm to be the most perfect extant." This was, to say the least, an exaggeration. For the story of the parliaments of Charles II was largely cribbed from the third volume of Laurence Echard's *History of England*. It was Echard who had performed the scrupulous gleaning now claimed by his plagiarist, whom from now on I shall call James Ralph; but Ralph gives almost no credit to Echard, whose name appears in his text very occasionally as the source of an anecdote, or as someone who makes mistakes! Ralph's procedure was to work through Echard, lifting out the sections on parliament, usually verbatim, and sewing them together. Thus his vaunted belief in truth did not extend to his scholarship. For 1667 he inserted Echard's account of the debates on Clarendon's impeachment, including the mistake of "Columbine" for Coleman! And his version of the debacle at the end of the twelfth session, which Echard had extricated from he scofflaw pamphlet *Votes and Addresses*, is word for word what he found in Echard.

A reader of the Preface might well also be startled, given its stated preference for the drama of speech, to discover that there are so very few debates recorded in the whole of the first volume. Indeed, it is rather a surprise to reach the 1677 parliament and find the contentious debates about foreign policy very fully reported—but without the names of the speakers. All is explained, however, in the first footnote to this part of *Proceedings* (which now, in the digitalized version, appears as an endnote): "We have this, and the following Debates, on the Authority of the celebrated Mr. Andrew Marvell, then Member for Kingston upon Hull." Echard, we remember, had cited Marvell as the source for his much-truncated account of the 1677 debates. Ralph, who seems to have been an even greater admirer of Marvell, took Echard's example as an incentive to go back to the *Account of the Growth of Popery* itself. Not only does Ralph transcribe, more or less verbatim, Marvell's extremely full account of these debates, but, warming to his task, he inserts partisan subheadings: "The Sense of the Ministers"; "The Sense of the Patriots"; "The Ministers Reply"; "Answered by the Patriots." Now at last we have reached a moment worthy of the advertisement in the Preface to *Proceedings*, whereby "we become Parties in the most important Debates, and have the Pleasure of approving, or opposing both Patriot, and Minister in turn."

From this point onwards, *Proceedings* commits itself to debates as the primary matter of parliamentary history. For the third, fourth, and Oxford parliaments of Charles II, there were several printed "records" of the debates, the issues discussed being so incendiary. And here the story takes a twist. For the Oxford parliament of 1681, Ralph could turn to either of two pamphlet accounts published by the Whig bookseller Richard Baldwin (see below, "The Printing Debate"), which were in turn taken almost word for word from Anchitell Grey's records, hitherto unpublished, though known to exist.

Grey's *Debates*

In a manuscript note inserted in his copy of Gilbert Burnet's *History of His own Time*, subsequently printed in the 1823 edition, Arthur Onslow, then speaker of the House of Commons, commented on the Long Prorogation: "I have seen a good MS. account of this debate, (in a collection of Mr. Anchistel [sic] Grey's,) which appears there to be very perplexed" (2:109). Tiny as it is, this note helps to explain why Grey's *Debates* was finally published. When it appeared in 1763, it carried a dedication to Onslow, who had apparently mentioned it, in its manuscript form, "with Approbation from the Chair," at some point during his long and outstanding tenure of that position. Ironically, Onslow's own reputation as an exemplary Speaker thus exempts the old debates from the legal restraints against those of the present day that he had himself insisted on.

We know nothing more of Onslow's intervention in this project; but in 1645 the *Gentleman's Magazine* (15:135–42) issued an extensive, eight-page proposal to publish, by subscription, the Commons debates recorded throughout the Restoration by Anchitell Grey, "Who was thirty years representative of the town of Derby, chairman of several committees, and decypher'd Coleman's letters for the use of the house." The journal supplied a powerful rationale for doing this, which would later appear verbatim as the Preface to the first volume, along with a tantalizing list of the subjects of all the debates, one by one, a list that itself eventually appeared at the end of the tenth volume, thus retroactively forming a table of contents. The proposal states that the task involves fourteen manuscript volumes, which, it says, would then be deposited "in some public office." (Their whereabouts today are not known, and they may have been dispersed.) This notice immediately follows one of Johnson's Magna Lilliputia contributions; and without making the contrast explicit, the proposal praises Grey for qualities that are precisely the opposite of those that Johnson displayed, paramount among which was his ability to invent what the speakers should have said, rather than record what they actually did say. No editor's name, however, was mentioned.

Why should this proposal have been made in 1745? For one thing, the series of *Proceedings* volumes had ended, with the suicide of Richard Chandler. For another, in 1745, James Ralph, Chandler's collaborator on the Restoration part of that project, had just published (anonymously) his own *History of England*, and was presumably looking for another project. For another, the last Jacobite rebellion, which had begun in 1745 with a French plan to invade England and reinstate the Stuart family, was a pressing invitation to revisit the relations between Charles II and Louis XIV that had so bedeviled the Long Parliament.

Grey's *Debates* was not, however, actually published until 1763. The dedication to Onslow was followed by an address "To the Reader" that exactly repeats the words of the proposal. *Debates* explains how the Revolution of 1688 came about, and the story is fraught with still pertinent issues:

the Struggles between Prerogative and Privilege, the Out-cries of Abhorrence and Prosecution, Efforts against Popery and arbitrary Power . . . Impeachments of Ministers, Attempts to set aside the Heir of the Crown, the expulsion of a King, and the Re-establishment of the Constitution . . . the Reader is led forward from Day to Day, and from Question to Question . . . observes the Birth, the Progress, the Maturity of Designs, sees the Colours of Party change before him, and Patriotism sink in one Year, and rise in another.

The style and principles of *this* prefatory manifesto are strikingly similar to those that had issued in *Proceedings* twenty years or so earlier; and, as in Volume 1 of *Proceedings*, the editor remained anonymous.

This unidentified editor also offers a shrewd account of what Anchitell Grey had personally contributed to the history of parliament. He asserts that Grey took his notes "without any View of Publication" and "only for his own Use or Amusement," a statement that was by now becoming formulaic, but in this case might have been true. Hence "he was under no Temptation either to suppress or misrepresent any Argument or Occurrence." Consequently, his versions contain

fifty Times more of the secret Deliberations of the House, than all the Accounts of Debates for the same Time yet published; for, were any part of them genuine, yet, for several Sessions, they have no Debate at all; whereas the Conviction which the Reader here finds that he is not misled, but enters on every Day's real Business, induces him to consider himself present in this active and honourable Assembly, partaking the Ardour and Anxiety of the unbiassed Englishman, and resenting the Subtleties and Evasions of his Opponent.

Thus whereas Johnson's eighteenth-century debates were written with high eloquence from second-hand information, Grey's seventeenth-century ones were written on the spot, with more concern for detail than elegance. It is worth noting that, even as the editor claims that Grey himself was unbiased, he also suggests that the reader will be able to choose sides between "the un-biassed Englishman" and the less candid, even disingenuous "Opponent" on the other side of the House; an invitation to decide from the beginning where, in partisan terms, the speakers stood, again remarkably similar to the invitation at the opening of *Proceedings* whereby we may "have the Pleasure of approving, or opposing both Patriot and Minister in turn, as Artifice or Prejudice discovers itself in either, to the Dishonour of Truth, and the Detriment of the Commonwealth."

The dedication to Onslow is merely signed "Your most Obliged, and Devoted Servant, The Editor." It has usually been assumed, no other name being circulated in connection with this fairly momentous publication, that this editor was Edward Cave himself. But Cave was a bookseller and publisher of other men's work, and had no obvious qualifications for the task, which required considerable historical scholarship. Besides, he died in 1754, nine years before *Debates* appeared; and from one of the footnotes we can determine that the editor was still at work in 1761, since he gives that date as the moment of his reflection on the great improvements the English have made in their navy.[5] And at the end of Volume 8, which takes the story up to the end of the last parliament of Charles II, we find the following editorial insertion: "To preserve connection, we have added the following Summary of the remaining part of King Charles's Reign." A footnote on the death of Lord Essex in the Tower refers to "a Book which is still extant, and now is, (1762) or lately was, in the possession of a Gentleman at Chelsea."

The Footnotes to Grey

The footnotes to Grey's *Debates* are a story in themselves. It has been said that Grey does not reveal his partisanship, another version of the anonymous editor's somewhat disingenuous claim that Grey was actually "unbiased." But this is not quite how *Debates* presents itself to us today—thanks to the footnotes. In Chapter 8, while setting out Grey's records of the latter part of the sixteenth session of 1677, I have several times drawn attention to the work the footnotes performed. One would not normally look to footnotes to identify the *tone* of a public record, as distinct from giving necessary explanations. This editor worked moderately hard. He collated Grey's records with the Journal of the House of Commons, indicating where events and speeches that Grey records do not appear in the Journal. He included the texts of speeches and other documents where necessary for clarity or continuity. But it is primarily in the footnotes that the work acquires a distinctive, indeed an ideological cast, and they may unconsciously have contributed to Rowlands's observation that "there is no doubt where [Grey's] political sympathies lay," a remark diametrically opposed to his statement that Grey never allows himself an evaluative comment. If Grey appears to be objective, the footnotes continuously nudge the work towards Whig historiography.[6]

Most of the footnotes consist of comments from previously published histories of England, most of which are what one would expect: in chronological order, Sir William Temple's *Memoirs of what past in Christendom* (1691), White Kennett's *Complete History of England* (1706), Echard's *History of England* (1707–18), Gilbert Burnet's *History of His own Time* (1724), Oldmixon's *Critical History of England* (1724), Sir John Reresby's *Memoirs* (1734), Roger North's *Examen* (1740), the letters of Algernon Sidney to Henry Savile (1742), Tindal's translation of Rapin de Thoyras's *History of England* (1732–47), and James Ralph's massive two-volume *History of England during the reigns of King William, Queen Anne, and King George I, with an introductory review of the reigns of the royal brothers Charles and James*, which had, we remember, appeared in 1745, the same year that the *Gentleman's Magazine* published the proposal to edit Grey's *Debates*. Ralph's *History* was therefore the most recent source available for the editor of *Debates*, and two-thirds of its huge first volume were devoted to the reign of Charles II.

A less expected source who appears frequently in the notes is Andrew Marvell, cited not only from the *Account* but also from his personal letters to his nephew William Popple, letters that had been published by Thomas Cooke in 1726 in an edition of Marvell's poems. In order of *importance*, the editor relied primarily on Marvell, Ralph, and Burnet. Burnet is a vital source for the character sketches the editor mentioned as a desideratum of the notes, and almost the only authority, except for Ralph, in the volumes that cover the post-Revolutionary years. After Marvell drops out of the story at his death in 1678, he is replaced by Temple, Algernon Sidney, and Reresby. Echard, Kennett, and Rapin rarely appear. And Roger North is usually cited in order to show his contrary bias. Let us note at this point that the only one of these historians who is still alive (just) when we know Grey's *Debates* was still in process of publication is James Ralph, who died on January 24, 1762.

I shall now begin to mount the case that the anonymous editor of Grey's *Debates* was in fact Ralph, to whom I have also attributed the first three volumes of *Proceedings*. The primary method of proof will be to show that the footnotes inserted by the anonymous editor are in fact derived, usually verbatim, from Ralph's *History*. The person most likely to have engaged in that peculiar form of plagiarism was Ralph himself, of whose habits of borrowing we have already learned. But before undertaking that fairly microscopic form of analysis, it seems pertinent to note that in Ralph's preface to his *History* he acknowledges having read, drawn on, and improved on Kennett, Echard, Oldmixon, North, Burnet, Rapin, Sidney's letters, Reresby's *Memoirs*, and North's *Examen*; that is, with the sole exception of Marvell, exactly the same list of historians as appear in the footnotes to Grey's *Debates*.

Let us start with a couple of salient examples of the use of Marvell. In March 1670, as we saw in Chapter 3, the Commons passed "An Act to suppress seditious Conventicles" which renewed the similar and now lapsed act of 1664. The new bill came up for its third reading on March 9 (Grey mistakenly has it as a second reading), and on this occasion Marvell only records six speakers, five against the bill (Serjeant Maynard, Colonel Birch, Sir Richard Temple, John Vaughan, and William Love, who would later speak on behalf of Protestant Dissenters in 1673), and one for it, Sir Henry

Coventry. What Coventry said, evidently replying to speeches not recorded, was as follows:

> There is nothing in this Bill but what is as arbitrary as in the Irish cattle Bill. He undervalues the Fanatics much, that thinks them not better worth than an Irish cow. If there be not power in the Ecclesiastics, it is fit it should be in the Law; therefore, never was there a more merciful Bill, that punishes, neither with blood nor banishment, a people that has punished us with both these.

If one were not paying close attention, one might miss the disparity between what Grey records of the debate and the results: "The Bill passed 138 to 78." But at the bottom of the page (in the 1763 edition—1:246) we find the following note:

> Marvell calls this Act "the Price of Money," adding, "The King told some eminent citizens, who applied to him against it, That they must address themselves to the Houses; that he must not disoblige his friends; and if it had been in the power of the Lords, he had gone without money."

And the note continues at some length, providing the details of what qualified as a conventicle, and what were to be the penalties for holding one.

What is this, what does it accomplish, and to whom do we owe it? First, of course, it introduces the interpretive commentary that Grey had withheld. It expands the story from parliamentary procedure to the realm of gossip, if not scandal, helping the reader to understand that the king, who inclined towards toleration, agreed to the Conventicles Act in exchange for the Commons voting him a Supply, which demand would engage them for all of October, November, and December of that year, as they projected taxes on everything (wine, currants, sugar, playgoing) and finally fell back on the tried and true, if hated, land tax. The anecdote gives us a picture of Charles II, laconic as usual, discussing with the very group at whom the Conventicles Act was aimed his own predicament and theirs. The ironic judgement of the footnote, part Marvell's, part the king's, overrides the give-and-take of debate, leaving us to assume nearly the worst, that the Conventicles Act is not merely oppressive, but an expedient in a larger game.

This remark of Marvell's came not from any contribution to the debate in the House that he made himself, though we know his views on it from his letters to his Hull constituents, but from one of his personal letters to William Popple, a letter dated March 21, 1670, as published by Cooke in 1726. What Marvell had actually written to Popple was slightly different:

> They [the Lords] are making mighty Alterations in the Conventicle Bill, (which, as we sent up, is the Quintessence of arbitrary Malice,). So the Fate of the Bill is uncertain, but must probably pass, being the Price of Money. The King told some eminent Citizens, who applyed to him against it, that they must address themselves to the Houses, that he must not disoblige *his* Friends; and if it had been in the Power of *their* Friends, he had gone without Money, (*P&L*, 2:315; italics added)

It is the editor who explains that "their Friends," that is, those who are friendly to the Dissenters, are the Lords, and that Charles now sees the Commons, at least for the moment, as "his Friends." So Marvell's comment, though disarmed of its most critical language, is altered to make it intelligible to a later and wider audience. In fact, when the Lords passed the revised Conventicles Act on March 26, seventeen members of that House recorded their dissent. These details may seem excessive as a gloss on what is *already* a gloss, Marvell's personal comment to his nephew now become footnote in a national archive, but they help to explain what lay behind the editor's choice of the footnote in the first instance.

Now, the intermediary source between Marvell's correspondence and the footnotes to Grey's *Debates* was in fact Ralph's *History of England*. In Volume 1, p. 180, n. 6, as Ralph purveys his account of the Conventicles Act, in which he is considerably interested, we find, verbatim, the note that begins "Marvell calls this Act 'the Price of Money,' " and, perhaps even more to the point, that the details about the act and its penalties come not from Marvell's letter to Popple but from the rest of Ralph's own footnote.

Ralph's interest in the Conventicles Act leads him to its next phase, though he does not clearly delineate the chronology. While it was working its way, with difficulty, through the House of Lords, the bill produced a crisis. The committee brought it back with several provisos, which caused an uproar in the Commons. At this point in *Debates*, the editor inserts the full text of the most troublesome proviso, with the following startling footnote:

> "In this Session," says Mr. Marvell, in his Letters, "the Lords sent us down a Proviso for the King, that would have restored him to all civil and ecclesiastical Prerogatives, which his ancestors had enjoyed at any time since the Conquest. There never was so compendious a piece of absolute, universal tyranny. But the Commons made them ashamed of it, and retrenched it." He adds notwithstanding, "the Parliament was never so embarrassed beyond recovery. We are all venal cowards, except some few."

For evaluative candor, this note is hard to beat. Its intermediate source, however, was Ralph's *History*, on the same page as the previous citation from Marvell, where it appears verbatim.

We must now consider some of the footnotes that do not feature Marvell. A telling note not attributed to anybody appears during the debates of October 1675, when the Commons had become deeply distrustful of the constant appeals to them for money without their seeing any of the promised results. A negative vote of 172 to 165 against further Supply passed on Tuesday, October 19 (Grey, 3:311). At the foot of the page we find the following:

> In comparison with the lavishness and extravagances of later times, these things have all the air of patriotism and public spirit; but if Mr. North, and all the other writers on the side of the Prerogative, deserve any credit, we are to conclude, that this excess of oeconomy did not arise from any tenderness to the public, but a settled resolution to distress the King.

In fact, this note derives verbatim from the text of Ralph's *History* (1:290–91), and it is full of mischief. The "later times" whose extravagances in supplying subsequent monarchs are here brought into comparison with the 1670s are Ralph's own times; and his suggestion that Roger North and "all the other writers on the side of the Prerogative" had a better view of things than the naïve person who might see the Commons' restraint as patriotic is unmistakably ironic. Now why would an editor include such a note in *Debates*, unnecessary as it is to a clear understanding of what was going on, were he not Ralph himself? And *as* Ralph himself, particularly enamored of such clever phrasing?

Most of the notes in *Debates* attributed to "Ralph" have both a judicial and an ironic flavor. Thus in 1676, when the House reconvened after the Long Prorogation, and the streets were full of pamphlets arguing that it was illegal and that parliament should be regarded as having been dissolved, the Commons heard that the Lords had imprisoned Dr. Nicholas Cary for having carried to the press the manuscript of *The Grand Question Stated . . . concerning the Prorogation*. One might say that "Ralph's" note was necessary to explain in more detail than did Secretary Henry Coventry why Cary had been committed:

> One Dr. Cary was brought to the Bar of the House of Lords, and questioned concerning a M.S. treating of the illegality of the Prorogation, which he had carried to the press; and because he declined answering such Questions as were put to him, and took sanctuary in the laws, which oblige no man to accuse himself, they fined him 1000.l. and sent him close prisoner to the Tower till it was paid. (Grey, 5:166; *History*, p. 314)

But the second part of this note, which Ralph had also included in his own text, was of a different color: "That the Lords, who had made so free with their own Privileges, by submitting the liberty of four of their body at once to the pleasure of his Majesty, should make thus free with both the liberty and property of a Commoner, is perhaps scarce to be wondered at." Both Ralph and the "Ralph" of the footnote in *Debates* thereby alluded to the imprisonment of the four lords who had, when parliament reconvened, argued strenuously that the Long Prorogation was illegal, and for their trouble had been sent to the Tower, to await the king's pleasure.

As *Debates* proceeds, as relations between Charles II and parliament worsen, the footnotes get longer. (The opposite will be true when we leave this reign behind.) In Volume 7, which deals with the parliaments of 1679 and 1680, long notes from Ralph's *History* are deemed necessary to fill in the historical events between sessions, including the prorogation of May 1679, which turned into a dissolution, and the calling of a new parliament for October, which, after several more prorogations, finally met in October 1680. In the interim Monmouth was deprived of his army commissions, and the duke of York returned to orchestrate affairs. When the Exclusion Bill was sent up to the Lords (where it would fail) the king once again demanded money for the protection of the isle of Tangier. At this point the editor inserted a particularly Ralphian note, disproportionate in its length to the tiny mention of Tangier in *Debates*:

> On the day the Exclusion Bill had been left with the Lords, his Majesty had by Message demanded a Supply for Tangier, without which, it was urged, that Place could not be much longer preserved. There was some truth in this, and some fallacy, as there is generally in all demands of the like nature. Tangier was indeed in some distress, but the king was in more, and whatever was given in relief of the first, would also have contributed to the relief of the last. But, on the other hand, the Commons very well knew that they had not been assembled to make fine Speeches in the House, or render themselves popular at the expence of the Royal Family. Like the fine Lady in the Comedy, there was but one thing they could do to pleasure the Court, which was, giving Money, and that being once done, they also knew, that an instant dismission would follow.

The source for this is Ralph's *History* (1:526). The tone is satirically comic, laced with sexual innuendo. "To pleasure the Court" is a particularly fine touch; and if Ralph and Grey's editor were indeed one and the same, we can easily see why this note was chosen for inclusion: not for the relevance of its information, but for its tone, and especially perhaps its allusion to the theater.

If James Ralph and the anonymous editor were one and the same, much that is otherwise odd can be explained—including an apparent attempt to conceal the extent of the notes' derivation from Ralph's *History*. Often a note is attributed to a previous historian, but if we check, we discover that the citation had already appeared in the *History*. In 1678, when the Lords sent down the bill excluding Catholics from parliament, with its proviso exempting the duke of York, the editor inserts as a note the comment from Burnet that we have seen before:

> The Duke spoke on this Proviso [in the House of Lords] with great earnestness, and with tears in his eyes. He said "he was now to cast himself on their favour in the greatest concern he could have in this world." He spoke much of "his duty to the King, and of his zeal for the nation;" and solemnly protested, "that, whatever his Religion might be, it should only be a private thing between God and his own soul, and that no effect of it should ever appear in the Government." The Proviso was carried for him by a few voices. And, contrary to all mens expectations, it passed in the House of Commons. *Burnet.*

In this case the irony results from comparing the duke of York's dramatics with what actually happened after his succession. But Grey's editor did not have to consult Burnet himself for this material, since it was, all but the last two sentences, available verbatim, including the quotation marks, in Ralph's *History* (1:396).

This strategy was used with almost comic abandon when the time came to comment on the brevity of the parliament that had been called after the dissolution of the Long Parliament. Summoned for what would be its last session on March 6, 1679, it was prorogued by the king on May 27, and though at first merely prorogued until August 14, it was dissolved on July 12. In *House of Commons*, Basil Henning comments: "Little is known about the circumstances surrounding the dissolution of the first Exclusion Parliament, except that it was ordered by the King against the advice of an overwhelming majority of the Privy Council, and nearly six weeks after the prorogation" (1:87). But the editor of Grey's *Debates* does his characteristic best to fill in this gap in our knowledge by supplying a flurry of information attributed to Sir William Temple, Algernon Sidney, Ralph, Temple again, Reresby, Sidney again, and Ralph. In fact, all of this material could be found, already collected, in Ralph's *History* (1:456–57), with the exception that the last long note by "Ralph" was from a later section of the *History* (1:472). The division of this material into separately attributed paragraphs might have been intended to deflect attention from the huge chunk of Ralph that had been marshaled to

deplore the king's tactics. The conclusion attributed to "Ralph" has the effect
we have by now come to expect, of supplying a particularly sardonic and well-
written overview:

> Thus in less than three months after his Majesty had publickly and
> solemnly promised to act no more by the advice of Favourites and Cabals,
> or without that of his Privy Council, was he twice induced to trespass as
> publickly on that engagement: First, by proroguing the Parliament without
> their knowledge, and now by dissolving it without their concurrence; and
> that this was the matter of fact, the very Proclamation stands witness, in
> which the King stands alone, and declares the Dissolution in his own name,
> and by his own authority, without the mention of any Council at all, "being
> resolved to meet his people, and have their advice, in frequent [i.e. newly
> elected] Parliaments.

Surely, only Ralph himself would have known of the presence of this overview
fifteen pages *after* his main discussion of the prorogation, and perceived its
value as the last word in the chorus of protests the footnotes to *Debates* had
displayed across the space of more than two pages (7:346–47).

James Ralph

So who was James Ralph? The new *Dictionary of National Biography* contains an
article by Laird Okie, author of *Augustan Historical Writing* (1991), which largely
depends for its material on an unpublished Columbia Ph.D. dissertation by
J.B. Shipley, "James Ralph, Pretender to Genius," (1963). One striking fact
about Ralph is that he is first heard of in America as a friend of Benjamin
Franklin, whom he accompanied to England in 1724, leaving behind a wife and
children. It is perhaps not surprising that Shipley's dissertation was never
published, since the whole of its first volume is devoted to Ralph's attempts
to establish himself as a writer in England, all of which met with scorn by
the public and contempt by his modern biographer. These attempts included a
satirical play, *The Fashionable Lady* (1730), which failed, and some drama criticism. In his second volume, however, Shipley provides valuable information
about Ralph's second career as a political journalist, in the course of which
he switched sides—dramatically—leaving Walpole's ministry to write for the
Opposition in 1737, collaborating with Henry Fielding in the Opposition
journal *The Champion* (1739–44), and in 1747–51, under the patronage of
George Bubb Dodington, the anti-court journal *The Remembrancer.* He also
wrote, in 1743, *The Critical History of the Administration of Sir Robert Walpole*, and
the next year *A Defence of the People*, and *Of the Use and Abuse of Parliaments*, which

appeared in two volumes, and had been heralded in a footnote on p. 60 of
A Defence. The letter was just a squib in the crossfire between the parties, but
Of the Use and Abuse of Parliaments attempted a serious blend of parliamentary
history and constitutional theory. Ralph never signed his name to any of these
works. In *The Champion* his contributions are recognizable by the signature
"Lilbourne." All this was minor in scale compared to his massive *History*, identified authorially merely as "By a lover of truth and liberty." In the 1750s, he
joined another Opposition faction led by William Beckford and the duke of
Bedford and, according to Okie, was "pensioned into silence by the Pelham
ministry" in 1753. Nevertheless, if I am correct in attributing to him the editor-
ship of *Debates*, this proved a very articulate silence. The appearance of *Debates*
in 1763 would have seemed to the recently deceased Ralph, had he been able
to look down at the England of George III, a fitting monument.

Ralph may have been working on *Debates* up to the last moment. Since the
footnotes decrease in number and complexity in the post-Stuart volumes, we
might infer that Ralph, who struggled with gout towards the end of his life,
was running out of energy as well as time. When he comes to the Williamite
volumes (although his own *History* was large on this period, especially its wars),
the presence of "Ralph" in the footnotes is on the face of it negligible—but
telling. On Wednesday, March 20, 1689, the Commons debated a bill from
the Lords for the regulation of trials of peers. In the course of the debate
William Williams mentioned the names of Lord Brandon and Lord Delamer,
who were both caught up in Monmouth's rebellion. In the footnotes, we find
the following account of Lord Brandon:

> In 1685, "for conspiring with other false traytors (Monmouth, &c.) to raise
> a Rebellion, Depose and put to death the late King, &c." of which being
> found guilty by the prostitute Juries of these times, he received sentence of
> Death; but by applying properly made a shift to obtain a Pardon; which Sir
> John Reresby celebrates as a signal Act of Grace, because that Lord had
> formerly been condemned for breaking a boy's neck in his cups, and had
> been admitted to mercy. Ralph.

The source for this note, verbatim, is Ralph's *History* (1:912). And the
following note on Lord Delamer—"Lord Delamer's charge was "for being an
Accomplice with Monmouth, in his late Rebellion"—though not attributed to
"Ralph," in fact appears in the *History* on the following page. Thus once again
the editor has known just where to go in the *History* (which of course has no
index) for a gloss on these figures, the first of which is really designed not to
fill us in on Lord Brandon, but to deliver a reproof to Sir John Reresby, a rival
historian of the era.

It is theoretically possible that another person than Ralph was the editor, and saw his task as an annotator primarily as one of plagiarism. But who could that possibly be? We have no other serious candidate, and, at the very least, this hypothetical figure must have known the pages of Ralph's *History* as well as their own author knew them. James Ralph had both the parliamentary experience to take on the task of editing Grey's *Debates*, and the political profile necessary to gain control of the manuscripts, which may have been held by the Grey family in Derbyshire. *Of the Use and Abuse of Parliaments*, though relatively superficial as both history and analysis, established his credentials as someone who believed that English parliaments, when not corrupted, could and should play a vital role in promoting what he referred to as "the true interest of the nation." His own *History*, though parliament was only a small part of its purview, greatly extended those credentials. And in editing *Debates* as a work of Whig or Country party historiography, he did something of much greater usefulness. Histories of England come and go, but the archives, if preserved and published, go on for ever. Ralph preserved Grey, in excellent condition. The footnotes he added make *Debates* considerably more than they were as naked reportage: a study in historiographical sophistication, and a game of scholarly hide-and-seek. Now that we have them online, we can play that game with considerable satisfaction.

Postscript: The Printing Debate

The story of how we got parliamentary history, as described above, is to some extent one of gamesmanship. Perhaps it is wishful thinking to suggest that those who kept the records and disseminated them were fortified by the political principles of openness and the public's right to know. One thing we can say for certain: parliamentary history evolved in defiance of parliament itself. It took a crisis to bring about a change of attitude. Towards the end of the Long Parliament there was a brief debate about leakage of votes. On Tuesday, October 29, 1678, "the Speaker acquainted the House with a person taken upon the Guard, with an account of all the Votes in the House, and transactions, &c." The person admitted to having received the material from "one Cole, who commonly distributed such papers," and that he, as a stranger, had purchased one of them. When Seymour asked: "Who employed you to look after Votes of the House of Commons?" the unnamed stranger replied:

> I did it to satisfy the curiosity of friends. I have had of those papers for one Mr. Osborn, from the same person, sometimes for 6d. sometimes for 12d. according as they were considerable. Cole delivered the Votes to one Smith, and I had them from him about five or six o'clock at night. Mr. Osborn is a

Counsellor at Law, and I brought them to him, but I make it not my business, only at the desire of persons.

This sounds like a very minor version of the trade of John Starkey. Seymour
proposed spoiling the trade, by tracing this case to its origins. To which
Sacheverell replied: "It is the right of every Member to take Votes out of the
Journal; and it is the right of any Commoner to see your Books." Then, after
a stage direction, "The Speaker reflecting upon Gentlemen that took notes,"
Sergeant Maynard (not yet the employer of Roger Morrice) declared: "No
man's memory can retain your Votes, and Gentlemen may take notes in your
House." According to Grey, "the thing went off without farther Proceeding."
And the editor observed in a footnote: "The only notice taken of this in the
Journal, is, an Order, 'That none of the Votes of the House be dispersed or
published in the coffee-houses.' " The security fences, and the attitudes that
erected them, were beginning to crumble.

The first general order for publishing the *votes* of a session was made on
October 30, 1680, in the context of the Popish Plot, and repeated on March 24,
1681 during the Oxford parliament, after a heated debate. This was a moment
in parliamentary history when what were called "appeals to the people" were
once more countenanced, as appeals *from* the people, in the form of petitions,
were accepted as part of the ferment. But this did not include debates. The
proceedings of the Oxford parliament were in fact published illegally in 1681
by the intrepid Richard Baldwin as a pamphlet, *The Debates in the House of
Commons Assembled at Oxford*, which includes the debate on printing the votes!
Remarkably, this pamphlet derives exactly from Anchitell Grey's debates, which
at that stage existed only in manuscript. Did Grey at this point, then, envisage
such a change in the climate that the notes he had been taking for over a decade
could now be released into the public sphere?

In a study of the Journals of the House of Commons[7] David Menhennet,
deputy librarian of the House, notes that in 1680 there were published, un-
officially, two "Journal Books," "corresponding fairly closely but not exactly"
to the official Journal for October 21 to December 1678 and from March 6
to May 27, 1679.[8] He concluded that in 1680 there was a demand for printed
and published copies of the Journal, which was further evidenced by a preface
to the second of these two books noting also, as proof of "the vallue curious
people sets upon them," a large scribal circulation. But Menhennet wondered
whether the order of 1680 to print the votes did in fact "mark a significant
change in the attitude of Members," and the later history of the issue would
suggest that, if it did, the change was both short-lived and limited in scope.

Unsurprisingly, no such resolutions were taken in the parliaments of James II,
and in the first Williamite parliament, in 1689, a motion to print the votes was

explicitly defeated, 180 to 145. It is worth listening to the reasoning, as Anchitell Grey painstakingly recorded it, on Saturday, March 9. When the motion was made, Sir Thomas Lee remarked, for the pragmatists, that it would "save the Gentlemen the trouble of writing to their Corporations." Sir Henry Capel said (for the liberals): "If you could keep your Votes out of the Coffee-Houses, and suppress the licentiousness of Printing [you might vote against this], otherwise you make secrets here of what all the World knows. . . . The World ought to know your Votes, and there is no harm in it." Sir Joseph Tredenham said (for the conservatives): "Those Rules and Measures our Ancestors left us, are the safest way. . . . When the King shall come to take notice what you do here, what becomes of your Liberty of Speech, and what becomes of your Freedom of Debates?" Richard Hampden gave a rather incoherent speech against printing the votes, arguing that it would show up their contradictions, and that the votes were no use without the reasons that produced them. He recalled the Oxford parliament: "I know the Wheels that moved it then. I know that printing your Votes sounded well abroad, and it seems a popular thing, like sitting at Charing Cross, but the People had much rather hear our Reasons than our Votes, and no more." He complained that the only reason to print the votes "is for the sake of the Booksellers, or that younger Gentlemen may be able, when the elder are in their graves, to know the Proceedings of Parliament; but they will see no reasons for them." Sir Richard Temple disliked all innovations, and said: "I hope we shall not imitate Holland, to go to our Principals for Instructions." Sir Thomas Littleton was, as one might expect, for printing. So was Sir Robert Howard, somewhat surprisingly:

> Methinks the Debate is, Whether you will publish your Votes tacitly, or expressly. If they are published without the Stamp of Authority, it seems you will rather permit it by an unjustifiable way, than a justifiable. If you will keep your Books secret, perhaps I shall be for that; but if you suffer them to be published by other means, then is not printing the honester and juster way[?]

But Sir William Williams, who as Speaker had been entrusted with the printing of the votes in 1680, and who believed himself to have been denied the Chair in James II's parliament as a result, distinguished between the practice in Holland, a commonwealth, and England, a monarchy, and again protested: "Your Reasons will not appear with your Votes; and the People will not apprehend the Reason of your Contradictions."

Sometime in 1689 Richard Baldwin returned to the fray. He printed *An Exact Collection of the Debates of the House of Commons, Held at Westminster, October 21, 1680, Prorogued the Tenth, and Dissolved the Eighteenth of January following. With the Debates of the House of Commons at Oxford, Assembled March 21, 1680,* a large 464-page volume that includes a vindication of both parliaments for their votes on excluding the duke of York from the succession. The account of the Oxford parliament is a reprint of the 1681 pamphlet as derived from Grey; the debates of the second Exclusion parliament are in a totally different style from those in Grey—more formal and seemingly less extempore. Baldwin wrote a preface "To the Reader" vindicating his own procedure, as follows:

It will appear in these following Sheets, upon what weighty Inducements and convincing Reasons, and after what free and mature Debates, those Bills came to be brought in and promoted, and under the influence of what Arguments and Motives these Votes and Resolves came to be made. These Papers, though exceeding worthy of the view of the Nation, had nevertheless remained confined to the Privacy unto which they were originally designed, had not the publishing some imperfect Notes of the Debates of a latter Parliament, relating to the same Matters, rendred it Indispensably necessary that the Kingdom should be better enlightned.... And as nothing can so vindicate or justifie the Proceedings of a Parliament, as a true and perfect Relation of their own Debates, ... so we no ways doubt, but that the Speeches here truly and fully subjoined, as they were *pro re nata* spoken, will at once rectifie the Opinions of some Men concerning the late Actings both of that and two other Houses of Commons, and fill the World with an esteem and admiration of an English Senate, where private Gentlemen, of which the Lower House of Parliament is constituted, can, concerning the greatest Affairs, and most abstruse parts of Policy, speak at such a rate *extempore.*

It looks suspiciously as though Baldwin, having heard what was said against printing the votes in this parliament, was directly answering the most cogent argument *contra*, that the votes were unintelligible without the debates, by showing what could be done for parliamentary history when debates, "as they were *pro re nata* spoken," were published for the edification of future readers. This high valuation of verbatim debates would reappear in the Preface to Grey's *Debates* when published in 1763.

In 1742, the Commons established a committee to consider whether the Journal should be printed. Menhennet emphasizes, however, that the motive was primarily conservationist—the manuscript journals were reported to be deteriorating—and the purpose was definitely not publication. Only one thousand copies were to be printed, for the exclusive use of members. On May 14, 1762, the House ordered the printing of the current volume of the Journal, and on April 26, 1769, the number of copies was increased to 1,500 and the restriction of their use to members was dropped. Menhennet suggests that the Commons were now "prepared to countenance a much greater publicizing of their business" (p. 23), a mild phrase that overlooks the challenges to their policy of secrecy that were now being made more boldly in the newspapers. In 1768, John Almon had started providing anonymous reports of the debates in current sessions in the *London Evening Post*, and other newspapers copied the practice. In 1771, the House of Commons attempted to take legal action against the printers of eight newspapers, including the *Post*, but their messengers were successfully charged with assault, and, as Almon put it in his *Memoirs*: "Parliament now finding its own impotency in this business, abandoned the whole question entirely."[9]

Notes

Introduction

1. Excellent use has been made of these images from 1624, 1628, and 1640 by Oliver Arnold, *The Third Citizen: Shakespeare's Theater and the Early Modern House of Commons* (Baltimore, 2007), pp. 18, 47–49, 70, 75, figs. 1–3.
2. D.T. Witcombe, *Charles II and the Cavalier House of Commons 1663–1674* (Manchester, 1966).
3. Paul Seaward, *The Cavalier Parliament and the Reconstruction of the Old Regime, 1661–1667* (Cambridge, 1989).
4. Steven Pincus, *Protestantism and Patriotism: Ideologies and the Making of English Foreign Policy, 1650–1668* (Cambridge, 1996).
5. Tim Harris, *Restoration: Charles II and his Kingdoms, 1660–1685* (Penguin, 2005).
6. This does not, of course, mean that there were not considerable differences of opinion and strategy within the two larger interest groups. A letter from Sir William Temple to the earl of Essex in Ireland in 1673, when tempers were heated in the Commons when the duke of York's plan to marry the Catholic duchess of Modena became known, differentiated between four separate parties within the Opposition, each with its own agenda. See *Essex Papers*, ed. Osmond Airy (London, 1890), 1:131–32.
7. Charles II's Declaration of Indulgence for persons who would not conform to the Church of England, announced on March 15, 1672, when parliament was not in session. This was the king's second Declaration of Indulgence: the first was published on December 26, 1662, also during a parliamentary recess.
8. Actually the Third Dutch War, declared on March 17, 1672, ended, for England, on February 19, 1674.
9. The Triple League was negotiated by Sir William Temple in January 1668, a military alliance between England, the United Provinces, and Spain for the defense of the Spanish Netherlands against France. It was almost immediately undermined by Charles's secret diplomacy.
10. The secret clauses in the Treaty of Dover, whereby Charles II promised to assist Louis XIV against the Dutch, in return for subsidies to endeavor to return England to Roman Catholicism.
11. Thomas Clifford, one of the five ministers in the Cabal, was promoted to treasurer in 1672 but resigned from office when parliament passed the Test Act of 1673 against Catholics.
12. *The Diaries and Papers of Sir Edward Dering*, ed. Maurice F. Bond (London, 1976), pp. 125–26.

Chapter 1

1. "An Act against malicious wounding or maiming" (22 & 23 Car. II, cap. I).
2. Arnold, *The Third Citizen*, pp. 47–75.
3. *CJ*, 2 (1640–1642), p. 604.
4. *CJ*, 8 (1660–1667), p. 639.
5. Gilbert Burnet, *Bishop Burnet's History of His own Time*, ed. M.J.R., 6 vols. (Oxford, 1823), 1:472.
6. For an argument that the *Gazette* also indicated support for the Anglican church by its selection of news and advertisements, see Thomas O'Malley, "Religion and the Newspaper Press, 1660–1685: A Study of the *London Gazette*," in Michael Harris and Alan Lee (eds.), *The Press in English Society from the Seventeenth to Nineteenth Centuries* (London, 1986), pp. 25–46.
7. For Samuel Pepys's rather full account of the anger caused by the speech, see above, p. 79.
8. That occurred on April 22, 1670, when in microscopic print it recorded the Address requesting the king to encourage the wearing of home-grown fabrics.
9. For a full account of the would-be monopoly over newsletters held by the secretaries of state, and long lists of those, abroad and at home, to whom Williamson sent his newsletters, see Peter Fraser, *The Intelligence of the Secretaries of State and their Monopoly of Licensed News 1660–1688* (Cambridge, 1956).
10. J.G. Muddiman, *The King's Journalist* (London, 1923), p. 172.
11. To judge at least from the long series held in the collection of the marquess of Bath at Longleat, MSS. 68, 77–88. Although there are moments when Muddiman reported royal speeches, bills passed, and even the occasional Commons Address, in general he seems to have assumed that his reader was more interested in foreign news. He did, however, include verbatim the king's angry speech to the Commons on May 28, 1677.
12. BL Add. MS. 36916, Aston Papers, Vol. 16.
13. Grey married Anne, daughter of Sir Henry Willoughby and widow of Sir Thomas Aston, ca. 1657. He thereby acquired Sir Willoughby Aston as a stepson.
14. This may be a misunderstanding. John Rushworth was at this time still struggling to complete his third volume, which would bring his documentary history up to 1644. To my knowledge there is no evidence that he intended a Restoration sequel.
15. *Letters . . . to Sir Joseph Williamson*, ed. W.D. Christie, 2 vols. (New York: Camden Society Reprint, 1965), 2:103.
16. Andrew Browning, *Thomas Osborne, Earl of Danby and Duke of Leeds 1632–1712*, 3 vols. (Glasgow, 1951), 3:2–3.
17. *Essex Papers*, 2:170. It is possible that the memorandum instead refers to March 1677, when Sir Gilbert Gerard moved for an Address to the king for an immediate declaration of war against France, and Danby himself, to gain time, persuaded the Commons to ask for the Lords' concurrence. The Lords amended the Address in ways that were not acceptable, and it never reached the king. See K.H.D. Haley, *The First Earl of Shaftesbury* (Oxford, 1968), p. 443.
18. Leicestershire RO, OG7, P.P. 42.
19. *Letters . . . to Sir Joseph Williamson*, ed. Christie.
20. These included Essex's private secretary in England, William Harbord; Edward, Lord Conway, who straddled English and Irish affairs; Francis, Lord Aungier, a member of the Commons throughout the Long Parliament; Sir Robert Southwell, MP and Court party supporter from 1673; and the famous diplomat Sir William Temple, one of whose letters in October 1673 offers a behind-the-scenes analysis of the heated conclusion to the eleventh session, and what was likely to come of the twelfth.
21. *Poems and Letters of Andrew Marvell*, ed. H.M Margoliouth, rev. Pierre Legouis, 2 vols. (Oxford, 1971), Vol. 2; subsequently referred to as *P&L*.

22. Basil Duke Henning, ed., *The Parliamentary Diary of Sir Edward Dering 1670–1673* (New Haven, 1940), subsequently referred to as Dering 1; Maurice Bond, ed., *The Diaries and Papers of Sir Edward Dering* (London: H.M. Stationery Office, 1976), subsequently referred to as Dering 2.
23. John Morrill,"Paying One's D'Ewes," *Parliamentary History*, 14 (1995), 179–86.
24. BL Add. MS. 28091, one of Danby's own manuscripts, contains the first half of Neale's parliamentary journal (ff. 29–76), which begins on Thursday, February 15, the first day of the session, and runs through March 20, 1677. The section from March 21 through May 28, 1677 appears separately in BL Egerton MS. 3345. After the adjournment on May 28, BL Add. MS. 28091 picks up the story again on February 5, 1678, no doubt because Neale was planning a major speech the next day.
25. Also still unpublished, in the National Archive, is the parliamentary journal of Joseph Williamson (SP 29/231, 253), who began recording, like Grey, in 1667, though Williamson did not enter the Commons until 1669, at which point, ironically, the journal stopped. Williamson began his journal-keeping as an under-secretary of state who professionally needed records of the Second Dutch War. He became interested in the business of the House of Commons when it started to investigate the "miscarriages" of that war in 1667, but his journal, maintained with the help of amanuenses, is barren of interpretation or commentary. He gives no more importance to the dealings of parliament than he does to the health and movements of notable persons, records no votes, and never even summarizes a debate, though he does reproduce from memory the king's speeches.
26. HMC, 9th Report, Appendix, pp. 69–79.
27. Arthur Bryant, ed., *The Letters, Speeches and Declarations of King Charles II* (London, 1935).
28. Witcombe, *Charles II*, p. 107, n. 4; doubtless he was misled by the appearance of both speeches in the printed version of the Lords Journal.
29. Grey, *Debates*, December 19, 1670: "To the Resolve of the Committee, 'That towards the Supply, every one that resorts to any of the Play-houses who sits in the Box shall pay one shilling, every one who sits in the Pit, shall pay six-pence, and every other person, three-pence,' the House disagreed." The tax was to have been pleasingly graduated, to fall most heavily on the wealthiest.
30. On March 7, John Starkey reported to Aston that the Lords passed the Subsidy Bill "on Tuesday last, but at the last reading there were 30 dissenters who were against passing the bill, but did not enter their protests."
31. Laurence Echard, *History of England*, 3 vols. (London, 1707–18), 3:263.
32. In his manuscript notes to his copy of the first edition of Burnet's *History*, Arthur Onslow remarked: "The duke of York's behaviour in this matter was like that of a great man, and the king's and duke of Monmouth's that of assassins" (1:470).

Chapter 2

1. BL Egerton MS. 3345, f. 19.
2. This and subsequent figures refer to the number of days in the Commons Journal that parliament actually sat to do business. They differ substantially from figures recorded by Abbott.
3. *His Majesties Declaration to All His loving Subjects, December 26, 1662, Published by the Advice of His Privy Council.*
4. For this and other quarrels over the Lords' appellate jurisdiction, see Swatland, *The House of Lords in the Reign of Charles II* (Cambridge, 1996), pp. 134–35.
5. HMC 7th Report, p. 484.
6. Pepys, *Diary*, 11 vols., ed. Robert Latham and William Matthews, Berkeley and Los Angeles, 1979, Vol. 5, pp. 102–03.

7. Bryant, *The Letters, Speeches and Declarations of King Charles II*, May 11, 1663: "If I do not write to you so often as I would, it is not my *faute*, for most of my time is taken up with the business of the Parliament, in getting them to do what is best for us all, and keeping them from doing what they ought not to do"; March 17, 1664 (the day after the fourth session convened); "I did not write by the last post, because I had so much business in order to the Parliament as I had no time"; November 21, 1664: "The Parliament being to meet on Thursday next, gives me so much business to put all things in a good way at their first coming together as I have only time to tell you"; November 30, 1667: "There can be nothing advanced in the Parliament for my advantage till this matter of my Lord Clarendon be over, but after that I shall be able to take my measures so with them, as you will see the good effects of it."

8. BL Add. MS. 25125, Coventry letters of April 1 and 8, ff. 25–29. This strategy was repeated on September 21, when he asked Charlton "if your affairs will permit [you to come to London] a day or two before the Meeting and I pray do me the favour to let me know of your arrivall that [I] may . . . acquit myself to my Master of having obeyed his Commands" (ff. 61–62).

9. *Essex Papers*, 1:174.

10. Browning, *Danby*, pp. 192–93, 205.

11. *Ibid.*, pp. 198–99.

12. Other prorogation tracts included *The Long Parliament Dissolved* (1676), attributed to Denzil Holles, which appeared in two separate editions; *Some Considerations Upon the Question whether the Parliament is dissolved* (1676); *The Grand Question stated and discussed* (1676), which resulted in the imprisonment of Dr. Nicholas Cary for refusing to divulge its authorship; and *A Seasonable Question and a useful Answer* (1676). After parliament convened in February 1677, there also appeared *A Narrative of the Cause and Manner of the Imprisonment of the Lords* (Amsterdam, 1677), whose contents show that it must have appeared after March 20; and *A Seasonable Argument to perswade all the Grand Juries in England to petition for a New Parliament* (Amsterdam,1677), sometimes attributed to Andrew Marvell, which appeared at the end of February 1677.

13. See also Marvell, *Account*: "But these frequent Adjournments left no Place for Divination, but that they must rather have been calculated to give the French more scope for perfecting their Conquests, or to keep the Lords closer, till the Conspirators Designs were accomplished; and it is less probable that one of these was false, than that both were the true causes" (2:371); Browning, *Danby*, notes a memorandum by the treasurer in favor of the adjournment at Easter 1677: "The lords continuation in the Tower" BL Add. MS. 28042, f. 36.

14. Witcombe, *Charles II*, p. 143, citing a letter from Musgrave to Williamson, October 20.

15. Nicholas Letters, Egerton MS. 2539, f. 157.

16. See Steven Pincus, " 'Coffee Politicians Does Create': Coffeehouses and Restoration Political Culture," *Journal of Modern History*, 56 (1995), 807–34.

Chapter 3

1. For example, Pepys reported on August 24, the day the Act of Uniformity took effect, that "there hath been a disturbance in a church in Friday-street; a great many young [people] knotting together and crying out 'porridge' often and seditiously in the church; and took the Common Prayer-Book, they say, away; and some say did tear it. But it is a thing which appears to me very ominous." "Porridge" was the Puritan name for the Book of Common Prayer.

2. *His Majesties gracious Speech To both Houses of Parliament, On Wednesday, February 18th 1662. Being the first day of their meeting after their Prorogation* (pp. 3–5). This speech did not find its way into the 1772 collection.

3. Although "jealousy" is a standard term for negative political feeling throughout this period, its appearance in the king's speeches has the effect of flagging dark spots in public opinion.

4. *His Majesties Speech at the Reception of the Petition* (London [?] 1663). The online version of this printed speech is missing its title-page. It uses the same ornamental capital as the speech at the opening of the session, so it may also have been printed by Bill and Barker. The version in The Commons Journal varies very slightly. It also does not appear in the 1772 collection, though the message of the next day does.

5. Ronald Hutton, *The Restoration* (Oxford, 1985), commented that the king's tone "almost provoked the MPs to defiance, for they resolved to supply him by only forty-eight votes in a House of nearly three hundred" (p. 198).

6. Seaward, *Cavalier Parliament*, p. 180, concludes that the court was lucky to get even this rather stingy concession.

7. Bryant, *Letters, Speeches and Declarations of King Charles II*, p. 158. Seaward, *Cavalier Parliament*, p. 119, agreed.

8. See also Seaward's important article, "The House of Commons Committee of Trade and the Origins of the Second Anglo-Dutch War, 1664," *Historical Journal*, 30 (1987), 437–52.

9. Marvell, however, sent the speech to Hull, along with Turnor's, "though perhaps you may have them from some other hand," without other comment (*P&L*, 2:53).

10. *Essex Papers*, 1:161. The editor, Osmond Airy, observed in a note that "Hitherto Charles II. in his speeches to Parliament had not told any open and deliberate lie. . . . Conway's note is the only record of his embarrassment."

11. *Ibid.*, 1:168.

12. See also Henry Thynne to Essex, *ibid.*, 1:317.

13. The Mock-King's speech appears in twelve manuscripts, of some considerable textual diversity, none of which is in Marvell's hand. See Peter Beal, *Index of Literary Manuscripts* (London and New York, 1980), Vol. 2, part 2, pp. 66–67. It was printed in *Poems on Affairs of State*, Vol. 3 (London, 1704), and there first ascribed to Marvell. Girolamo Alberti, Venetian secretary to the doge and senate, reported its circulation on March 1, 1675 (*CSPD Venetian* 1675, p. 366). It is one of the most startling features of the Newdigate newsletters that, for April 13, 1675, one letter summarizes the actual royal speech at the opening of parliament, and another of the same date but in a different hand transcribes the whole mock speech, without comment or context (L. c. 170). This copy was unknown to Beal.

14. See Marvell, *Prose Works*, 2 vols. (New Haven, 2003), 1:460–64.

15. Marvell began sending Hull the royal speeches in 1667 (the prorogation speech of January 21), and continued as follows: opening speech, October 10, 1667, summarized; October 28, 1669, sends "papers," probably including the speech of October 19; February 15, 1670, sends both king's and lord keeper's; October 25, 1670, summarizes lord keeper's speech and promises to send it if printed, but doubts it will be; November 1, writes that both speeches "are prohibited printing but you will receive a written copy"; January 24, 1674, sends a MS. copy of king's speech, "which I hope you can read"; April 13, 1675, summarizes both king's and lord keeper's speeches, urging his constituents "not by this summary relation . . . to conceive of it accordingly; When printed I will send it to you." This dutiful letter is in flagrant conflict with Marvell's private account of the speech and its real meaning as recounted to William Popple on July 24; June 4, 1675, an intermediary speech about differences between the Houses: "The Kings Speech I shall send you by the next Post"; June 10, 1675, sends the king's speech at the prorogation; February 15, 1677, at opening after Long Prorogation; summarizes the king's speech and promises to send it as soon as printed; May 23, 1677, cites the king's entire speech, which was not published; May 28, 1677, cites the king's entire speech of rebuke, subsequently recited

in the *Account*; January 28, 1678, sends a copy of king's speech, possibly in manuscript; April 29, 1678, sends Finch's speech, "(his Majesty being present but not speaking)."

16. *Hatton Correspondence*, ed. E.M. Thompson, 2 vols. (Camden Society, 1878; repr. New York, 1965), 1:164.

17. See C. Brinkman, "Charles II and the Bishop of Münster in the Anglo-Dutch War of 1665–6," *English Historical Review*, 21 (1906), 686–98.

18. See also the speech of April 5, 1664 (SP 29/96/44), which thanked the Commons for repealing the Triennial Act, where "your so unanimous" is inserted before "concurrence," and "harte" is substituted for "head" as the location of the king's "designes" for the holding of future parliaments (a softening of the potentially sinister meaning). The autograph speech of November 24, 1664 (SP 29/105/79), delivered as prologue to the Paston move for Supply, along with Pepys's inflated estimate of the naval costs, raises the "jealousy" "that when you have given me a noble and proportionable supply for the support of a war, I may be induced by some evill councellours (for they will be thought to thinke very respectfully of my owne person)," and replaces "respectfully" with "respectively," an alteration rejected in the printed version, despite the fact that at this time "respectively" could be used in precisely that sense. In the next line the king inserts "suddaine" before the peace that these malicious whisperers suspect, and replaces "nothing" with the more moving "no blessing in this world" as the extent of the king's desire for an *eventual* "firme peace betweene all Christian Princes." It seems obvious that Charles was aware he was skating on thin ice.

19. BL Add. MS. 34362, f. 55.

20. I have found no evidence of this speech being as well known as Marvell's, however. It is not included, as the 1675 Mock-King's speech was, in *A New Collection of Poems relating to State Affairs*, the 1705 volume that gathered up all the political satires of the past and present.

Chapter 4

1. See *Autobiography* in *Supplement to Burnet's History*, ed. H.C. Foxcroft (Oxford, 1902), pp. 451–52. The autograph manuscript of the *Life* is in the Bodleian, Add. MSS. D.24, ff. 195–218. Burnet may, however, have gotten the idea of including character sketches in both the *History* and the *Life* from Clarendon's *History*.

2. All students of Clarendon are indebted to the three great articles, all entitled "Clarendon's *History of the Rebellion*," by C.H. Firth, in three consecutive issues of the *English Historical Review*, 19 (1904), 26–54, 246–62, 464–83. Firth sorted out the compositional strata of both the *History* and the *Life*, and made it possible for others to describe the evolution of these texts with some economy.

3. See also HMC, 6th Report, pp. 364–65, and 7th Report, p. 536.

4. Coventry Papers, BL Add. MS. 32094, ff. 24–27.

5. Witcombe, according to his index, confused him with Edward Vaughan.

6. BL Egerton MSS, 2539, f. 137v.

7. Haley, *The First Earl of Shaftesbury*, tackles this question and arrives at an answer only slightly more forgiving than Burnet's: "The speech was said [by his grandson] to have been prepared by the foreign committee for him reluctantly to deliver, and he was supposed to have been so disturbed that he had to have Locke standing at his elbow with a written copy, ready to prompt him . . . it is sufficient here to say that the apparent vehemence was purely tactical. . . . His real opinions were not necessarily so extreme, and certainly the policy he defended in the speech was not one which he had first devised" (pp. 282–83).

8. What must have been the speech in question exists as a manuscript among Shaftesbury's papers: "1675 The Earle of Shaftesbury's Speech in the H. Of L. against the Test," Malmesbury papers, Hampshire RO, 9M73/G201/1. In editing

the *Letter from a Person of Quality*, J.R. Milton and Philip Milton not only showed the similarity between this speech and the *Letter*, but pointed out that "other copies seem to have been in circulation—one was certainly available to the Whig historian John Oldmixon, writing just over fifty years later." See John Locke, *An Essay Concerning Toleration and Other Writings on Law and Politics*, ed. J.R. Milton and Philip Milton (Oxford, 2006), pp. 90–91.

9. The Miltons publish the *Letter* in an edition of Locke's works, but divide the authorship between (perhaps) Locke and Shaftesbury himself. They assume that Shaftesbury "took the completed manuscript with him when he returned to London shortly before the opening of the new session of Parliament on 13 October" (p. 92), implying that Shaftesbury feared the Test would be reintroduced in that session. The *Letter* itself warned at its close that the consolidation of the new Danby-led party "must be the work of another Session" (p. 32). The *Letter* appears to have gone on sale during the first week of November, probably not merely to pre-empt such a reintroduction, but to alert the Commons fully as to the court's plans for the muzzling of any opposition.

10. *Memoirs of Sir John Reresby*, ed. Andrew Browning, 2nd edn., ed. M.K. Geiter and W.A. Speck (London, 1991), p. ix.

11. Sir William Temple, *Works*, 4 vols. (London, 1814), 2:316–17.

12. In a note attributed to information in the *Hatton Correspondence*, 1:164, Browning (*Danby*, 1:279) states that it was Charles's speech of May 23, 1678 that was prepared by Temple. This is clearly a mistake, since it was the summary of international negotiations for which Temple's assistance was needed, not the short speech of the 23rd asking for money which required no informational backup except on the state of the budget.

13. For details about the French subsidy as it was renegotiated, half-paid, withdrawn, and then renegotiated between Danby and Montagu, see Browning, *Danby*, 1:271–72.

Chapter 5

1. See Nigel Smith, ed., *The Poems of Andrew Marvell* (London and Harlow, 2003), p. 361.

2. BL Add. MS. 72602, in the Trumbull Papers, contains a fair copy of these proceedings, which matches the 1700 imprint, except in having the names of speakers given in full. The British Library dates it to 1700, but how it relates to the imprint remains unclear.

3. Echard, *The History of England*, 3:268–69.

4. *Letters . . . to Sir Joseph Williamson*, 2:83.

5. An ironic echo of Shaftesbury's warlike speech about the Dutch at the opening of the eleventh session.

6. BL Add. MS. 28045, a later collection of materials about impeachments, several in Danby's hand, contains a partial transcript of this tract, including not only the impeachment attempts, but, more surprisingly, the sardonic address to the reader (ff. 32–38).

7. John Locke, *An Essay Concerning Toleration and Other Writings on Law and Politics 1667–1683*, ed. J.R. Milton and Philip Milton (Oxford, 2006).

8. This list obviously circulated in manuscript as a highly significant document. Newdigate received a copy in a newsletter (L. c. 258) entitled "A List of the Lords who voted in the vote for an addresse to the King for dissolving the Parliament November 22d 1675." For another manuscript version see BL Add. MS. 35865, Hardwicke Papers, ff. 224.

9. See HMC, 9th Report, pp. 69–70; reports of inquiries into the origins of *The Long Parliament Dissolved* involved the press of Nathaniel Thompson, whose types "agreed in everything" with the tract, "there being no letter in the book which Thompson had not in his press"; the bookshop of John Hancock, Jr.; and the elusive Mrs. Brewster, from whom Hancock bought his copies. The investigation came to a dead end with the disappearance of Brewster.

10. *Ibid.*, p. 73: part of this tract was seized at Thompson's press, which he co-partnered with Thomas Ratcliffe, on January 30.
11. *Ibid.*, pp. 70–73: the report of inquiries into the origins of *The Grand Question* also involved the press of Nathaniel Thompson, who was sent to Newgate prison for it. These accounts variously show that Cary was trying to find a publisher in January, and saying that the pamphlet must be printed before parliament met. On Sunday, February 4, Thompson received the manuscript, with the caveat that "if the impression were not finished by Friday night [February 9] it was as good not have it done at all" (p. 73).
12. In BL Add. MS. 25124, Coventry Papers, Secretary Henry Coventry wrote to Sir John Robinson, the governor of the Tower, on February 14, 1677: "His Majesty is informed that Dr. Carey lately by order of Counsell sent to your Custody is willing to speak with his Majesty in private. I pray goo you and speake with him and if you find him in that temper bring him as secretly as you can to Mr. Chiffins his Lodginge and His Majesty will do him the Grace to hear him in private himself".
13. Sawyer's father had been a member of parliament in the 1620s, but was expelled for complicity in unparliamentary taxation.
14. This phrase echoes the title-page of *The Long Parliament Dissolved*, which carried a quotation from Deuteronomy 27:17: "Cursed be he that Removeth his Neighbours LandMark: and all the People shall say, Amen."
15. Bodleian MS. Carte 79, ff. 31–60. The importance of these Wharton drafts has been obscured by miscalendaring.
16. Bodleian MS. Carte 80, ff. 785–87.
17. The speech by Anglesey, however, must have come from another source. It is not too difficult to guess what that source might have been; all the more important since one of the drafts (f. 42v) reported incorrectly that "My Lord Privy Seale argued against it [the dissolution] long."
18. Nicholas von Maltzahn, ed., *An Account of the Growth of Popery*, in *The Prose Works of Andrew Marvell*, 2 vols. (New Haven and London, 2003), especially 2:207–14.
19. *LJ*, 13:161.
20. Von Maltzahn, *Account*, pp. 196–97, citing *Historical Manuscripts Commission Ormonde*, NS 4:407–08.
21. *CSPV 1669–70*, pp. 259 and xxvi; the second reference was found by von Maltzahn, *Account*, 2:244, n. 120.
22. Bodleian MS. Carte 8, f. 774.

Chapter 6

1. The most important exception is Douglas Lacey, *Dissent and Parliamentary Politics in England, 1661–1689* (New Brunswick, 1969), which provides an invaluable set of brief biographies of those who were either themselves Presbyterians or who were sympathetic to Dissenters. See also, from the opposite perspective, Walter G. Simon, *The Restoration Episcopate* (New York, 1965), which exhaustively details the views and behavior of the Anglican bishops, a majority of whom were in favor of rigid conformity.
2. Simon, *Restoration Episcopate*, p. 94.
3. Charles sent them a capitulatory message on April 2.
4. G.F. Trevallyn Jones, "The Composition and Leadership of the Presbyterian Party in the Convention," *English Historical Review*, 79 (1964), 307–54; *Saw-Pit Wharton: The Political Career from 1640 to 1691 of Philip, Fourth Lord Wharton* (Sydney, 1967), pp. 177–86. The lists exist in Bodleian MS. Carte 80, f. 559, and MS. Carte 81, ff. 79–81. There is disagreement among historians as to whether these lists reveal Wharton to have been naïve and over-optimistic about the degree of potential support, or whether they were

merely open-ended canvassers' lists. The heading "friends" does not appear on any of the lists, and seems to derive from the nineteenth-century calendar.

5. Swatland, *The House of Lords*, p. 105.

6. Jones, "Composition and Leadership," p. 318.

7. *Dissent and Parliamentary Politics*, p. 61; in Bodleian MS. Carte 77, f. 592 and Carte 81, f. 331, there are drafts of what look like a speech Wharton intended to give in the Lords, arguing against the "exorbitant power" that the act gave to a single justice of the peace.

8. Bodleian MS. Carte 81, f. 337 contains "A Bill for the ease & security of Protestant Dissenters," marked on the back in Wharton's hand, "Being as is supposed that it was presented by the Duke of Bucks at the prorogation. Nov. 1672." F. 346 contains "Certain Proposals [or Motives], for Comprehension and Indulgence" (?1672), drawn up by Wharton in his own hand.

9. John Spurr, *Oxford Dictionary of National Biography*, citing Bodleian MS. Carte 45, f. 151.

10. The speech was edited from MS. Carte 80, ff. 757–59, by Caroline Robbins, *Bulletin of the Institute of Historical Research*, 21 (1946–48), 212–14.

11. Simon, *Restoration Episcopate*, pp. 160–61; he cites a manuscript introduction by Bishop Thomas Barlow to the Bodleian copy of *Several Tracts Relating to the Great Acts for Comprehension* (London, 1680).

12. Simon, *Restoration Episcopate*, pp. 158–62.

13. See *ibid.*, p. 162; John Spurr, "The Church of England, Comprehension and the Toleration Act of 1689," *English Historical Review* 104 (1989), 933–35.

14. Not February 10, as Simon reported on the basis of Pepys' *Diary*; the pre-meeting was crucial.

15. There are no entries in Grey till February 13.

16. Pepys, *Diary*, 7:292, somewhat rearranges these events.

17. Sir Charles Wheeler had entered parliament in a narrow by-election victory in 1667. His "invective speech" was probably an early attempt to impress that did not truly match his beliefs, since by March 2, 1670 he had come out strongly in favor of the new Conventicles Bill.

18. This must be Thomas Jones I, registered by Henning as "a great countenancer of the Presbyterian party."

19. See also Milward on March 30: "This day the bill was brought in for continuing the act against conventicles; it was opposed by Mr. Marvell, but it was ordered to be read to-morrow" (p. 238).

20. See HMC, 8th Report, March 26, 1670 pp. 142–43. This takes note of Marvell's report to Hull on the unamended bill.

21. Marvell carefully followed its fortunes for Hull. On December 8, he wrote that the new bill makes conventicles "riots & orders that who can not pay his 5s. or who shall refuse to tell his name or abode shall worke it out in the house of correction. Also that Constables may break ope house by day, by warant for a distresse" (*P&L*, 2:120). On March 23 (after the distractions of the "nose" bill), he reported that "the clause that makes them riots is thrown out & severall other clauses softned so that the most materiall thing now left in it is onely indemnity to such as have exceeded in prosecuting the law" (*P&L*, 2:137). On April 6, he recorded the final vote, and that when the bill went up to the Lords they "red it once & divided for throwing it out, but it was retaind *by the odds of two voices*" (*P&L*, 2:138; italics added).

Chapter 7

1. Browning, *Danby* 1951, 1:146.

2. *The Diaries and Papers of Sir Edward Dering*, ed. Bond.

3. *A Collection of King's Speeches* (London, 1772), pp. 128–31. The quotations are from Sallust, *Catiline*, 21.1 and Tacitus, *Histories*, 2:10.1.

4. Given Mallet's record of anti-Catholic activity, it looks as though Dering misremembered what he said. Perhaps he said "Protestant Dissenters."

5. On October 19, after the prorogation, it had to be reintroduced, and was committed the next day. It was engrossed on November 12, but again lapsed with the next prorogation. In the 1677 session it was resuscitated; Daniel Finch wrote to his uncle that "it is to be hoped it will never pass, at least not in the form in which it was presented" (Leicestershire RO, Finch Papers, P.P. 42, p. 25).

6. Browning, *Danby*, 1:155–57.

7. *Ibid.*, 1:156. For example, he states that "Colonel Birch was confident that from all his accusers could say the Treasurer 'would come out purified like gold.' " In fact, what Birch said, on April 26, was this: "That the Treasury is gone is certain [the money has vanished], but as to the Treasurer's being in fault, [he] *hopes* he will come out purified like gold." It does not appear that Browning consulted Dering's *Diary*. On the other hand, he found a very full account of the entire impeachment proceedings in the Lindsey MSS., and a fragment of the rough notes for that account in the Leeds MSS., Packet 6. See also BL Add. MS. 28047, f. 142, which gives a list of speakers identified as pro or con.

8. Dering had in fact given rather a long speech which he claimed in his *Diary* supported adjournment but which actually supported a graceful acceptance of the royal answer: "I showed them that in petitions and addresses of this nature the matter was wholly in the King's power. Where no positive law was broken, no one man of the Kingdome could say he was personally injured, sooner or later we must acquiesce in the King's pleasure, and then the sooner we did it and the more decently we approached it, still the better" (p. 81).

9. Marvell, writing to Hull, has this slightly wrong: "The Tellers not agreeing of the Numbers upon dividing" (*P&L*, 2:154). Grey also seems to have it wrong: "The Tellers . . . differing in their account of the Yeas and Noes some called, 'Tell again,' others, 'Report.' " Note that Dering disagrees with Grey on the teller for the Noes, for Grey has instead Sir John Hanmer, and Edward Rowlands accepted his version for *House of Commons*.

Chapter 8

1. Leicestershire Record Office, Finch Papers, P.P. 42, p. 19.

2. BL Add. MS. 28091, one of Danby's own manuscripts, contains the first half of Neale's parliamentary journal (ff. 29–76), which begins on Thursday, February 15, the first day of the session, and runs through March 20, 1677. The section from March 21 through May 28, 1677 appears separately in BL Egerton MS. 3345. After the adjournment on May 28, BL Add. MS. 28091 picks up the story again on February 5, 1678, no doubt because Neale was planning a major speech the next day.

3. *A Seasonable Argument* claimed: "he has a promise his son shall marry Moll Davis's daughter and he made a viscount and maintained if his brew-house fail [again]. Formerly called Golden Neale, now Brazen Groom Porter."

4. See also Marvell to Hull, on February 27, March 3, and March 6.

5. Thomas Neale was also extremely interested in Harrington. He reports the debate very fully, including Harrington's own speech. BL Add. MS. 28091, ff. 47–51.

6. BL Add. MS. 35865, ff. 135r–156v. This discovery was made by Nicholas von Maltzahn.

7. Marvell's *Account* and its source say the Address was presented on the 30th. The *Account* summarizes debates pro and con which show no connection with Grey on the 29th, and so must refer to the 30th, which Grey does not record. Nor does he record March 31 or April 2 and 3, but by that time the Address was in the king's hands. See also "heads of the Arguments in the House of Commons *against* the last Addresse . . . Aprill 16. 1677," Middle Temple, Treby MSS., Sub item 27.

8. The division was actually on whether "this particular of a League *Offensive and Defensive with the Dutch* should be left out of the Address." By 182 to 142 it was agreed to retain this new specific demand.

9. See Temple, *Memoirs*, 2:438–41; Temple does not give the slant that Grey's editor derives from his account, but he had in fact refused to be the agent of the treaty with Holland alone, as being inadequate to the task of bringing France to the table, and had proposed instead Laurence Hyde, an ambassador at Nijmegen who was then at The Hague.

10. BL Add. MS. 35865 contains another manuscript account of this part of the session, from March 1 to early May, entitled "A Journal beginning March. 1677 [i.e. 1678] in which are the severall Votes and Addresses to his Majestie for making Alliances with the Confederates in order to the making of a Warr against France." This account contains no debates, almost no dates, and very few numerical votes; it is obsessive about procedure, and hence repetitive; its chief interest, apart from its testimony to the reportorial instinct at this time, is its focus on the texts of the treaties finally released to the House at the beginning of May.

11. BL Add. MS. 28091, ff. 65v–66r.

12. See P.A. Bolton's article in *House of Commons*, which states that, having been a Court party supporter, Gerard, with his cousins, went over to the Opposition after the Long Prorogation. The four years' silence was occasioned by his humiliation in January 1674 when he utterly failed to substantiate charges of popery against Arlington.

13. Haley, *The First Earl of Shaftesbury*, p. 443.

14. Here BL Add. MS. 35865, "A Journall," does give the division (f. 183).

15. It is, ironically, also a reprise of the scene Marvell paints in *Last Instructions to a Painter* in 1667, when the Court party rose early to caucus on the excise tax ("They feign a parly, better to surprise . . ./ Thick was the Morning, and the House was thin"), but were foiled by Strangeways, "fighting it single till the rest might arm." Other echoes show how history was repeating itself: "The close Cabal . . . secretly for Peace decrees,/ Yet as for War the Parliament should squeeze." But by this time the two Coventrys, "Hector Harry" and "Will the Wit," were on opposite sides of the question.

16. Grey's editor, still carefully comparing texts, remarked in a footnote that the king's answer was not recorded in the Journal, "but is preserved in Sir Thomas Webster's *Collection* . . . and is also confirmed by Sir John Reresby, in his *Memoirs*, p. 62."

17. *King Charles's Speech against Tacking . . . With part of the Lord Chancellor (Finch's) Speech, delivered the same day to both Houses of Parliament.* Darby added an explanatory note on what had occasioned the speeches, and a *Query*: "Whether it would not be an unpardonable Sin in Whigs, and such as are Friends to the late Revolution, and consequently to her present Majesty Q. Anne, to run so counter to the Opinions of those two Great Persons above nam'd, as some Gentlemen of late have done?"

Chapter 9

1. The classic study is John Kenyon's *The Popish Plot* (London, 1972), which exhaustively follows Oates until his trial for perjury, but devotes little space to parliament. Kenyon was interested in Coleman as a peculiar character, almost as peculiar as Oates, but the more damning testimony of the Darby/Montagu letters is passed over in two pages.

2. From "Miscellaneous Papers," in Dering 2, pp. 184–85 (italics added). The vote Dering refers to was taken on November 1. The king's message was delivered on November 9 (*CJ*, 9:536). The phrases in square brackets were inserted as interlineations.

3. This phrase was deleted by Dering.

4. The Latin phrase had been deployed by Finch as lord keeper, in his speech opening the new session of parliament on April 13, 1675, subsequently published.

5. Coventry Letter Book, BL Add. MS. 25124, ff. 155–56.

6. BL Hargrave MS. 149, ff. 37–38. The manuscript is entitled "Speeches made in Parliament by severall Persons," and the name Russell Robartes appears on f. 1. It was identified as Booth's journal by Mark Knights, *Representation and Misrepresentation in Later Stuart Britain* (Oxford, 2005), p. 93. The most interesting fact about the journal, however, is that it starts with the debate on improper adjournments of the House by Seymour, a debate that took place on Saturday, February 9, 1678, before Booth's arrival. Booth looked backwards, evidently, by consulting Grey's notes.

7. Seaward, *Cavalier Parliament*, pp. 141–51.

8. *LJ* 13: he told the Lords and Commons "That he did not refuse to pass this Act for the Dislike of the Matter, but the Manner, because it puts out of his Power the Militia for so many Days. If it had been but for Half an Hour, He would not have consented to it, because of the ill Consequences it may have hereafter, the Militia being wholly in the Crown; and so far as He is enabled by Law to raise the Militia, if they will enable Him with Money to pay them, He shall employ such of them as He thinks fit, and are necessary for the Safety of Himself and the Kingdom."

9. Mark Jones, *Medals of the Sun King* (London, 1979), pp. 18–19. There is no trace of it in Josèphe Jacquiot, *La Médaille au temps de Louis XIV*, the catalogue of the 1970 state exhibition. It was bad enough, perhaps, that one of the French medals celebrating the Treaty of Nijmegen in August 1678 carried the message "Pace in Leges suas confecta" (Peace made on his own terms).

10. Browning, *Danby*, 1:312–13.

11. BL Add. MS. 28047, f. 47. For Netterville's history of informing, see Alan Marshall, *Intelligence and Espionage in the Reign of Charles II, 1660–1685* (Cambridge, 1994), pp. 211–12.

12. This was in fact addressed by the Commons in May 1679—scarcely the first item of business, so taken up they were with the impeachment of Danby.

13. BL Add. MS. 34362, "Satires of Charles II," attributed to Sir Samuel Danvers (of Cudworth), 1681, ff. 48–49; *POAS, Second Part*, pp. 11–13.

14. Compare the debates on this bill in April 1675, pp. 69—70 above; but the Commons returned to it in the 1677 session.

15. BL Add. MS. 34362, ff. 70–71. This collector was particularly interested in satires about the Long Parliament, but those he selected were by no means all supportive of it. "Upon a Prorogation of the Parliament before the last Prorogation was expired," which dates from 1674, complains: "Have we more Mony given in twelves yeares space/Then Norman Bastard had and all his Race . . . And all for this?"

16. Echard, *History of England*, 3:511–12.

17. [James Ralph,] The *History of England during the reigns of K. William, Q. Anne, and K. George I. With an introductory review of the reigns of the royal brothers, Charles and James, in which are to be found the seeds of the revolution*, 2 vols. (London, 1745), 1:424.

Chapter 10

1. For this speech, see Haley, *The First Earl of Shaftesbury*, p. 510, who, though not equipped with Echard's information, points out that the endorsement on the copy in BL MS. 38847, f. 76b., and indicates that it was available for printing and distribution in London and Norwich.

2. As Andrew Browning observed of those who published Reresby's *Memoirs*, "a general election was imminent, and the long anticipated second volume of Burnet's *History* . . . was holding out an immediate promise of historical ammunition for the Whigs" (Reresby, p. ix).

3. BL Add. MS. 1739, ff. 83–84: May 30, 1739: "If you have any further lights for my undertaking I have engaged in with respect to the debates in Parlt. you will oblige me

greatly"; August 26, 1739: "In my undertaking with Regard to the Proceedings of Parliament, I find I shall be indebted to the advice and assistance of all my Friends. The Journals of Sir S. DEwes I have bought, but I find them too imperfect to set out upon anew. Farther Lights therefore are necessary, which may be certainly found, I am told, in my Lord Oxford's, Doctor Meed's, or the Cotton Library."

4. Thomas Erskine May, *Constitutional History of England* (Boston, 1862–63), pp. 390–94.

5. Grey, *Debates*, 3:329. "To set the contrast between those times, and the present, in a striking light, let it be remembered, that we have now in commission, from forty guns and upwards, above 130 ships, while so vigorous and successful have been our efforts that the French at this time [1761], have scarce thirty left, and such has been the supineness of the Dutch, that their once formidable fleets are now scarce heard of."

6. I am grateful to Stuart Handley for directing me to the short essay on Grey by E.S. de Beer, *Bulletin of the Institute of Historical Research*, 5 (1927–28), but puzzled by de Beer's bland statement that the annotation of *Debates* is "adequate."

7. Menhennet, *The Journal of the House of Commons: A Bibliographical and Historical Guide*, House of Commons Library Document, No. 7 (London, 1971).

8. *Ibid.*, p. 18. These then may have preceded and influenced the official order to print the votes of October 30, 1680.

9. John Almon, *Memoirs of a Late Eminent Bookseller* (London, 1790), p. 120; Annabel Patterson, *Nobody's Perfect: A New Whig Interpretation of History* (New Haven, 2002), pp. 64–67.

Index